MODERN TECHNOLOGY OF ACID SLURRY, SURFACTANTS, SOAP AND DETERGENTS WITH FORMULAE

MODERN TECHNOLOGY OF ACID SLURRY, SURFACTANTS, SOAP AND DETERGENTS WITH FORMULAE

Written By :
EIRI Board of Consultants & Engineers

ENGINEERS INDIA RESEARCH INSTITUTE
4449, Nai Sarak, Main Road, Delhi-110 006 (India)
Ph.: 91-11-23918117, 23916431, 45120361, 23947058
* **E-Mail**: eiribooks@yahoo.com & eiriprojects@gmail.com
* **Website**: www.eiriindia.org, www.eiribooksandprojectreports.com

Printed and Published by :

ENGINEERS INDIA RESEARCH INSTITUTE

4449, Nai Sarak, Main Road, Delhi-110 006 (India)

Ph.: 91-11-23918117, 23916431, 45120361, 23947058

★ **E-Mail**: eiribooks@yahoo.com & eiriprojects@gmail.com

★ **Website**: www.eiriindia.org, www.eiribooksandprojectreports.com

Marketed By:

EIRI PROJECT CONSULTANTS & PUBLISHERS

Roop Nagar, Delhi—110007

ISBN : 978-93-80772-03-5

Printed in New Delhi (India)

Rs. 850/-

Printed and Published by Sudhir Gupta for "Engineers India Research Institute", 4449, Nai Sarak, Main Road, Delhi-110 006 and Printed at Swastik Offset, Delhi

Preface

The Book **Modern Technology of Acid Slurry, Surfactants, Soap and Detergents with Formulae** covers almost all the basic and advanced details to setup own Unit. The Book Covers Soap, Fatty Acids and Synthetic Detergents, Detergent Componentsg, Surfactants, Builders, Raw Materials, Analysis and Testing, Manufacture of Acid Slurry, Manufacture of Soap, Surfactants, Manufacture of Synthetic Detergents, Detergent soap and Additives.

The book has been written for the benefit and to prove an asset and a handy reference guide in the hands of new entrepreneurs & well established industrialists.

ENGINEERS INDIA RESEARCH INSTITUTE

4449, Nai Sarak, Main Road, Delhi-110 006 (INDIA)

E-mail : eiribooks@yahoo.com

www.eiriindia.org

Contents

1

Soap, Fatty Acids and Synthetic Detergents

SOAP

Introduction

The origin of the word "soap" is traced to sacrificial Mount Sapo of ancient Roman legend. The mixture of fat and wood ashes that reacted to form soap was carried by rain to the banks of the Tiber river and found as a clay deposit useful for cleaning clothes.

The boiling of fats with ashes was recorded as early as 2500 B.C. Commercial soapmaking was a widespread art in the Middle Ages in Europe. The invention of the soda ash process by Leblanc in 1791, and the discovery by Chevreul in 1811 that soap was composed of a mixture of fatty acids paved the way to modern soap manufacturing processes.

Chemistry

The modern definition of soap relates to cleansing agents derived from fats, oils, and other fatty derivatives: the soaps are alkali and ammonium salts of fatty acids containing from 8 to 22 carbon atoms. These fatty acids are generally a mixture of saturated, unsaturated and polyunsaturated moieties:

$CH_3(CH_2)_{10}COOM$: saturated soap

$CH_3(CH_2)_6CH_2CH=CHCH_2(CH_2)_6$-COOM: mono-unsaturated soap

$CH_3(CH_2)_3(CH_2CH=CH)_2CH_2(CH_2)_6$-COOM: di-unsaturated soap

$CH_3(CH_2CH=CH)_3CH_2(CH_2)_6$-COOM: poly-unsaturated soap

$[M = Na, K, (HOCH_2CH_2)_3NH^+]$

In general, two types of chemical reactions are utilized in the manufacture of soap: the saponification of triglycerides (fats and oils) and the neutralization of fatty acids (which themselves are produced from the triglycerides by a variety of methods, most notably by the splitting of fats and oils with steam). Sodium hydroxide, potassium hydroxide, sodium carbonate, and triethanolamine are the most commonly utilized alkaline moieties in these processes (Fig. 1.1).

In recent years, soap manufacture by an alternate route, the saponification of fatty methyl esters, has been under development, most

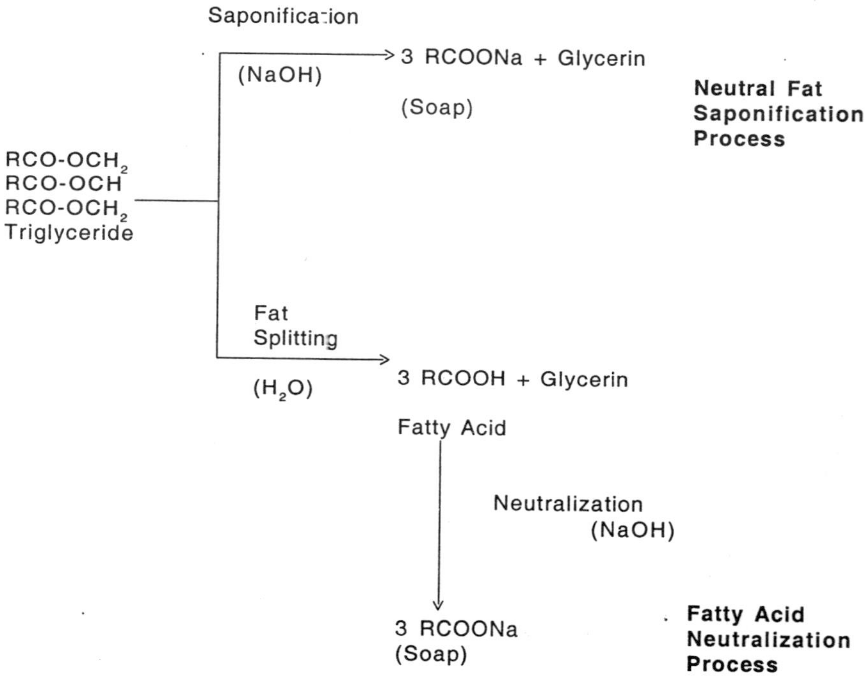

Fig. 1.1. The Chemistry of Soap manufacture.

notably in Japan (Lion Corporation) and Italy (Ballestra). The fatty methyl esters are obtained from the methanolysis of tri-glycerides; inorganic alkali, quaternary ammonium salts, and enzymes (lipase) have been used as catalysts for methanolysis in commercially practiced processes (Fig.1.2).

Manufacturing Technology

Several designs of commercial equipment, based on the two processes described in Fig. 1.1, are available for the manufacture of soap.

Neutral Fat Saponification

- *Kettle Processes*
  - Semi-boiled
  - Boiled
- *Modern Processes*
  - Mazzoni SCNC-N
  - Alfa Laval Centipure
  - Hitachi
  - Dial Saponiflex

Fatty Acid Neutralization

- Mazzoni SC and SCC
- Alfa Laval
- Sato
- Dial Saponiflex

A critical review of these designs is beyond the scope of this chapter. However, the processes themselves are described in a subsequent section.

Raw Materials

The triglycerides (triesters of fatty acids with glycerin) are the basic raw material for the manufacture of soap utilizing a variety of processes. The triglycerides, as a renewable resource, occur widely throughout the plant and the animal kingdoms.

Soap products in the United States are produced almost exclusively from tallow fat and coconut oil or their fatty acid derivatives. The utilization of palm oils, palm kernel oil, and their derivatives for soap manufacture is more commonly practiced in many other parts of the world, especially in Asia. Among other triglycerides cottonseed oil, ricebran oil, castor oil, neem oil, sunflowerseed oil, fish oil, and olive oil also have been used as indigenous feedstocks in many developing nations. The fatty acid composition and analytical characterization data of some of the key fats and oils utilized for soap production are given in Table 1.1.

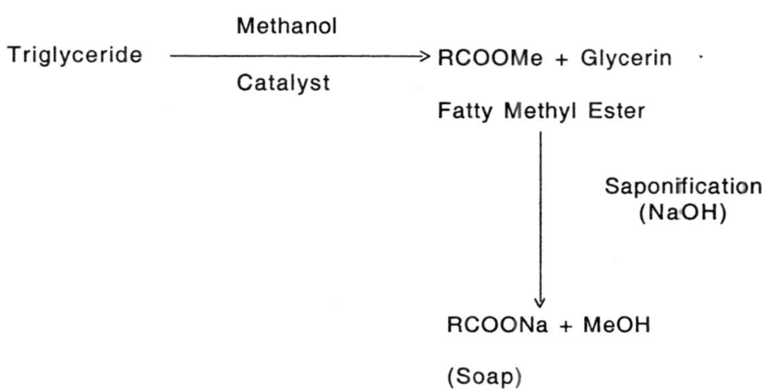

Fig. 1.2. Fatty methyl ester process for soap manufacture..

Most of the fats and oils utilized for soap manufacture require a combination of degumming, deodorization, refining, and bleaching steps, which are discussed further in the section on fatty acids.

For both the saponification and the neutralization reactions, sodium hydroxide is the most commonly utilized base. In some special situations, such as the manufacture of transparent and translucent soaps, potassium hydroxide and triethanolamine also are employed.

Functional Properties of Soap

Almost as a rule, the solubility of soap in water increases with an increase in the size of the monovalent cation (base); an increase in the size of a divalent cation (Mg, Ca) results in a decrease in the solubility,

TABLE 1.1 Fatty Acid Distribution and Analytical Characterization of Soap Base Fatty Acids

Fatty Acid Distribution	*Coconut*	*Stripped Coconut*	*Palm Kernel*	*Palm*	*Tallow*
Caprylic ($C_8H_{16}O_2$)	7	1	4		
Capric ($C_{10}H_{20}O_2$)	6	1	5		
Lauric ($C_{12}H_{24}O_2$)	48	55	50		
Myristic ($C_{14}H_{28}O_2$)	19	22	15	2	2.5
Palmitic ($C_{16}H_{32}O_2$)	9	11	7	42	27
Stearic ($C_{18}H_{36}O_2$)	2	2	2	5	20
Oleic ($C_{18}H_{34}O_2$)	8	7	15	41	42
Linoleic ($C_{18}H_{32}O_2$)	1	1	1	10	5
Linoleic ($C_{18}H_{30}O_2$)					1
C_{20}/C_{22} isomers				1	2.5
Characterization Data:					
Titer, °C	26	29	25	40	40
Iodine value (IV)	10	5	18	55	55
Color, Gardner, max.	5	1			5
Acid value (AV)	270	255			205
Saponification value (SV)	270	255			205
Color, Lovibond, 5-¼	10Y/1R	4.5Y 0.6R			

however. An increase in the chain length of the fatty acid moiety of soap results in a decrease in the solubility of soap, whereas the presence of unsaturation results in an increase in its solubility. In general, an increase in the water solubility is accompanied by a increase in the softness and mushiness properties of soap.

For lathering attributes, the use of fatty acids of C_{10} to C_{12} chain length is most preferred. The fatty acids of longer chain length, from C_{16} to C_{18}, contribute to the cleansing properties of soap. A combination of coconut (C_{10}-C_{12}) and tallow (C_{16}-C_{18}) fatty acids thus is most suitable from the viewpoint of consumeracceptable lathering and cleansing properties of soap.

Manufacturing Processes

The following is a description of the neutral fat saponification and the fatty acid neutralization, two principal processes used for manufacture of soap in the world markets today.

Neutral Fat Saponification. In the saponification of triglycerides with an alkali, the two reactants are rather immiscible. Because saponification is a bimolecular nucleophilic substitution (Sn^2), the kinetic rate enhancement of this reaction is achievable by both a high-shear mixing and an increase in the reaction temperature during the processing. The saponifiction reaction is self-catalyzed to some extent: the formation of soap product effects the emulsification of the two immiscible reactants, causing an acceleration of the reaction rate.

The amount of alkali required to saponify a triglyceride blend is calculated by the following equations:

$$\text{Triglyceride} + 3NaOH \rightarrow 3RCOONa + \text{Glycerin}$$

$$NaOH = [SV \times 0.000713] \times 100/NaOH(\%)$$

$$[SV/1000] \times [MW(NaOH)/MW(KOH)] \qquad (26.1)$$

where *SV*= saponification value and *MW*= molecular weight.

The process flow diagram of a typical triglyceride saponification plant is illustrated in Fig. 1.3. The essential components of this plant include proportionating pumps for introducing correct quantities of reaction components into a reactor autoclave, which operates at temperature and

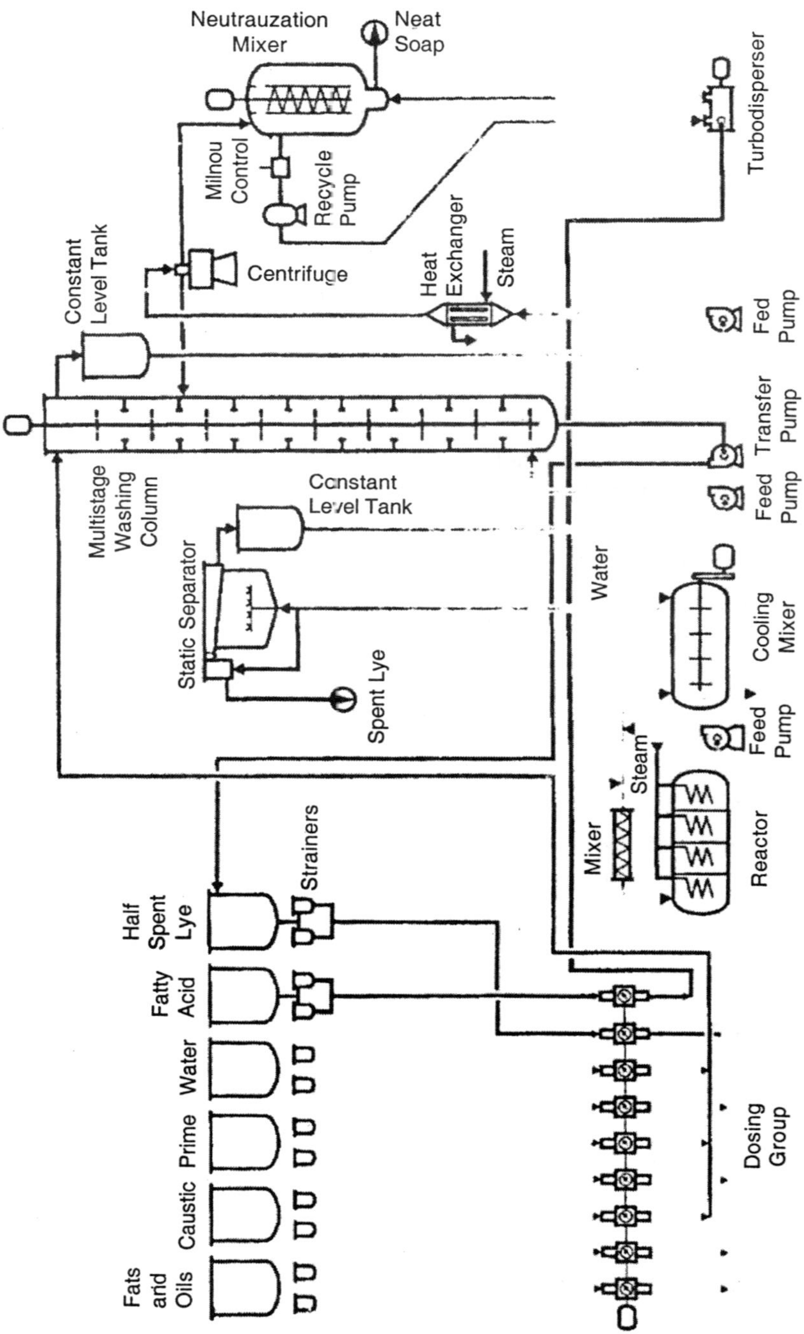

Fig. 1.3. Continuous neutral fat saponification plant.

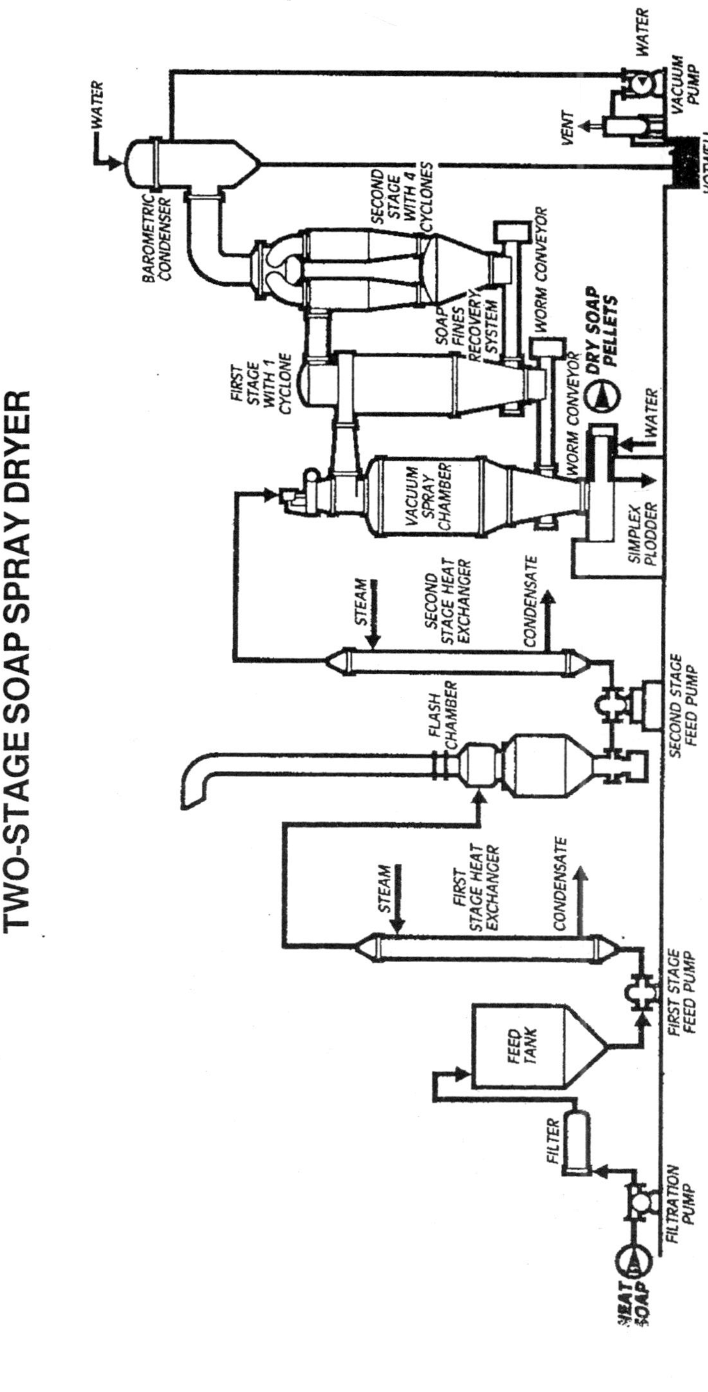

Fig. 1.4. Two-stage toilet-soap spray dryer.

CONTINUOUS FATTY ACID NEUTRALIZATION PLANT

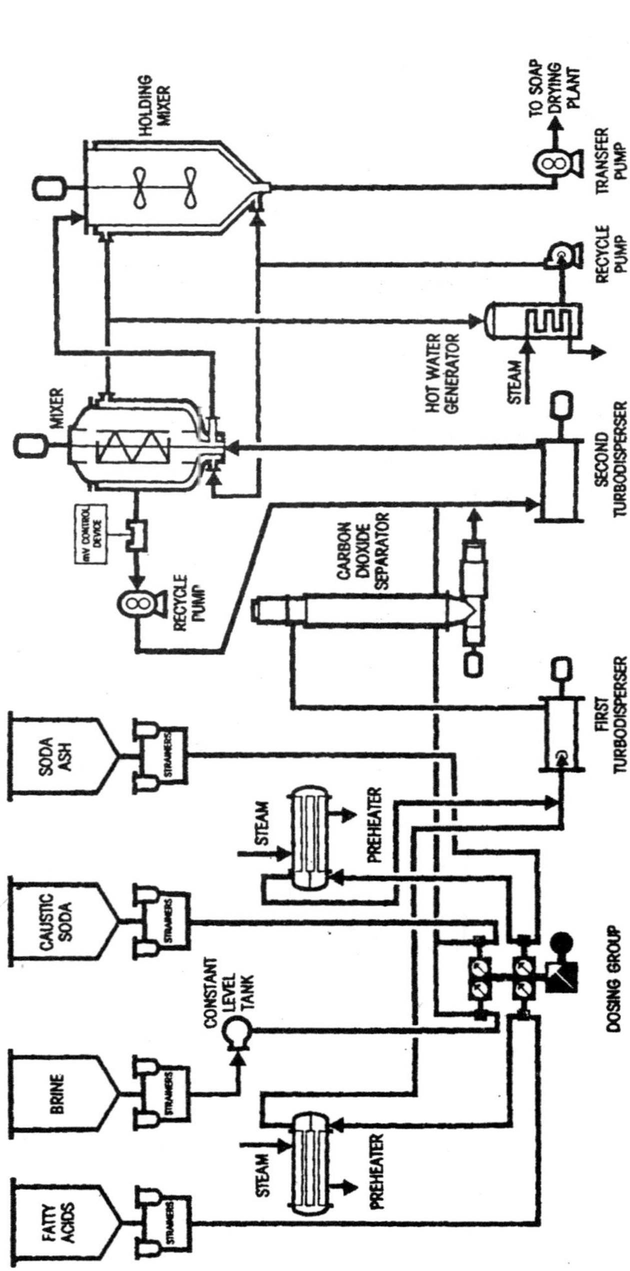

Fig. 1.5. Continuous fatty acid neutralization plant.

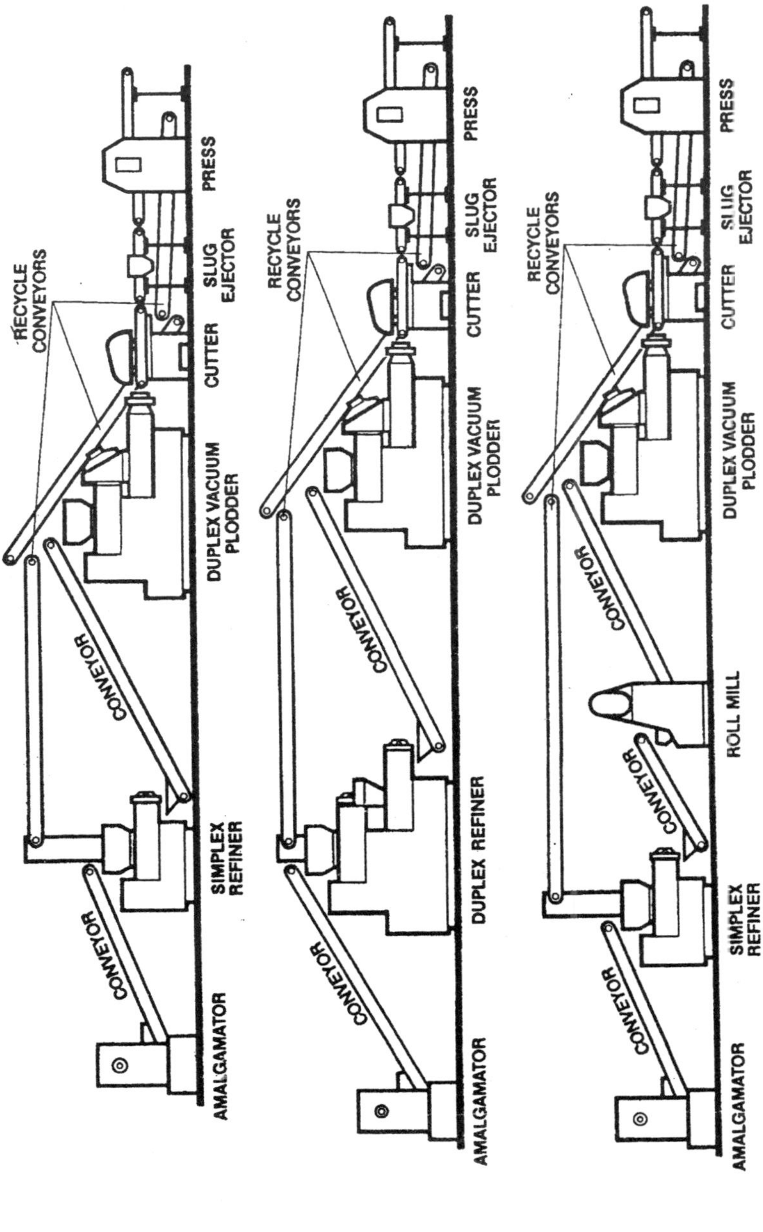

Fig. 1.6. Toilet soap finishing line.

pressure conditions appropriate for a rapid and complete reaction. The saponification mixture is recirculated within the autoclave. The temperature of the saponified mass is lowered in a cooling mixer; then the mass is pumped to a static separator for separation of the unwashed soap from the spent lye solution. The soap then is washed with washing lye counter-currently in a washing tower to separate glycerin (as spent lye) from it. Centrifugal separators remove the traces of lye from the soap. The neat soap (60-63% total fatty matter) is neutralized and sent to vacuum spray dryers to produce soap as pellets (78-82% total fatty matter), ready for processing into the finished product on finishing lines.

Soap Drying. The soap mass obtained after the completion of saponification (neat soap) is most commonly dried by a vacuum spray dryer. The water content of soap is thus reduced from 30 to 35 per cent in neat soap to 8 to 18 per cent in soap pellets or flakes. A variety of vacuum spray dryers, from single-stage to multi-stage designs, are available from several manufacturers. The operation of a single-stage vacuum spray dryer involves the pumping of neat soap through a shell-and-tube heat exchanger where the soap is heated by steam passing through the outside tube in a countercurrent manner. The preheated soap is sprayed onto the walls of a vacuum chamber through a revolving nozzle. The thin layer of dried and partially cooled soap deposited on the walls of the vacuum chamber is removed by rotating scrapers and falls to the bottom of a plodder, which extrudes the soap mass in the form of noodles or pellets.

The multi-stage dryers (Fig. 1.4), which are expanded versions of the single-stage dryers, permit more efficient drying of a wider range of soap formulations than the single-stage dryers.

Fatty Acid Neutralization. The acid-base reaction of fatty acids with alkali to produce soap (below) is much faster than the corresponding reaction of triglycerides with alkalis.

$$RCOOH + NaOH \rightarrow RCOONa + H_2O$$

The amount of alkali (NaOH) required to neutralize a fatty acid blend can be calculated as follows:

$$NaOH = [\text{weight fatty acid} \times 40] / \text{MW fatty acid} \quad (.26.3)$$

The average molecular weight of a fatty acid blend is calculated from the following equation:

$$\text{MW fatty acid} = 56.1 \times 1000/AV \quad (26.4)$$

where AV(acid value of fatty acid blend) = mg of KOH required to neutralize 1 g of fatty acid.

A typical Mazzoni fatty acid neutralization soap plant is illustrated in Fig. 1.5. The operation of this plant involves the pumping of the reactants through preheaters to a turbodisperser where the contact of the reactants with each other initiates the formation of neat soap. The soap mass, which is partially reacted at this stage, then proceeds to the mixer where it is recirculated until the neutralization is complete. The completion of neutralization process is monitored by an electric potential (millivolt, mV) measurement for alkalinity. The neat soap then is dried by vacuum spray dryers, as descri-bed earlier, to produce soap pellets ready for finishing into soap bars.

Soap Finishing. For the manufacture of bar soap products, the soap pellets are mixed with color, perfume, and other additives in a mixer (amalgamator). The mixed soap mass then proceeds to a series of plodders/roll mills to refine the entire mixture into a uniform, homogeneous product. The finished product is extruded from the last plodder as a continuous slug. A chain cutter with blades cuts it into individual pieces that are stamped with a press into soap bars of the desired size and shape.

The wrapping, cartoning, and end packaging machinery complete the bar soap finishing lines. The schematic diagrams of a variety of soap finishing configurations are illustrated in Fig. 1.6.

FATTY ACIDS

The fatty acids are produced industrially from the triglycerides; this processing involves the steps shown in Fig. 1.7.

Refining involves the purification of triglyceride to remove impurities (phosphatides, polyethylene, chlorophyll, heavy metals, off-odors, off-color) by a combination of acid alkali washing, clay/activated silica bleaching, deodorization, and hydrogenation steps.

Splitting of triglycerides usually is performed by high pressure steam, resulting in the formation of split fatty acids and glycerin. The production of fatty acids by special "splitting" processes, such as hydrolysis of fatty methyl esters, ozonolysis of unsaturated fatty acids, and chemical oxidation, is practiced in special situations.

Distillation of split fatty acids results in the improvement of chemical, color, and odor quality of the finished product.

Triglyceride

↓

Refining — Washing, Bleaching, Deodorizing, Hydrogenation

↓

Splitting — Hydrolysis to produce split fatty acids and glycerin

↓

Distillation — Purification of split fatty acids

Fractionation
Distillation to separate lower molecular weight (C-6 to C-14) fatty acids

Example:
Coco fatty acid→ C-8 (Caproic acid)
C-10 (Caproic acid)
C-12 (Lauric acid)
C-14 (Myristic acid)

Separation
Physical separation of higher molecular weight (C-16 to C-18) fatty acids

Example:
Tallow fatty acid→ Stearic acid
Oleic acid

Fig. 1.7. Production of fatty acids from triglycerides.

Fractionation and Physical Separation

Distilled fatty acid streams are separated to obtain individual components of those fatty acid streams in a higher state of chemical purity. Fractionation is performed to separate the more volatile lower molecular weight fatty acids (C_8-C_{14} chain length); physical separation is practiced to obtain higher molecular weight, less volatile or thermally unstable fatty acids (C_{16}-C_{18} chain length). Hydrogenation is utilized to reduce the unsaturation and poly-unsaturation of fatty acids. Hydrogenated fatty acids also can be produced by the hydrogenation of triglycerides followed by split-ting of the resulting fat/oil blend. The selective reduction of di- and poly-unsaturation often is accomplished by the use of nickel-based specialized catalysts, by a process often called touch hydrogenation.

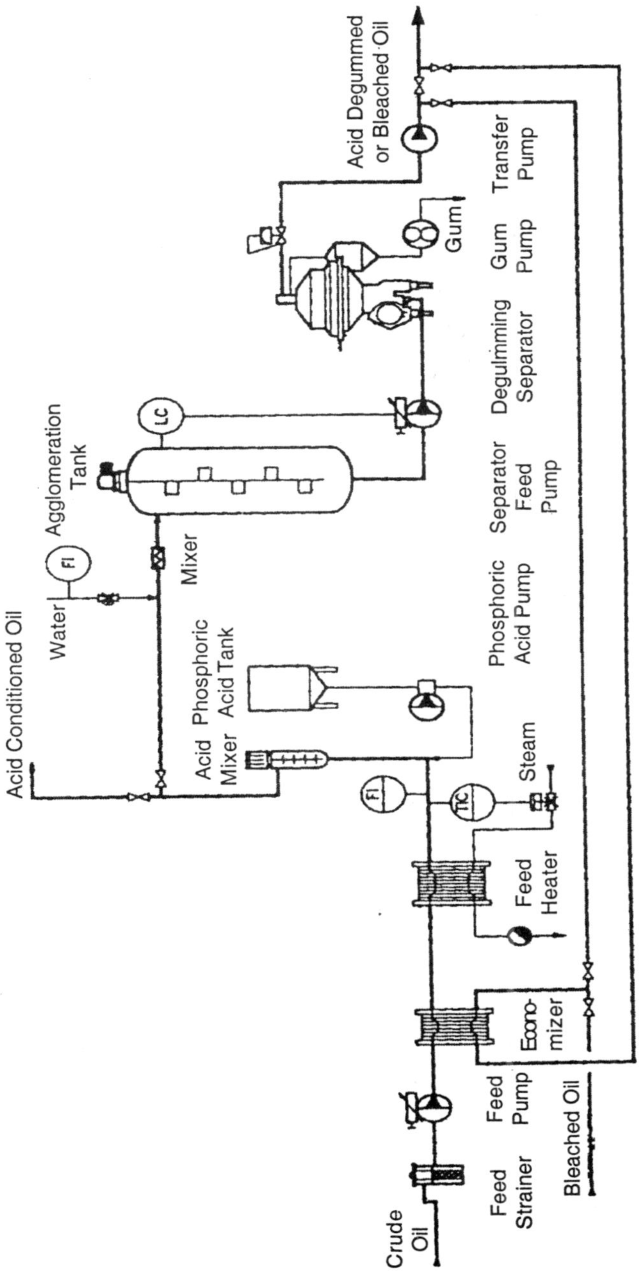

Fig. 1.8. Acid degumming plant for acid washing of fats and oils.

CONTINUOUS FATTY MATTER BLEACHING PLANT

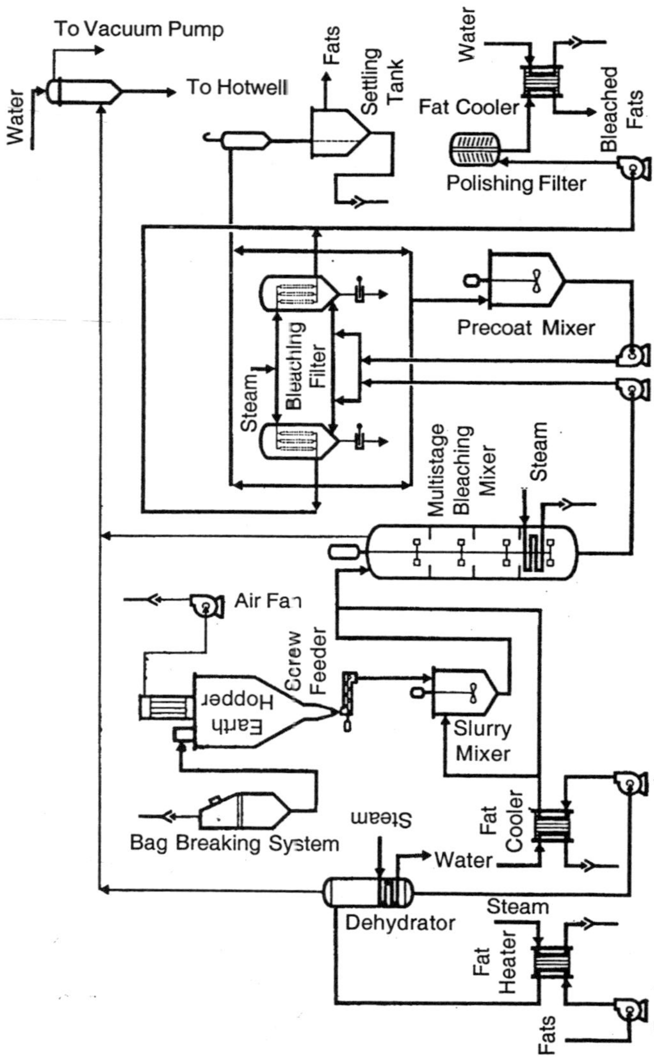

Fig. 1.9. Continuous fatty matter bleaching plant.

In the partial hydrogenation of the unsaturated moieties the isomerization of the double bonds of mono-unsaturated components is a common occurrence; it results in the transformation of the *cis* to the corresponding *trans* stereoisomer. As the physical properties of these isomers may vary significantly, their impact on the properties of the final product should be evaluated rather carefully, for little information is available on this subject at present.

Fat Refining

A typical fat refining plant (Alfa-Laval process) for the acid washing of fats and oils, is illustrated in Fig. 1.8. The triglyceride is degummed to

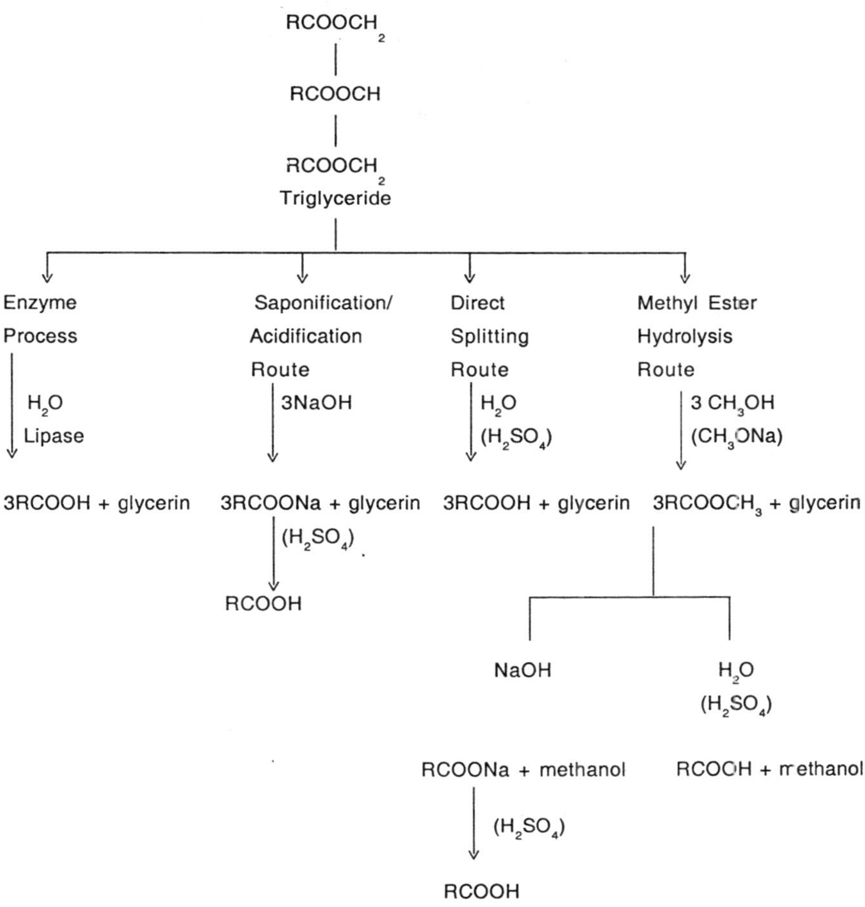

Fig. 1.10. Fat splitting processes.

remove phosphatides by acid washing, and then is sent to a bleaching plant where it is dehydrated and treated with an activated clay for the removal of heavy metals, chlorophyll, polyethylene, and color (Fig. 1.9).

Fat Splitting Processes

The direct reaction of triglycerides with alkali followed by acidification or the treatment of triglyceride with water (with or without an acid catalyst) results in the splitting of fats into fatty acids and glycerin. The splitting of fats with water also can be performed by using various lipase enzymes as catalysts. The enzyme process is still in the developmental stages. The inter-esterification of triglycerides with methanol followed by acid or alkali cleavage of the resulting fatty methyl ester is used for the production of certain lower molecular weight (C_8-C_{10}) fatty acids; those methyl esters are generally the by-products of fatty alcohol production (Fig. 1.10).

The splitting of fats can be done either in a batch (Twitchell process) or in a continuous (Colgate-emery process) mode; the enzyme-based processes are still under development for commercial applications. A comparison of these processes follows.

Process	*Hydrolysis Time, hr*	*Conversion, %*
Twitchell batch	8-24	95
Continuous	1-3	98-99
Enzyme	72	98

The manufacture of fatty acids from trigly-cerides via their reaction with alkali followed by acidification is not used commercially. However, the recovery of fatty acids from alkali refining of fats (to produce acid soaps) and soap reboiling operations (the recovery of fatty acids from the acidification of soap waste streams) still are practiced in special situations.

Industrially, the fatty acids are produced predominantly by the high pressure, high temperature splitting of triglycerides. Both batch and continuous processes are available, the continuous process being in greater worldwide use today.

Batch Process. The triglyceride is heated with water at 150 to 250°C and 10 to 25 bar pressure. The splitting is achieved in from 6 to 10 hours, depending on the nature of the triglyceride feed: the higher the molecular weight of the triglyceride, the slower the splitting reaction. The reaction can be accelerated by increasing the temperature; under high pressure and at 225 to 260°C, no catalyst is required.

A typical commercial batch fat splitting plant (Lurgi) operates at 230°C/ 400 psig with over 96 per cent split yields achieved after two changes of water to remove the glycerin by-product. The sweetwater (glycerin water mixture) is circulated continuously from the base to the top of the autoclave in this process.

A number of other batch fat splitting plants also are available.

Continuous Fat Splitting Process. Continuous fat splitting currently is the most widely used process in the industry. In the single-stage splitting process, fat and water are fed countercurrently into a continuous flow column at up to 260°C/60bar pressure conditions. The glycerin by-product (sweet-water) produced in the splitting process is removed by water, thus accelerating the reaction equilibrium toward completion (Fig. 1.11). The high splitting temperature ensures adequate dissolution of the water phase in the fat to the extent that mechanical forces for contacting the two reactants are not required. The fat phase passes from bottom to top through the tower, the void volume of the tower acting as a reaction chamber. The water phase travels downward through the mixture of fat

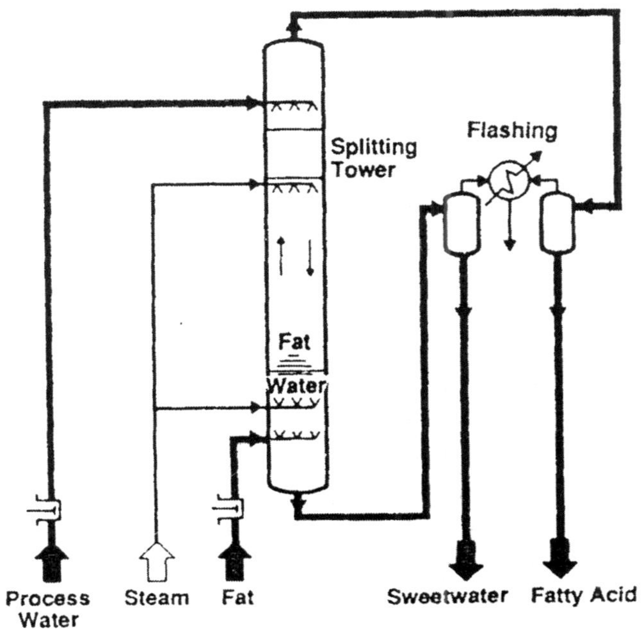

Fig. 1.11. Single-stage countercurrent fat splitting plant.

and fatty acid. The top and bottom sections of the tower also are designed to effect the transfer of heat from the products to the incoming reactant streams. Split yields of up to 99 per cent can be achieved by the use of pre-purified fats.

In summary, the continuous high pressure splitting of fats involves:

- The use of excess water to drive the reaction to completion and for removal of glycerin from the reaction zone.
- The use of a proper combination of temperature and pressure conditions to increase the solubility of water in the fat phase while maintaining the boundaries of the fat/water interface. These conditions also result in an increase in the rate of splitting.
- The possible use of an acid catalyst to accelerate the reaction rate.

Saponification/ Acidification Process. The recovery of fatty acids from soapstocks and soap reboil operations is of commercial value:

$$\underset{\text{(unrefined)}}{\text{Triglyceride}} \xrightarrow{\text{caustic refining}}$$

$$\underset{\text{(refined)}}{\text{Triglyceride}} + \underset{\text{(soapstock)}}{\text{RCOONa}} \xrightarrow{(H_2SO_4)} \text{RCOOH}$$

$$\underset{\text{(impure soap)}}{\text{RCOONa}} \xrightarrow{\text{reboiling}}$$

$$\underset{\text{(purified neat soap)}}{\text{RCOONa}} \xrightarrow{(H_2SO_4)} \underset{\text{(purified fatty acid)}}{\text{RCOOH}}$$

The recovery of fatty acids from soapstocks by a continuous process has been described: soapstocks obtained from degumming and alakli refining operations is subjected to a saponification step followed by controlled acidification for cost efficiency and pollution control.

The saponification/acidification route is used for the manufacture of fatty acids that are sensitive to excessive heat. The splitting of castor oil with NaOH at 100 to 220°C followed by acidification has been used to produce castor fatty acids.

Enzymatic Processes. The enzyme hydrolysis of triglycerides is catalyzed by lipases:

$$\text{Trigiyceride} + 3H_2O \xrightarrow{\text{enzyme}} 3RCOOH + \text{Glycerin}$$

Enzyme-based splitting of triglycerides is under active development and offers the following advantages over modern steam hydrolysis plants:

- The hydrolysis occurs under mild conditions (35-37°C, ambient pressures).
- The color quality of the products is superior.
- The capital investment may be lower.
- The split yields are equivalent.

The selection of a suitable lipase for a commercial viable process is based on the following criteria:

- It should be nonspecific and nonselective as to the structure of the triglyceride.
- It should be stable at above ambient processing temperatures, typically 45 to 65°C.
- It should be economically viable. (This aspect has initiated a number of ongoing studies on the recycling and immobilization aspects of lipase utilization for triglyceride hydrolysis.)

Methyl Ester-Based Processes. The fatty methyl esters are produced predominantly by the transesterification of fats and oils with methanol in the presence of an alkaline catalyst under very mild reaction conditions. They are used in the production of lauric-type (C_{12}) alcohols. The short-chain fatty methyl esters (C_8—C_{10}), produced as by-products via the fractional distillation of crude lauric-type (coconut, palm kernel) methyl esters, are converted to fatty acids via acidic or alkaline hydrolysis (Fig. 1.12). The hydrolysis of short-chain fatty methyl esters by steam splitting or Twitchell-type processes is not very efficient because of unfavourable equilibrium constants.

Fatty Acid Distillation

The removal of contaminants (unreacted triglycerides, odor and color bodies, polymerized matter, and decomposition products) from split fatty acids is achieved by simple distillation. The products obtained from such straight distillations are called "whole cut" fatty acids (whole coconut fatty acid, for example).

Triglyceride + CH_3OH ——> 3 $RCOOCH_3$ + glycerin

↓

(Fractionation)

C-8/C-10 Methyl Esters → (hydrolysis) → C-8 / C-10 Fatty Acids

C-12+ Methyl Esters → (hydrogenation) → C-12+ Fatty Alcohols

Fig. 1.12. Fatty acid production via methyl esters.

The separation of individual fatty acid components from whole fatty acid distillates is achieved by fractional distillation. However, fractional distillation cannot efficiently separate C_{16} to C_{18} saturated from the corresponding unsaturated fatty acids. In such cases, the melting points vary considerably with the degree of unsaturation; and this property is used for their separation via a number of industrial processes.

Distillation. Straight distillation is used for the removal of low-boiling (top cuts) and high-boiling (pitch) impurities from the split fatty acid stock. The distillation can be done either in a batch or a continuous manner. The batch distillation generally is employed for small-capacity manufacturing; continuous distillation is utilized for large-scale manufacturing and is highly automated (Fig. 1.13).

The split fatty acid (deaerated and preheated) is sent to a distillation column (Fig. 1.13), where it is vaporized rapidly by flowing over heated trays under vacuum (10mbar) with the addition of live steam (for fatty acid circulation and reduction of the partial pressure). The high boilers are removed by two stages of entrapment: the high boilers and bottoms from the distillation column pass through additional heated trays and a reboiler section to vaporize residual fatty acids from the bot-toms; the light end condenser traps the low boilers and the product. The heavy "bottoms" distillate is collected at the bottom portion of the still.

The distillation process is not used for the narrow-cut fractionation. However, by passing a second time through the distillation tower the main-cut distillates may be separated into a light and a heavy fraction; the light end is collected at the top products sections, whereas the heavy end is collected at the bottom residue section of the still. The separation of light and heavy fractions in the first pass is possible for high lauric-type split fatty acids (coconut and palm kernel fatty acids, for example).

The operation of a Lurgi fatty acid distillation system proceeds as follows. The crude fatty acid is dried and degassed in a vacuum dryer/degasser. It then is pumped into the distillation chamber (vacuum of 10-12 mbar) that is divided into 5 to 10 chambers by vertical plates. Each chamber is equipped with a heating element and a baffle. Steam is passed into the system to effect recycling of the liquid between the heating elements and the baffles by the principle of an air-lift pump. The fatty acid is sprayed on the baffles as a fine mist to allow it to evaporate easily; non vaporized liquid is recycled from the bottom. The fatty acid passes through each chamber in succession, the nondistillable residue being collected in the last chamber, from which it is discharged continuously. The fatty acid vapor is condensed in surface condensers. The typical yields of head cut, refined fraction, and residue are 1 to 5, 85 to 91, and 7 to 11 per cent, respectively.

Fractionation. The separation of individual components of a fatty acid mixture into high purity fraction (98% +) is achieved by fractional distillation. In a continuous fractionation still, the fractionation column can be equipped with trays, in the "Thormann" system, or with traditional packing to effect contact between the upward-moving vapors and the downward-flowing condensing liquid states.

A typical high-efficiency fractionation system (Fig. 1.14) consists of one continuous straight distillation and one or, preferably, two fractionation columns. This system is very efficient for the separation of low-boiling fatty acid components; a C_{12} fraction of 99.5 per cent purity from coconut fatty acid or a C_{22} fraction of 95 per cent purity from rapeseed fatty acid is readily obtained.

From an operational viewpoint, in rectification column 1 of Fig. 1.14, crude fatty acid is dried and vapourized with the addition of steam under a vacuum of 8 to 40 mbar. A mixed fraction is withdrawn from the column top. The product from the bottom of column 1 is vaporized in rectification column 2 with steam under a pressure of 6 to 8 mbar. The low-boiling fraction is collected in downstream scrubbers after the vapor has been condensed in surface condensers.

The separation scheme for coconut fatty acid is shown in Fig. 1.7. A variety of alternate fractionation schemes can readily be devised.

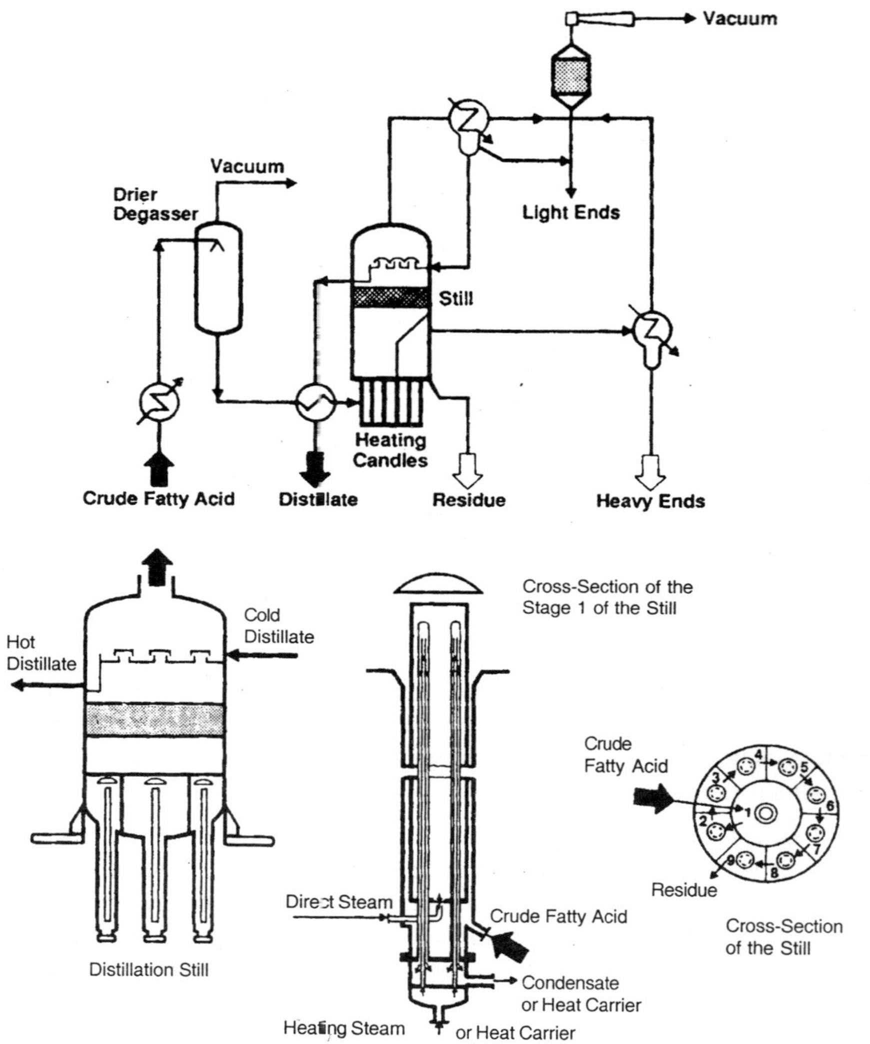

Fig. 1.13. Continuous fatty acid distillation plant.

Fatty acid distillation has been done for over 100 years. However, most of the currently practiced art has originated in the past 25 years. The majority of the recent work falls in the following areas:

- Improvements in the column design to reduce residence time.
- Enhancements of system design to minimize pressure drops.
- Demister designs for better air/effluent water pollution control.

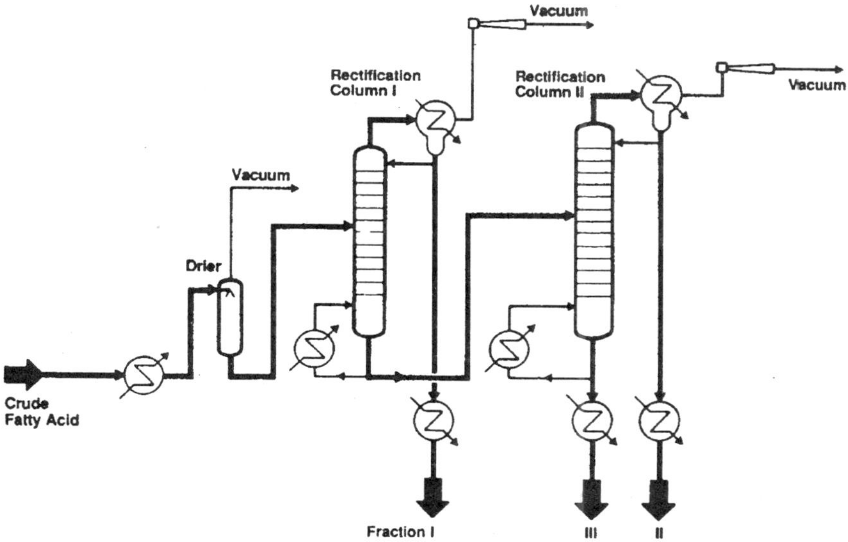

Fig. 1.14. Fatty acid fractionation.

Special Separation Methods

The separation of long-chain saturated fatty acids (C_{16}-C_{18}) from the corresponding unsaturated fatty acids by distillation is not practical because of the proximity of their boiling points. However, both the melting points and the solubility (in organic solvents) of these two types of fatty acids are vastly different. These properties are used to advantage for separating mixtures of saturated and unsaturated fatty acids into fractions that are rich in either saturated (stearin) or unsaturated (olein) components.

$$\text{Tallow fatty acid} \xrightarrow{\text{separation}} \underset{\text{(Stearin)}}{\text{Stearic acid}} + \underset{\text{(Olein)}}{\text{Oleic acid}}$$

The following processes are used commercially for the separation of such fatty acids: mechanical pressing, solvent crystallization, and hydrophilization.

Mechanical Pressing. This method, also called panning and pressing, is the simplest and oldest method, and is still practiced in many Third World countries. In the method, fatty acids is melted in shallow pans and then allowed to cool. The material transforms into a crystalline solid, with a liquid phase trapped between the crystals of the solid phase. The liquid portion (olein) is squeezed out by the application of mechanical force, separating it from the solid (stearin) component.

The pressing can be done by hydraulic presses in either a batch or a continuous mode. A multiple number of melting/crystallization/pressing cycles is utilized for obtaining fractions of increasing purity:

$$\text{Tallow fatty acid} \xrightarrow{\text{first pass}} \underset{\text{(Stearic acid)}}{\text{Single press}} \xrightarrow{\text{second pass}}$$

$$\underset{\text{(Stearic acid)}}{\text{Double press}} \xrightarrow{\text{third pass}} \underset{\text{(Stearic acid)}}{\text{Triple press}}$$

The unsaturation, as determined by the iodine value (IV), decreases from an IV of 10.0 for a single press to an IV of 1.0 for a triple press stearic acid grade.

Solvent Crystallization. Two processes, one utilizing acetone (Armour) and the other methanol (Emery), are well known. Using the latter, fatty acid is dissolved in 90 per cent aqueous methanol in a 1:2 acid/solvent ratio by the application of heat. The resulting solution then is cooled to — 15°C in a multi-tubular crystallization chamber equipped with scrapers for efficient heat transfer. The crystallized fatty acids are removed by filtration. The filter cake is melted and stripped of any residual solvent to give the refined stearin fraction, and then the liquid stearin is converted to flakes or

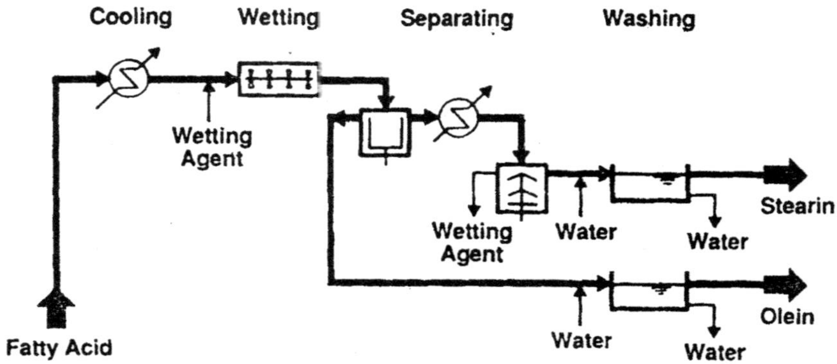

Fig. 1.15. Hydrophilization process for separation of olein and stearin.

powder by a variety of processes. The mother liquor from the above nitration is stripped to obtain the olein fraction. The separated stearin and olein fractions have a variety of commercial applications in both chemical and food industries.

Hydrophilization Process. In this process, olein and stearin are separated by forming a suspension of the stearin moiety in water with the aid of a surfactant followed by filtration to remove the stearin (Fig. 1.15). The mixture of fatty acids is melted and then partially crystallized by cooling. The resulting slurry, which is a mixture of olein (liquid) and stearin (crystalline solid), is mixed with water containing a wetting agent (sodium dodecyl-benzene sulfonate, sodium lauryl-sulfate). After mixing for a specified period, the slurry is centrifuged; the light fraction provides the liquid olein moiety, the middle fraction is a suspension of solid stearin in water, and the bottom portion is water/surfactant solution.

Thermodynamically, the fatty acid crystals, after being wetted by the surfactant solution, transfer from the liquid oil into water solution. The oil droplets then coalesce to give the lighter olein phase. The separated stearin is remelted to remove residual water/surfactant, and then reprocessed to the desired level of purity.

Although the quality of the final product from these three processes is fairly comparable, hydrophilization currently is the most widely used process for the separation of stearic and oleic acids.

SYNTHETIC DETERGENTS

Introduction

Synthetic detergents initially were developed as soap substitutes in an economy that was running short of edible fats and oils. These synthesized compounds were more resistant to calcium salt formation in hard water and generally provided improved wetting, cleansing, and surfactancy over soaps. The term "synthetic detergents" has been shortened to "syndets" to describe detergent compositions that are comprised of the synthetic active ingredient, water hardness control agents (builders), and other detergent additives. "Surface active agent" has been shortened to "surfactant" to describe the surface active principal or active ingredient (AI). Since their introduction in the 1940s, synthetic detergents have continued to grow in both total volume and percentage of detergent use.

Whether in liquid or in powdered forms, present detergent products are complex mixtures of several ingredients. The formulations consist primarily of surfactants, builders, and other additives designed to maximize performance for the consumer while maintaining reasonable raw material and manufacturing costs. Recent trends in both liquid and powdered product forms show increased utilization of mixed builder and surfactant systems. Also, performance additives such as bleaches, bleach activators, softeners, and enzymes often are present in the detergent to boost overall performance. However, in all products, the backbone of the detergent is the surfactant/builder system.

Surfactant Hydrophile-Hydrophobe Balance

As the term indicates, surface active agents are active at surfaces by preferential orientation of the molecule. This suggests that some built-in characteristic of the surfactant controls or contributes to molecular activity. Surfactants can be tailored for effective use in either aqueous or non-aqueous systems, depending upon their solubility characteristics. An optimum hydrophile-hydrophobe balance generally exists for a specific detergent application and for the compound class used. This optimum composition often is developed through evaluation of required hydrophil-hydrophobe characteristics of the application. For example, alkylbenzene is slightly surface active in non-aqueous media but insoluble and ineffective in water. Addition of a single SO_3H group through alkylbenzene sulfonation provides high water solubility and excellent surfactant characteristics in water, but insolubility in petroleum solvents. If alkylbenzene is di- or trisulfonated, the compound becomes more water-soluble and loses much of its surface activity, operating essentially as an additional electrolyte in the system. In both cases, the hydrophile balance is exceeded, with insufficient hydrophobe influence to increase the preferential orientation necessary for surfactancy. However, neutralization of the SO_3H group of highly water-soluble alkyl benzene sulfonic acid with a long chain amine produces an effective nonaqueous surfactant. A similar effect of decreasing water solubility and increasing non-aqueous surfactancy can be achieved by increasing the alkylbenzene carbon side chain length from C_{12} to C_{18} or higher.

Non-ionic surfactant systems depend upon a multiplicity of oxygen and hydrogen bond linkages to effect hydrophile-hydrophobe balances similar to those exhibited by SO_3 solubilizing groups in alkylbenzene sulfonate. Ethylene oxide-adduct types of nonionics can be varied in chain length to impact hydrophobe characteristics. Additionally, adjustments in degree of ethoxylation can be used to modify the hydrophile balance.

In studying the literature, one might believe that lauryl sulfate, sodium stearate, dodecyl-benzene sulfonate, and so on, are pure compounds. Commercially available compounds are mixtures of homologs, with lauryl sulfate being a generic designation for a mixture of sulfates whose largest fraction is derived from the C_{12} alcohol; the remainder come from higher and lower alcohols. The total distribution of homologs is dependent upon the degree of fractionation in the original alcohol production. The same is true for alkylbenzene derivatives and nonyl-phenol compounds, while soaps are mixtures of the various fatty acids natural to fats and oils. Non-ionic ethylene oxide adducts are further examples of mixtures; the non-aethylene glycol ether designation suggests that this compound is the primary constituent, but ethylene oxide adds to individual hydrophobe molecules in a manner that can yield a normal Poisson distribution of adducts, with the 9-molar adduct representing the distribution mean. Although it might seem that a competitive edge could be gained by supplying a highly purified product, mixtures frequently permit usage where pure compounds are less effective. Long experience with soaps and synthetics shows that except for highly specialized purposes, pure compounds are not competitive with properly chosen soap or synthetic mixtures.

Anionic Surfactants

Alkylaryl Sulfonates. Alkylbenzene sulfonates have been the "workhorse" of the detergent industry for more than 25 years. They account for approximately 50 per cent of the total synthetic anionic detergent volume used in liquid and spray-dried formulations. Three basic grades of alkylate (alkylbenzene) are manufactured, with molecular weight ranges of approximately 235, 240, and 260. In general, the C_{10-12} range alkylates are used for light duty liquid systems. The C_{12-14} range alkylates are used in heavy duty liquid and spray-dried detergents. The alkylate is sulfonated and neutralized, primarily to a sodium salt, prior to use in detergent formulations.

Prior to 1965, alkylbenzene production was synthesized from petroleum tetrapropylene reacted with an aluminium chloride or hydrogen fluoride catalyst and benzene. The resultant alkylate was a "hard" branched-chain compound that was considered slowly biodegradable. A straight-chain alkylate, termed LAB (linear alkylbenzene), has been produced since 1965 in the United States. Extensive research has demonstrated biodegradation effectiveness in sewage treatment plants in excess of 95 per cent.

Three basic processes have been practiced for linear alkylbenzene manufacture. The most prevalent route of alkylbenzene manufacture is by partial dehydrogenation of paraffins, followed by alkylation of benzene with a mixed olefin/paraffin feedstock, using liquid hydrogen fluoride catalyst. A second route is via partial chlorination of paraffins, followed by alkylation of the chloroparaffin/paraffin feedstock in the presence of an aluminium chloride catalyst. The third process uses partial chlorination, but includes a dehydro-chlorination to olefin step prior to alkylation with aluminium chloride or hydrogen fluoride.

Distillation is used in all processes to separate alkylation reaction products into the targeted detergent alkylate homolog distributions. A coproduct stream of high molecular weight linear alkylbenzene and dialkylben-zenes also is produced, for use in lubricant detergents and industrial applications.

Products with low 2-phenyl isomer content (13-22%) are produced by hydrogen fluoride alkylation of internal olefins from paraffin dehydrogenation. High 2-phenyl products (25-35%) are produced from aluminium chloride alkylation of chloroparaffins. Generally, high 2-phenyl products are preferred for use in liquid detergent applications because of the improved solubility found with the higher 2-phenyl level. Low 2-phenyl alkylates also can be used for this application, with additional usage of hydrotropes.

Sulfonation. For detergent use, the alkylate must be sulfonated to an acid form and then neutralized with a base such as sodium hydroxide. The major uses of the neutralized slurry are in the production of spray-dried detergent and both light and heavy duty liquid detergents. The slurry also can be drum-dried to a powder or flake, or spray-dried to light-density granules. Dried forms are used primarily for institutional and industrial cleaning applications and car washing compounds. The sulfonation reaction is quite exothermic and almost instantaneous. In order to prevent decomposition and maintain optimum color of the resultant sulfonic acid, an efficient reactor heat removal system is necessary.

Oleum and sulfur trioxide are used routinely for sulfonation, with the latter growing in popularity in recent years. Oleum sulfonation requires relatively inexpensive equipment and can be accomplished by either batch or continuous processes. However, the oleum process has major disadvantages in the SO_3 cost/lb (as H_2SO_4), the need for spent acid stream disposal, and potential corrosion problems due to sulfuric acid generation. The oleum process typically yields an 88 to 91 per cent purity sulfonic acid with the remainder consisting of approximately 6 to 10 per cent H_2SO_4, 0.5

to 1.5 per cent water, and 0.5 to 1.0 per cent unsulfonated oils. Reactions involved in oleum sulfonation are shown below.

Sulfonation:

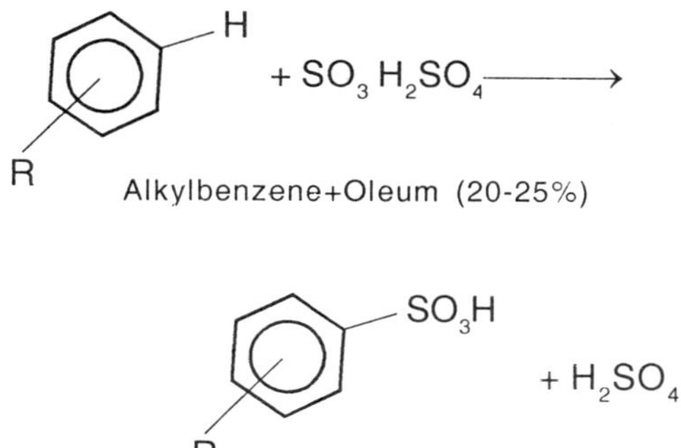

$+ SO_3\ H_2SO_4 \longrightarrow$

Alkylbenzene+Oleum (20-25%)

$+ H_2SO_4$

Sulfonic acid + 96% Sulfuric acid

Neutralisation:

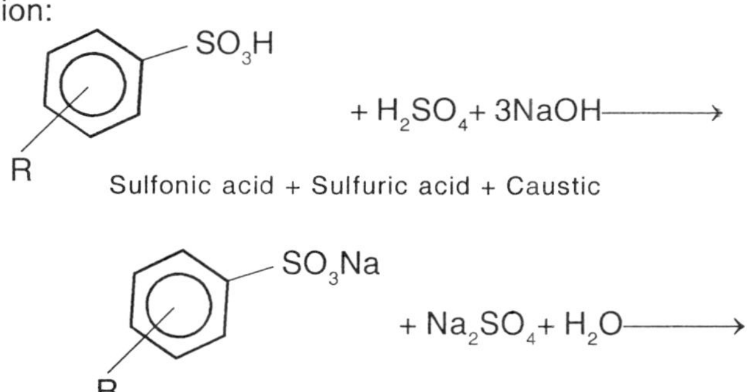

$+ H_2SO_4 + 3NaOH \longrightarrow$

Sulfonic acid + Sulfuric acid + Caustic

$+ Na_2SO_4 + H_2O \longrightarrow$

Sodium alkylbenzene sulfonate + Sodium sulfate + Water

A typical batch oleum sulfonation process is shown in Figure 1.16. Four basic processing operations are utilized prior to neutralization: sulfonation, digestion, dilution, and phase separation. Mixing of the alkylate and oleum is done in the sulfonation stage. Heat removal from the exothermic reaction is achieved by reactor jacketing and/or recirculating heat exchanger loops. Key variables in controlling alkylbenzene conversion and acid color are the temperature, acid strength, reaction time, and oleum-to-alkylate ratio. The product leaving the sulfonation zone is aged or digested 15 to 30 minutes to allow reaction completion; at this point, the reaction product is a mixture of sulfonic acid and sulfuric acid. Following digestion, the mixture is diluted with water to quench the reaction. The reaction mass then is fed to a separator to allow gravity settling of the spent sulfuric acid

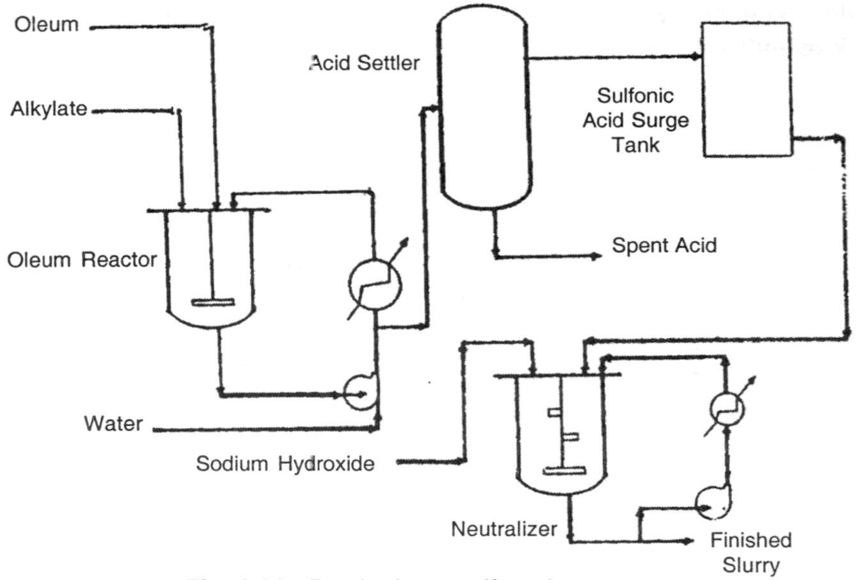

Fig. 1.16. Batch oleum sulfonation process.

layer from the lighter sulfonic acid. The lower spent acid layer contains approximately 75 to 80 per cent sulfuric acid; and the upper layer consists of approximately 88 to 91 per cent sulfonic acid, 0.5 to 1 per cent

Sulfonation:

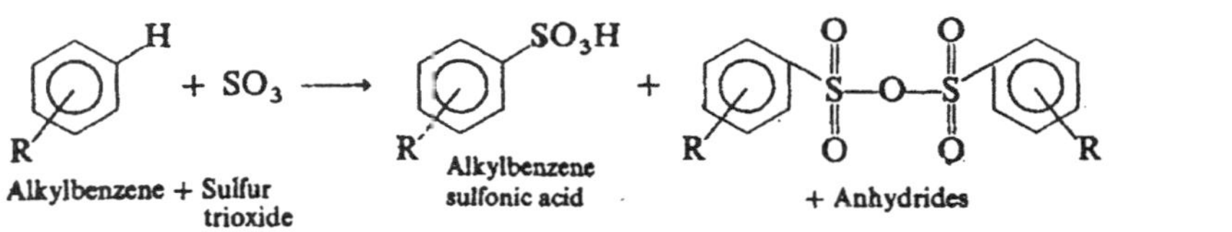

Hydration:

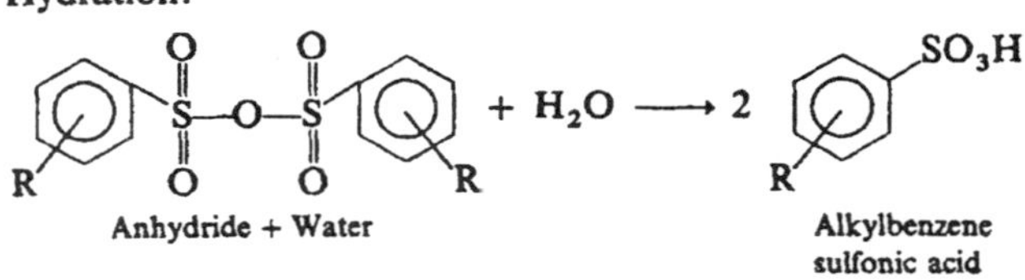

Neutralization:

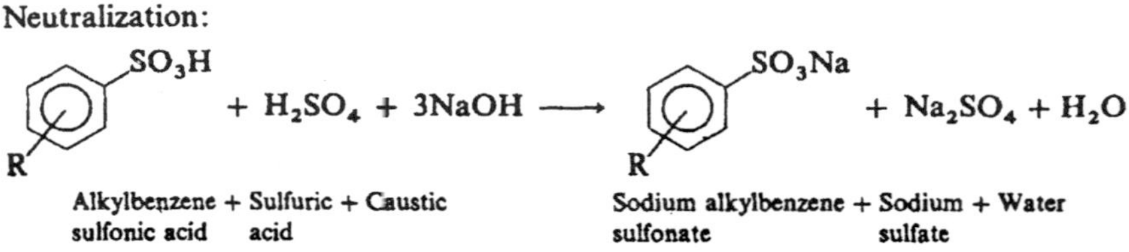

unsulfonated oils, and 6 to 10 per cent sulfuric acid. The separation time is dependent upon the separator vessel configuration, sulfonic acid viscosity, temperature, and degree of aeration in feed streams.

The gaseous air/SO_3 sulfonation process normally generates a product composed of 95 to 98 per cent purity sulfonic acid with 1 to 2 per cent sulfuric acid, 0.5 to 1.5 per cent water, and 1.0 to 2.5 per cent unsulfonated oils. Although the initial capital investment costs are much higher than those for an oleum process, relative sulfonic acid yields and spent acid disposal costs are substantially lower. The chemical reactions involved in air/SO_3 sulfonation are as follows:

A typical continuous air/SO_3 sulfonation process is outlined in Fig. 1.17. Sulfur trioxide for the sulfonation reaction is either produced from vaporization of liquid SO_3 or generated on-site by burning sulfur and then

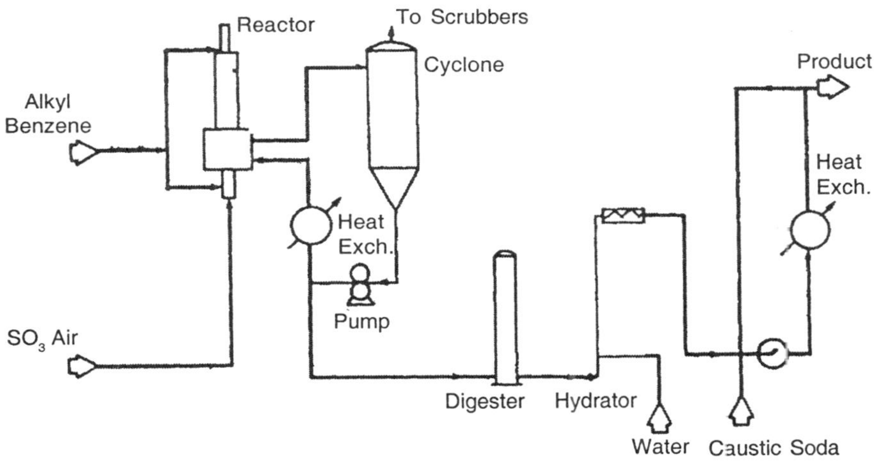

Fig. 1.17. Alkyl benzene sulfonation schematic flow diagram.

catalytically converting SO_2 to SO_3 over a vanadium pentoxide catalyst. Increased shipping regulations and sensitivity to storage of the highly hazardous liquid SO_3 have increased the trend toward on-site sulfur trioxide generation. The vaporized sulfur trioxide is diluted to 4 to 8 wt. % in dry air prior to sulfonation. The air serves as a diluent and heat sink for the highly exothermic sulfonation reaction.

In the sulfonation reactor, the molar ratio of SO_3/alkylate is controlled between 1.03/1.0 and 1.06/1.0 to achieve optimum conversion to sulfonic acid without increased side reactions or color degradation. The Chemithon, Ballestra, and Mazzoni units have unique falling film reactor designs to provide intimate mixing of the alkylate and air/SO_3 streams. The reactor temperature is controlled between 110 and 150°F, depending upon the desired production rates and product quality targets. Digestion and hydrolysis temperatures are controlled between 110 and 125°F, During hydrolysis, approximately 2 parts of water per 100 parts of reaction product are added to convert acid anhydrides to sulfonic and sulfuric acid.

Sulfur trioxide sulfonation also is practiced in processes that use liquid SO_2 as a refrigerant and a solvent. The product quality is high, and the sulfonic acid color is low because of low temperatures and rapid removal of the reaction exotherm via SO_2 vaporization. Equipment consists of fairly simple glass-lined reactors equipped with gaseous SO_2 recovery. Control of SO_2 recovery, frothing, and purging of SO_2 from the reaction products are keys to achieving a high-quality product. As in the case of air/SO_3 sulfonation, this process can be used for all detergent-grade surfactants, including alkylbenzene, alcohol ethoxylates, and alcohols.

A novel venturi reactor has also been patented by Chemithon Corporation. The organic reactant is sulfonated by injection into a stream of gas containing sulfur trioxide at a venturi. The reaction mixture is quenched and recycled downstream until sulfonation is complete. This reactor design is utilized primarily for highly viscous, high molecular weight specialty surfactants for industrial applications such as lubrication oil additives.

Neutralization of sulfonic acid is similar in the case of either an oleum or a SO_3 sulfonation process. The sulfonic acid can be neutralized with aqueous solutions of base; that is, KOH, NH_4OH, NaOH, or alkanolamines. The sodium salts are used for formulating spray-dried detergents for household laundry consumption. Ammonium and alkanolamine neutralized salts generally are used in light duty liquid detergents. In general, neutralized salts from oleum sulfonation contain approximately 8 to 10 per cent sodium sulfate, where as those from air/SO_3 sulfonation contain only 2 to 3 percent sodium sulfate.

Sulfation. For sulfation of alcohols or ethoxylated alcohols, falling film reactors also are used, but cooling water and sulfation temperatures are adjusted to lower values for these raw materials. The digestion and hydration steps are not required in sulfation, and these systems are bypassed. The acids are neutralized immediately to minimize degradation and side reactions in storage.

Typical sulfation reactions for alcohols and alcohol ethoxylates are shown in the following equations:

$$R\text{—}OH + SO_3 \rightarrow R\text{—}O\text{—}SO_3H$$

$$R\text{—}(OC_2H_4)_n\text{—}OH + SO_3 \rightarrow R\text{—}(OC_2H_4)_n\text{—}O\text{—}SO_3H$$

Typical processes for air/SO_3 sulfonation of alpha olefins are shown in Fig. 1.18 (alpha olefins), Bleaching often is required in the post-hydrolysis steps to remove color bodies prior to neutralization.

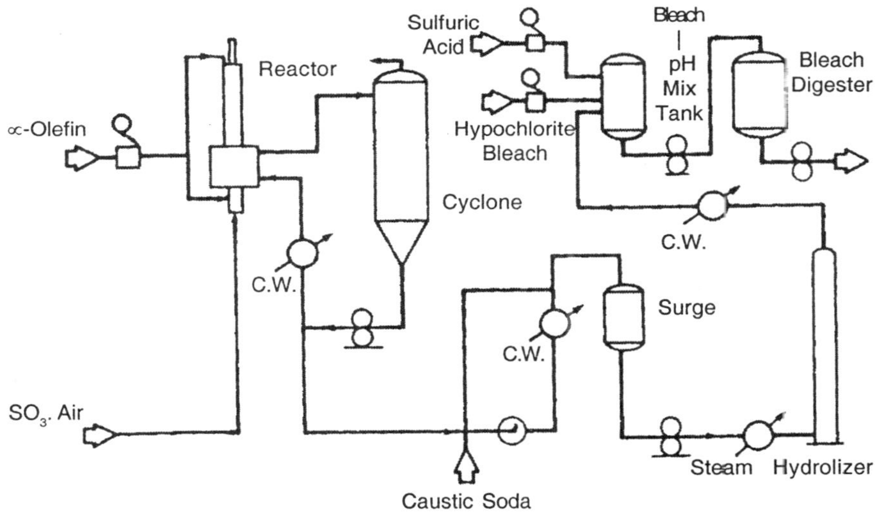

Fig. 1.18. Alpha-olefin sulfonation schematic flow diagram.

For laundry detergents containing mixtures of alkylbenzene sulfonate, alcohol sulfates, or alcohol ethoxy sulfates, sulfonation reactions are either campaigned or produced in two separate units—one for sulfonation, one for sulfation. The respective acids can be blended prior to neutralization to yield a superior product to one made by post-blending of the neutral salts.

Neutralization. Sulfonic acid also can be processed to a dry powdered form by stoichiometric neutralization with a base salt, such as sodium carbonate. The neutralized mixture is slightly moist at this stage, and requires blending with other detergent additives to complete its transition to a dry free-flowing powdered detergent. The Ballestra process mixes the acid and salts together, whereas the Staffer process meters the acid and caustic streams into a tumbling product bed. The A. G. Hoechst process degasses the sulfonic acid prior to neutralization. Removal of SO_2 or SO_3 gas and improved temperature control produce a neutralized paste of excellent colour quality.

Non-ionic Surfactants

Non-ionic surfactants are increasingly popular active ingredients for liquid heavy duty laundry detergent formulations. The majority of non-ionic surfactants are polyoxyethylene or polyoxypropylene derivatives of alkylphenol, fatty acids, alcohols, and amides. It has been estimated that approximately one ethylene oxide unit is required to solobilize each methylene unit. Thus, by changing the ratio of ethylene oxide to fatty acid, the nature of the surfactant can be modified from an oil-soluble to a water-soluble product. This versatility makes applications possible in numerous areas, such as detergents, agricultural products, metal protection, emulsion polymerization, textile applications, deinking, and penetrants. The reaction of ethylene oxide with fatty acids was described initially in 1928. Shick and Jungermann have edited very thorough volumes concerning non-ionic surfactants.

Ethoxylation. In processing, the fatty acid and catalyst are charged to a reactor and purged with an inert gas such as nitrogen. The partial pressure is adjusted so that the explosive limits, of the gas mixture in the reactor during and after addition of ethylene oxide are not exceeded. The mass is heated to reaction temperatures of 115 to 200°C, and ethylene oxide is added until the desired pressure is reached. Heat removal rates control the rate of reaction. Excessive cooling can result in excessive absorption of ethylene oxide into the reaction mixture, which can result in sudden reaction followed by overpressure. The reactor temperature and pressure are controlled until the desired quantity of ethylene oxide has been added. Then the ethylene oxide addition is discontinued, the batch is cooled, and the catalysts are removed by filtration.

Other examples of non-ionics commonly used in syndets are glycols, glycerols, sugar esters, and alkanolamides. Polyethylene glycol esters of fatty acids are produced by reaction with ethylene oxide or by esterification of the fatty acid with polyethylene glycols. The reaction with ethylene oxide is described as:

$$RCOOH + nC_2H_4O \rightarrow RCOO(C_2H_4O)_nH$$

Laurie, palmitic, stearic, and oleic acid also are ethoxylated and widely used as detergents and emulsifiers.

Amphoteric Surfactants

These surfactants contain both cationic and anionic groups. The products are relatively expensive because of the raw materials involved and processing costs. Typical applications include shampoos, bubble baths, and other toiletries and cosmetics where mildness is a major concern. A typical product is shown below:

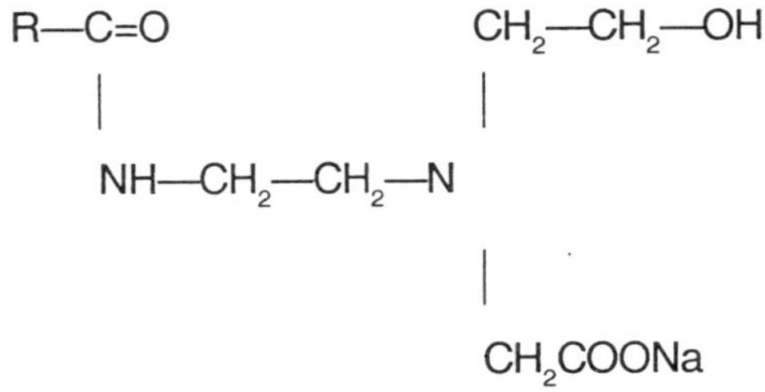

N-Beta-hydroxyethyl-NV-beta-carboxymethyl fatty acid amidoethylamine, sodium salt

Other examples of fatty amine oxides include dimethylcar-boxymethyl coconut fatty acid, propylamide ammonium betaine, alkylamide betaine, and cocamidopropylamine oxide. Additional varieties are cited by McCutcheon.

Alkylolamides

A wide variety of amine condensates can function as foam boosters, wetting agents in aqueous/nonaqueous systems, emulsifiers, and dispersants. These are mainly reaction products of diethanolamine (DEA) or mono-ethanolamide (MEA) with fatty acids at a 2:1 ratio. Excess DEA converts both the amino and the amido ester to an active 2:1 product, N,N-bis(2-hydroxyethyl) lauramide. In detergents, alkylamides are used at 1 to 2 per cent levels as foam stabilizers. The general formula for alkylanolamide is:

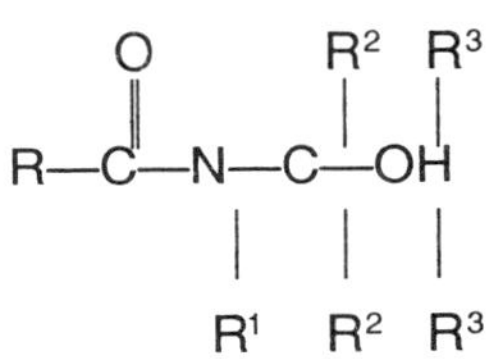

R^1 = alkyl; R^2 = hydrogen, alkyl, or hydroxyalkyl; and $R^{2\text{-}3}$ = hydrogen or alkyl

Cationic Surfactants

Cationic surfactants tend to be specialty items that are tailored for diverse uses: germicides, textile applications, sensitizers, flotation agents corrosion inhibitors, and fabric softeners. Their primary growth has been in fabric softeners for home laundry detergent. Because cationics are antistatic agents, they perform well in removing static charges associated with synthetic fabrics.

These surfactants have at least one hydrophobic group attached directly to a positively charged nitrogen molecule. Cationic surfactants may be formed from nitriles, amines, amide-linked amines, or quaternary nitrogen bases. Significant literature reviews cover this subject in detail.

Detergent Builders

Builders typically are added to a detergent formulation- to extend or improve the formulation cleaning performance across a wide range of use conditions. The combination of builders and surfactants exhibits a synergistic effect to boost total detergency and cleaning efficacy, as compared with an equal amount of either compound alone. The major properties and characteristics that are desirable for a compound to be considered a detergent builder include:

1. The ability to control water hardness and other metal ions.
2. A contribution to final product alkalinity.
3. Buffer capacity in the proper pH range.
4. Deflocculation capability.
5. Compatibility with other formulation ingredients and detergent additives.
6. Consumer safety.
7. Environmental acceptability.
8. Processibility.
9. Adequate cost/performance.

In today's detergent products, a variety of builder materials are used singly or in combination with other builders to contribute unique properties for final product performance enhancement.

Phosphates. Tetrasodium pyrophosphate ($Na_4P_2O_7$—TSPP) became commercially available in the mid-1930s and soon gained acceptance as the preferred builder for soap-formulated products. The combination of TSPP and sodium carbonate was more effective than either ingredient used separately. By the mid-1940s sodium tripolyphosphate ($Na_5P_3O_{10}$—STP) was commercially available and had supplanted TSPP as the preferred builder because of superior detergent processing, solubility, and hardness ion sequestering characteristics. Sequestration is defined as the reaction of a cation with an anion to form a soluble complex. The sequestration of Ca^{++} and Mg^{++} ions leads to softened water and is the most important function of any detergent builder.

Sodium tripolyphosphate is the major builder ingredient in heavy duty laundry detergents, automatic dishwashing compounds, and industrial and institutional cleaners. In liquid consumer laundry detergents, sodium citrate has displaced tetrapotassium pyrophosphate ($K_4P_2O_7$—TKPP), but TKPP use in industrial and institutional liquids is preferred because of its superior solubility and sequestration characteristics.

Other possible builder salts include sodium trimetaphosphate, trisodium and tripotassium phosphates, and sodium acid pyrophosphate. Each has a unique property whose utility is dependent upon the particular detergent system or application. The book *Phosphorus and Its Compounds* presents a complete assessment of phosphates and their role in detergents.

Silicates. Both sodium and potassium silicate solids or solutions have valued functional characteristics such as emunification, buffering, deflocculation, and anti-redeposition ability. Silicates also provide corrosion protection to metal parts in washing appliances, as well as to the surfaces of china patterns and metal utensils in automatic dishwashers. Silicates are manufactured in either liquid, crystalline, or powdered form; and they also vary in degree of alkalinity. The alkalinity of the silicate provides buffering capacity in the presence of acid soils and enhances the sequestration ability of the builder system in the formulation. The silicate/alkali ratios of the silicate are selected by the formulator to meet specific product requirements. Silicate ratios of 1/1 commonly are used in dry blending applications, with liquid silicates with silicate/alkali ratios of 2/1 and higher commonly used in laundry and automatic-dishwashing applications.

In using liquid silicates, it is essential that the proper silicate ratio be selected for various process and performance parameters. For example, liquid silicates containing a high SiO_2/Na_2O ratio are susceptible to forming insolubles if overdried. In agglomeration processes, the use of lower SiO_2/Na_2O ratios of liquid silicates requires additional mixing, aging, and drying to obtain a crisp, free-flowing product.

Carbonates. In certain areas of the United States, phosphate sales have been legislatively banned from use in laundry detergent products. In these areas, sodium carbonate (Na_2CO_3) or a combination of sodium carbonate and zeolite has replaced STP as the builder in granular laundry products. Sodium carbonate softens water by precipitating the hardness minerals, and it is one of the most economical sources of alkalinity for detergents and provides some degree of soil dispersion and suspending action. Sodium carbonate is commonly used in powdered laundry detergent, automatic-dishwashing compounds, hard surface cleaners, and presoak formulations.

Sodium Citrate. Sodiumcitrate($Na_3C_6H_{25}O_7$) has builder characteristics due to its ability to sequester water hardness ions and deflocculate soils. Sodium citrate's principal use is in liquid laundry products, with limited use in dry powders.

Zeolites. An important alternative builder for powdered laundry detergents in regions where phosphate salts have been legislatively banned for laundry product use, zeolites are crytalline hydrated aluminosilicates of Group I and Group II elements. They are sodium, calcium, magnesium, potassium, strontium, and barium salts, and appear in natural or synthesized forms. Zeolite Type 4A (empirical formula—$Na_2O \bullet Al_2O_3 \bullet 2SiO_2 \bullet 4.5H_2O$, commonly called Zeolite A) is the most widely used form for laundry detergents.

Zeolites are not water-soluble, but they reduce calcium water hardness by ion exchange. The calcium ion passes through the zeolite pore openings and exchanges with the sodium ion. Magnesium ions are not significantly removed by zeolites because of the large radius of magnesium; therefore, zeolites are used in conjunction with other builders such as sodium carbonate to control magnesium and other ions present in the wash water.

Sodium Nitrilotriacetate. One of the first compounds developed as a replacement for sodium tripolyphosphate was sodium nitrilitriacetate ($N(CH_2COONa)_3 \bullet H_2O$—NTA), which has excellent sequestration and/or chelating ability. This product was quickly accepted by the detergent industry as an alternate builder, bat its use in detergents was suspended in the United States in December 1970, when three major detergent manufacturers voluntarily agreed to discontinue its U.S. usage because of preliminary evidence indicating that the compound could be teratogenic. Subsequent assessment by the EPA, culminating nearly 10 years of extensive safety studies, indicated that the risk to persons exposed to

NTA from detergents is not significant. However, the EPA stated that NTA should not be used in products such as shampoos, hand-dishwashing detergents, foods, or other consumer products designed for direct dermal or oral exposure. Although NTA has not been used in U.S. household laundry products since the voluntary ban except in brief test markets, it has been widely used as a detergent builder in Canada since 1970, and in the United States in industrial and institutional cleaning products. NTA normally is used in liquids as the primary builder or as a supplement to phosphates in spray-dried detergents.

Detergent Additives

In addition to detergent builders and surfactants, there are numerous additives that perform other specific functions in detergents. A few of the most widely used materials are described below.

Sodium Sulfate. Although considered a builder by some manufacturers, sodium sulfate (Na_2SO_4) contributes little to detergent performance. It is commercially available from natural sources and as a by-product from rayon processing. In dry mix and agglomerated type products, sodium sulfate is used to improve finished product flow characteristics. In spray-dried products, sodium sulfate acts as an inert "filler" and aids in density control and flow characteristics.

Sodium Chloride. Sodium chloride (NaCl) still is used by some formulators in detergent manufacture, its main function being as an inert "filler" or diluent. In spray-drying applications, NaCl is used to control slurry viscosity and the density of the spray-dried bead or graules. Although salt is used to some extent in automatic dishwashing formulations, its use is not recommended because of potential machine and dishware corrosion.

Sodium Carboxymethylcellulose (NaCMC). The surfactants employed in synthetic detergents are very effective in removing soil and stains from the surface of the washed fabric. Under heavy soil loading, there is a tendency for these soils to redeposit on the fabric. NaCMC is effective in reducing soil redeposition at formulation levels of 0.1 to 0.5 per cent.

Optical Brighteners. Although the surfactant system in detergents cleans clothes effectively, white fabric tends to "gray" or lose its white appearance after numerous washes. Optical brighteners are added to detergent formulations to visually improve the "whiteness" or brightness of the fabric.

All major liquid or powdered detergent products contain one or more fluorescent whitening agents. Substantive to most fabrics, these materials absorb ultraviolet radiation and convert it to a visible blue-white reflectance range. This characteristics masks the natural yellowing or graying of the fabric. Most brightener systems are more effective on cotton than on synthetic fabrics. The usage range varies from 0.05 to 0.2 per cent in the detergent formulation.

Hydrotropes. Hydrotropes are used primarily in liquid detergents to increase the solubility of less soluble ingredients and improve storage stability. They also are used occasionally as viscosity modifiers in the slurry phase of manufacturing spray-dried detergent powders. Reduction of the detergent slurry viscosity improves its processing characteristics, reduces product bulk density, and ensures crisp, free-flowing granules. The most common hydrotropes are the ammonium, potassium, or sodium salts of toluene, xylene, or cumene sulfonates.

Enzymes. Proteolytic and amyolytic enzymes have been designed for use as adjuvants in detergent systems to remove stains. These complete proteinaceous molecules act as catalysts and tend to break down particular soils and stains to a form more readily removed from fabrics. These ingredients are used in presoak detergent systems and some liquid and powdered laundry detergents.

Pearlescent-Opacifying-Thickening Agents. These compounds are used in liquid detergent systems to produce a specific aesthetic effect. Pearlescent compounds (bismuth, titanium dioxide-coated mica) normally are insoluble in water or alcohol, but are dispersed in emulsion systems. Opacifying agents (e.g., water-soluble salts of styrene and maleic anhydride) are used to reduce translucence, modify the viscosity characteristics of the liquids, and provide a creamlike texture or pearlescent effect to the product.

Thickeners such as bentonite clays are used in providing rheological modification for automatic-dishwashing liquids. The clays impart a thixotropic nature to the liquids that allows sufficient yield stress to prevent premature dispensing into the automatic dishwasher. The use level in automatic-dishwashing liquids is at 0.5 to 1.0 per cent.

Anticaking Agents. Because of the reduced phosphate levels and use of nonphosphate builders in some powdered laundry detergents, flow characteristics and caking tendencies have changed. Products formulated with increased anionic active levels and higher sodium carbonate content tend to exhibit compaction caking in the detergent carton. Anticaking agents have been added to the formula to reduce this tendency, especially in warm humid climates. A wide range of products are available, including sodium benzoate, tricalcium phosphate, colloidal aluminium oxide, silicon dioxide, magnesium silicate, calcium stearate, and microcrystalline cellulose.

Spray Drying

A major portion of the powdered laundry detergents today are spray-dried. In this process, the detergent raw materials are mixed with water to form a thick paste or slurry, atomized into spherical droplets, and dried to produce a crisp, free-flowing granular product. The art of spray drying was first patented in 1883 but was not practiced to any extent until the 1930s. With the advent of synthetic detergents in the 1940s spray drying became the dominant method of detergent processing. The advantages of spray drying are numerous; for example, the product density can be varied from 0.20 to 0.80 g/cc, the detergent granule solubility is significantly improved, the production rates are increased, and multiple formulations can be prepared using the same equipment. The major disadvantages of spray drying are the initial capital investment required, its relative inflexibility in varying products sizing and density in some units, and the energy-intensive nature of the process. Spray drying is divided into several process steps: selection of formulations, slurry preparation, atomization, drying, conditioning of the product, post-additions, packaging, waste reclamation, and pollution control.

Spray-dried detergents are manufactured for use in locations where various legislative restrictions may limit phosphate use. Typical formulations are shown in Table 1.3.

Slurry preparation of the detergent formulation is considered to be the single most important factor in spray drying. Control of the raw material order of addition, slurry solids level, slurry temperatures, viscosity, and aeration enables manufacturers to deliver the desired final product characteristics. Essentially, the spray tower itself is simply a contained heat source that removes moisture at a uniform rate dependent upon the quality and the quantity of feed to the dryer. If feed variables are not controlled, variability in the density, moisture level, aging, and/or packaging characteristics increases. For example, if the slurry solids level is not constant (±2%), the evaporative load, production rate, particle sizing, and moisture levels of the spray-dried granules will vary. Compensating for non-uniform feed to the spray tower is difficult because of the interaction of controllable variables such as tower temperature, pump pressure, gas velocity, and so on. Although some minor tower adjustments sometimes are necessary to control process conditions, the major control for routine operations is the preparation and uniformity of the detergent slurry.

Slurries are prepared via batch, semi-continuous, and continuous crutching units. A continuous slurry preparation system is shown in Fig. 1.19. Solids levels normally are kept as high as possible (64-72%) to reduce the heat requirements and maximize the tower throughput. With the introduction of "soft" (biodegradable) alkylbenzene, the sodium tripolyphosphate used in processing slowly changed from low temperature rise (TR) grades to high TR grades. Low TR sodium tripolyphosphate tends to form more "lumps" and "grit" during hydration from the anhydrous to the hexahydrate phase in the mixing stage than the high TR grade. It is advantageous to maximize sodium tripolyphosphate hexahydrate ($Na_5P_3O_{10}$-$6H_2O$) formation, as this water is "bound" and will be retained in the final product. The bound water acts as an inert filler and contributes to the free-flowing characteristics during conveying, storage, and packaging.

TABLE 1.3 Spray-Dried Detergent Formulations

Ingredients (100% Active Basis)	*Phosphate-Built Detergent, % in Formula*	*Non-Phosphate-Built Detergent, % in Formula*
Sodium tripolyphosphate	20-35	0
Sodium carbonate	5-10	10-40
Zeolite A	0	15-25
Sodium alkylbenzene sulfonate	0-15	0-20
Sodium alcohol ethoxylate	0-15	0-20
Sodium alcohol ether sulfate	0-5	0-5
Sodium silicate	3-6	3-6
Sodium sulfate	10-30	10-30
Sodium CMC, optical brightener	1-2	1-2
Enzymes	0-2	0-2
Bleaches	0-8	0-8
Water	3-8	1-8

After the detergent raw materials are mixed, the slurry is charged to a homogenizer, and any large lumps or gritty particles are desized and screened to prevent plugging of the spray nozzle. The slurry then is charged to a booster pump, deaerated, and sent to a high pressure pump (300-1200 psig) for atomization. Most detergent slurries are atomized into **spherical droplets** via high pressure nozzles. The nozzles produce a hollow

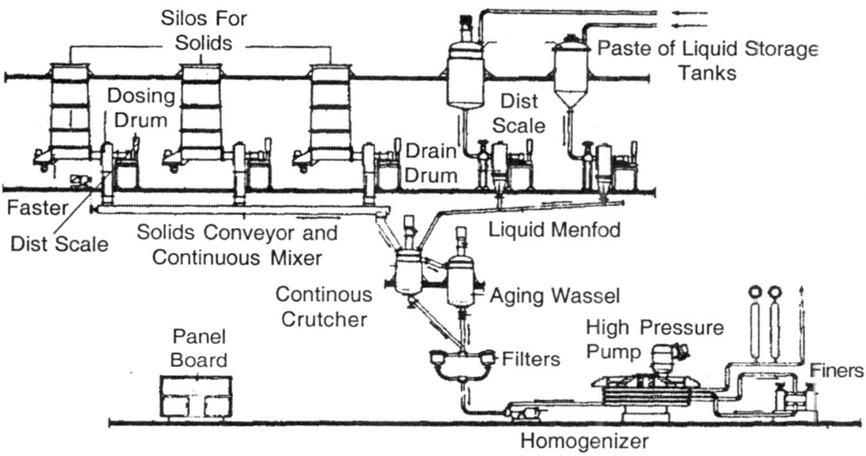

Fig. 1.19. Countinuous slurry preparation system.

conical pattern with a spray angle of 45 to 90°. The slurry emerges from the nozzle as a film, which is sheared into droplets by the centrifugal force developed by specially grooved cores inserted into the nozzle before the discharge point. A series of spray nozzles (2-25) is placed near the top of the spray tower and angled so that one edge of the desired spray pattern is vertical to the spray tower side walls. Pump pressures of from 300 to 1200 psig may be used to atomize the slurry. Some spray towers use two or three rings of nozzles, depending upon the formulation and drying capacity of the unit. Production rates of detergent spray towers range from 5000 to 80,000 lb/hr. In most cases, the rates are controlled by the slurry feed facilities, solids levels, and drying capacity. Figure 1.20 shows a typical schematic for a spray-drying facility.

Spray towers vary in size from approximately 10 to 35 feet in diameter, and range from 40 to 200 feet in height. A majority of detergent spray towers use countercurrent air flow patterns although some are cocurrent in design. In general, a tower of countercurrent design will produce a higher-density particle than the cocurrent type. In countercurrent systems, the heated gas stream (250-270°C) is uniformly dispersed into the lower section of the tower through a series of plenum chambers or baffles equally spaced around the unit's periphery. The hot gases are cooled as they exhaust from the top of the tower by the drying of atomized detergent droplets upon contact with the hot air stream. Because of the relatively low temperatures (110-140°C) at this point in the tower, the particles do not expand to their full capacity as water evaporates. This lower expansion rate results in a bead with increased bulk density and a thicker shell. If a similar formulation were dried in a cocurrent spray tower, the higher initial air contact temperature (250-370°C) and increased drying rate would increase the evaporative rate and result in a thin-walled bead of lighter density.

In most spray towers, the air flow rate and the temperature are adjusted at the inlet ports to maintain balanced air/temperature patterns. When the atomized slurry is sprayed into the drying chamber, the air flow pattern is disturbed and becomes very turbulent. This effect can cause localized temperature gradient zones ("hot or cold spots") and impact the particle drying characteristics. For example, it is possible to have both over and underdried particles discharged at the same time from the tower because of maldistribution of the air flow in the tower. Adjustment of the air flow patterns, as well as sending a balanced spray into the tower, can help counteract short-circuiting. Increased impingement of the product on tower walls is another negative effect of excessive turbulence, and of excessive spray nozzle velocity. A "ring" of product may form approximately 10 to 20 feet below the spray nozzles and build in size until it cracks or scales off the walls. Ring-removal methods such as periodic cleaning using air or water lances, vibration or sonic shocks, or mechanical cleaning rings sometimes are used to prevent a buildup that could result in blockage of the tower discharge.

After drying in the spray tower, the detergent granules are conveyed to storage silos prior to carton packaging. In some processes, product storage is preceded by fluid-bed conditioning.

The product from the tower is very warm (75- 120°C) and typically contains free surface moisture levels of 1 to 3 per cent. Conditioning is employed to prevent caking or product flow problems due to either the high temperature or excessive free moisture content. Following conditioning, perfume and other heat-sensitive ingredients (enzymes, surfactants, bleaches) may be added to the product. Post-addition is accomplished by metering the additives into the spray-dried base beads in a rotary drum or other mixing device. The post-additions normally comprise 2 to 15 per cent of the total detergent product. An excellent review of major spray-drying patents was provided by Sittig.

Agglomeration Processing

Agglomeration is a technique of binding a mixture of granular and/or dry powdered non-uniform raw materials into an attractive granular form

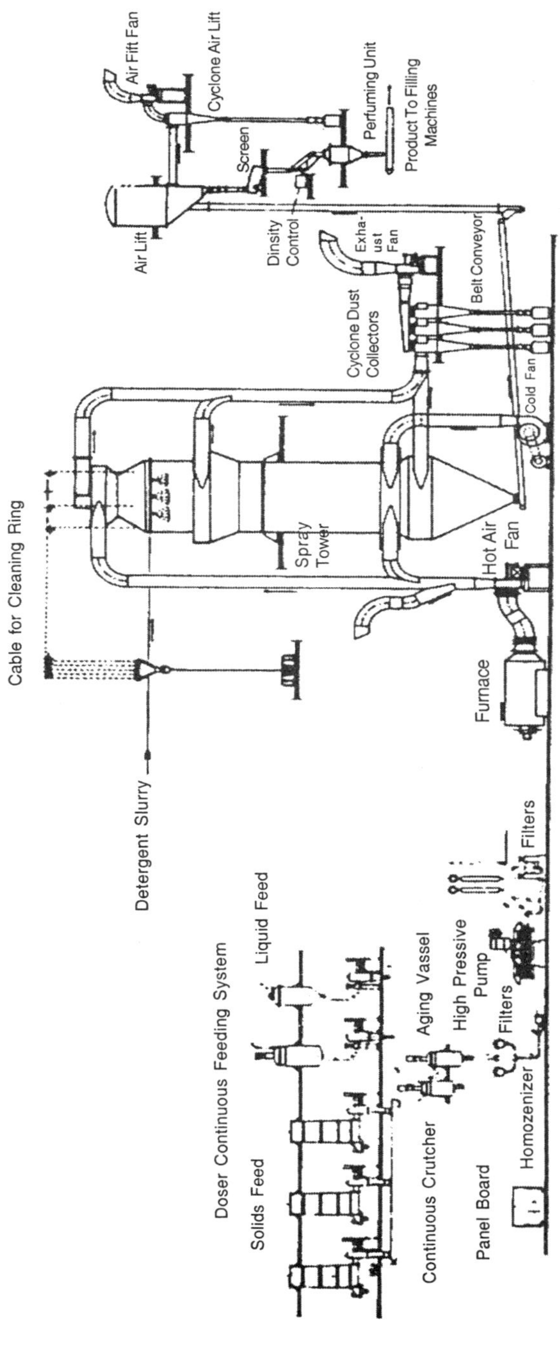

Fig. 1.20. Spray-drying facility; the detergent slurry feed can come from a plant like the one in Fig. 26.20.

with enhanced aesthetic and flow characteristics. The majority of granular automatic-dishwashing compounds (ADWCs) and some laundry products manufactured today use agglomeration processes. The advantages of agglomeration are centered around low capital costs relative to spray towers and reduced energy consumption. Also, agglomeration generally yields a higher-density product, which can result in reduced packaging costs. The primary disadvantage of agglomeration processing is a limitation in surfactant loading due to raw material absorption characteristics, particularly in laundry applications. As energy costs assume increasing importance and higher-density products gain wider acceptance, agglomeration or combinations of agglomeration and spray-drying technologies will find wider use.

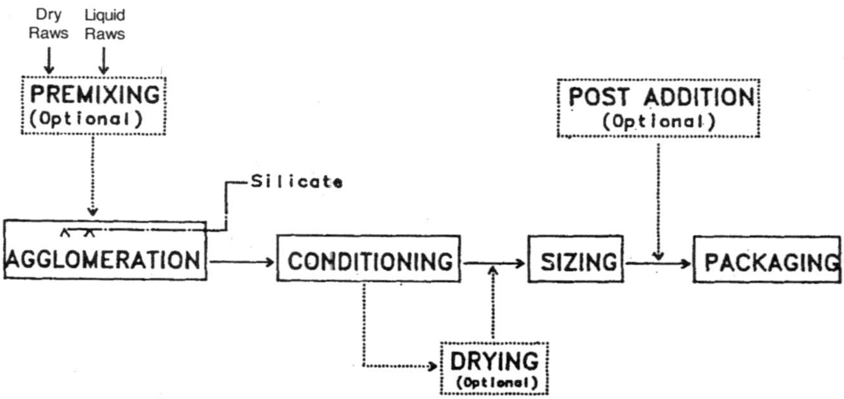

Fig. 1.21. Unit processes in agglomeration.

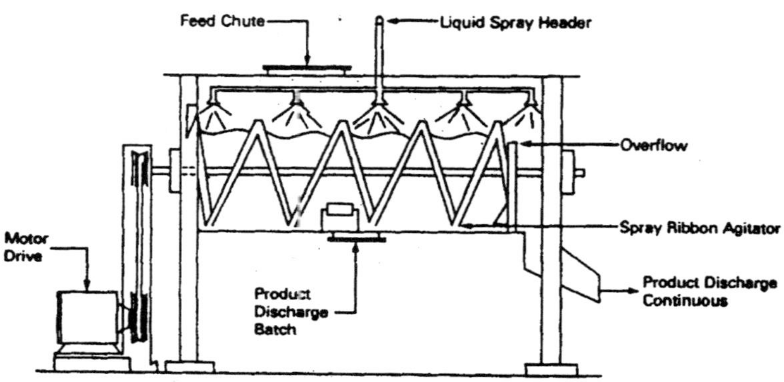

Fig. 1.22. Batch or continuous ribbon mixer.

The typical process steps for formulating a laundry detergent or ADWC product usually are defined in the laboratory prior to continuous plant processing, but they generally follow the scheme shown in Fig. 1.20. Frequently the dry raw materials are premixed and then metered into the agglomeration equipment. In the agglomerator, the dry raw material surface is exposed to atomized sprays of surfactant or silicates to begin building the agglomerated particle. Following addition of liquids to the dry raw materials, the product has a wet or pasty texture and requires conditioning to remove excess water prior to storage or packaging. Conditioned agglomerates are screened to remove oversize particles, and then are blended with additives such as chlorinated isbcyanurates, bleaches, enzymes, dyes, or perfumes that would not be stable under agglomeration conditions.

Numerous equipment types can be used for agglomeration, including horizontal ribbon and vertical mixers, rotary drums, zig-zag mixers, and pan agglomerators. Horizontal ribbon mixers (Fig. 1.22) are used primarily for "dry mix" formulating, where only limited agglomeration occurs. They are comprised of a U-shaped trough and a ribbon or paddle-type agitator. Liquids are sprayed onto the surface of the dry material bed and slowly dispersed into the mix. Mixer operation can be either batch or continuous. Vertical mixers have become more commonly used due to low space requirements and high efficiency of operations. The vertical mixer (Fig. 1.23) utilizes high speed agitation to intimately mix and uniformly blend liquids and dry raws prior to discharge. The contact time is reduced to less than 5 seconds. The rotary drum units generally contain baffles that "roll" or "lift" the product for uniform dispersion of liquid feeds. Pan and zig-zag agglomerators generally are used for limited, specialty product manufacture.

The vertical and the rotary drum agglomeration equipment finds most widespread use in the detergent industry because of improved agglomeration, increased liquid feed dispersion levels, and optimized product uniformity. In addition to agglomeration of detergents and automatic dishwashing compounds, these units can be used for hydration of sodium tripolyphosphates, dry neutralization of sul-fonic acids, post-addition of raw materials and fines to spray-dried products, and particle encapsulation. An excellent review of detergent agglomeration has been provided by Dolan.

Liquid Detergent Processing

Liquid heavy duty laundry products accounted for approximately 40 per cent of the 1990 U.S. heavy duty laundry detergent market. The growth in heavy duty liquids began in 1974 as the result of phosphate-banning legislation. Unbuilt liquids based on non-ionic and anionic/nonionic active combinations gradually increased in volume for various reasons including convenience, solubility, and improved performance of these types versus

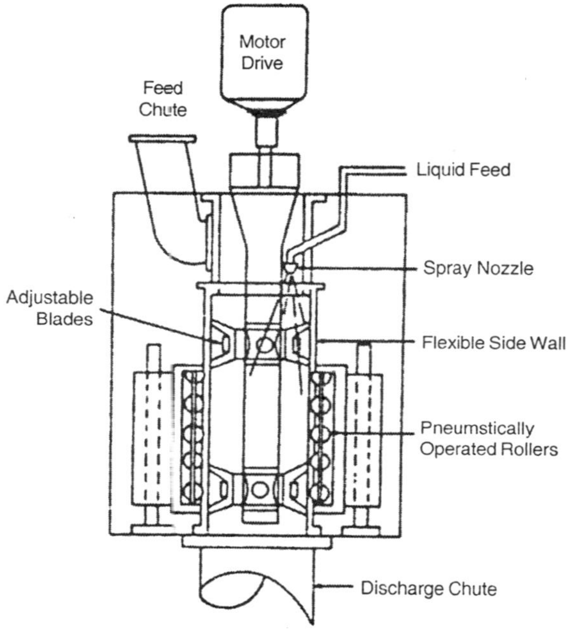

Fig. 1.23. Continuous in-line vertical agglomerator.

non-phosphated powdered detergents. In the mid-1980s the introduction of higher-performance liquids accelerated growth in this segment, with the market share essentially doubling from 1984 to 1990.

Liquid products are approximately 50 to 60 per cent water, with the remainder being a combination of surfactants, builder, foam regulators, hydrotropes, anti-redeposition agents, whitening agents, corrosion inhibitors, colorants, and perfume. Several formulations also contain antistatic and fabric-softening ingredients. Liquid systems require careful selection and blending of raw materials to achieve a stable product. Special attention is necessary for the following items:

- *Viscosity.* The product must be pourable and must retain the same viscosity characteristics from batch to batch. This variable can be controlled by proper solvent or hydrotrope selection.

- *Clear-cloud point.* The composition should have sufficient solubility to prevent "hazing" or separation of product when subjected to storage in cool temperatures.
- *Freeze-thaw stability.* The formulation must be compounded to prevent phase separation or solidification at freezing temperatures.

Many light duty liquid detergents are formulated with linear alkylbenzene sulfonate. Heavy duty liquid detergents often use a combination of actives such as LAS, sodium alcohol ether sulfate, alcohol ethoxylates, and olefin sulfonates. The manufacture of light and heavy duty formulations requires relatively basic equipment for blending of the various ingredients. The raw materials are added batchwise to a large mixing vessel or proportionated to in-line mixers before being directly fed from the mixer to the filling lines.

In 1986, liquid automatic-dishwashing detergents were introduced. These products used the principle of thixotropic slurries to address product form issues such as machine cup dispensing rates and product physical separation. The slurries were generally homogenous in nature and sufficiently viscous to prevent premature dispensing into the dishwasher prior to the wash cycle. Although the market share had grown to approximately one-third of the automatic-dishwashing market by 1988, product issues of cleaning performance, unused product remaining in the package, and unwanted bleaching of kitchen fabrics now have (decreased product market share to less than 20 per cent. Unique ingredients in this product are bentonite clays, which are used to thicken formulations and provide their characteristic viscosity. High-shear mixing equipment such as homogenizers is used for this application in batch or continuous stirred tank systems. Product types and processing techniques are covered in patents.

Detergent Trends

To date, no new detergent builders have been developed that have the functional characteristics and cost advantages of phosphates. A variety of builders (previously discussed) presently are being formulated in non-phosphate-legislated detergent products, but these salts are not as effective as phosphates. This performance differential s being compensated by increased use levels of synthetic surfactant and other detergent additives.

The major worldwide detergent product trend is introduction and sale of powdered detergent concentrates. These laundry products, which achieved widespread market dominance in Japan in 1988, have captured sizable market acceptance in Europe, were test-marketed in the United States, and since then have been claiming an increasing share of the market in the United States. These dense products permit reduced use levels of one-third to one-half cup per load and provide a significant reduction in product packaging, warehousing, and shipping costs. The product type requires process changes that utilize combinations of spray drying, agglomeration, and sometimes granulation technologies.

Although growth in liquids appears to have plateaued, liquid detergent formulations are expected to maintain their position in the detergent market. Current and future energy considerations as well as water conservation suggest that a movement toward reduced water temperatures and water consumption will occur. These factors, coupled with high consumer performance expectations, will continue to challenge the detergent industry during the coming decade.

2

Detergent Components

Substrates, the objects to be cleaned by soap or detergents, vary very widely in both chemical composition and surface configuration. With relatively few exceptions, however, they can generally be divided into two great classes — fabrics and fibrous materials, and "hard surface." The fabrics present a highly complex configuration capable of holding soil mechanically even though the soil may be physicochemically removed from the surface. Most of the important fabrics are organic polymeric materials, swellable by water and permeable to small molecules and ions dissolved in aqueous baths. Many of the most widely encountered ones, cotton, rayon, wool, nylon, cellulose esters and synthetic polyesters, contain ionogenic or polar centers capable of localizing electric charges.

Soils are extremely variable in composition. They may consist of a single solid or liquid phase, but usually two or more phases are present, intimately and randomly mixed and irregularly disposed over the substrate surface, In a surprisingly large number of important cleaning systems, the nature of the soil and even the quantity present in quite well known. This is the case, for example, in most textile mill operations such as raw wool scouring, the boil-off and scouring of loom-state woven goods, and the soaping of printed cottons.

Soil particles occur in a more or less continuous range of sizes. Particle size is one of the most important factors determining the ease with which a solid soil can be removed from a substrate. Particles above about 5 u (5×10^{-4} cm) in diameter are generally quite easy to remove, even from an intricate fabric. Particles less than 10^{-4} cm tend to be irremovable by ordinary detersive processes once they become intimately attached to a typical textile fibre. These particles are responsible for the gradual irreversible graying of white goods with continued wear and laundering. Fortunately, particles in this size range tend to form clumps and clusters with one another before they reach the fibre surface. These clusters tend to behave like individual large particles. Particles (or clusters) in the range of 10^{-4} cm tend to resist removal by simple agitation in liquids that are not surface active, but these particles are removable by normal detersive processes. This is the size range of most interest. From the practical point of view, "undesirable foreign matter" may include material that is soluble in the bath, such as encrusted sugar residues, and molecularly dispersed material such as fruit juice stains. Removal of these soils is an important aspect of the cleaning art.

Baths considered in this book are aqueous solutions. Among bath components, the solute that is effective in cleaning, usually a mixture of several components, is called the **detergent.** The term detergent is also used quite frequently in the restricted sense to mean a surfactant of high detersive power. Nonsurfactants such as alkali silicates and phosphates also exert a detersive effect. In the great majority of fabric systems, the most important detersive component in the bath is a surfactant. Nonsurfactant components that augment the cleaning effect in these systems are called **builders.** Many of the materials that act as builders in fabric systems, e.g., phosphates and silicates, are primary detergents in hard surface systems.

Detergents are formulated to suit the requirements of the soiled substrate to be cleaned and the expected range of washing conditions. Some detergents, for example, the familiar bar or toilet soap, consist essentially of only one component. There are relatively few cleansing systems, however, in which a suitably formulated detergent consisting of several components will not outperform the best single component detergent. The numerous materials which are used as ingredients of laundering detergent formulations for fabrics may be divided into the following groups :

(a) **Surfactants,** including the various synthetic surfactants and soaps.

(b) **Inorganic salts, acids and bases** : materials of this class that are not builders, i.e., that do not contribute to detergency, are referred to as "diluents" or "fillers".

(c) **Organic builders** or additives which enhance the detergency, foaming power, emulsifying power, or soil-suspending effect of the composition.

(d) **Special purpose additives,** such as bleaching agents, brightening agents, bactericides or emollients, which modify or improve the physical form or the stability of the detergent, but which have no direct effect on soil removal.

Surfactants : The surfactant types which are most widely used as primary cleansing ingredients in detergent compositions include (a) soaps (i.e., sodium or potassium salts) of fatty acids, rosin acids and tall oil; (b) alkylarylsulphonates; (c) alkyl sulphates, including surfactants with both branched-chain and straight-chain hydrophobes, as well as primary and secondary sulphate groups; (d) sulphates and sulphonates containing an intermediate linkage between the hydrophobic and hydrophilic groups, such as the fatty acylated methyl taurides and the sulphated fatty monoglycerides; (e) long-chain acid esters of polyethylene glycol, particularly the tall oil ester; (f) polyethylene glycol ethers of alkyl phenols; (g) polyethylene glycol ethers of long-chain alcohols and mercaptans; (h) fatty acyl diethanolamides; (j) block copolymers of ethylene oxide and propylene oxide.

Inorganic compounds : The more important inorganic detergent constituents may be grouped into the following six categories: alkalies, phosphates, silicates, neutral soluble salts, acids and insoluble inorganic builders.

Alkalies : Sodium carbonate, either in anhydrous form (soda ash) or in hydrated form, is used as a builder or filler with soaps, synthetic surfactants. Sodium bicarbonate ($NaHCO_3$), sodium sesquicarbonate ($NaHCO_3Na_2CO_3$), and sodium borate ($NaB_4O_y.10H_2O$ borax) are used in place of soda ash when a lower pH is desired. Potassium analogs of the above salts are sometimes used for formulations of high solubility.

The alkalies have no sequestering effect on heavy metal ions, and they have little if any suspending effect on most solid soils. They are effective in maintaining a high pH, and are, therefore, useful as true builders for soap in fabric detergency. They have little building effect on the synthetic surfactants, which do not tend to hydrolyze in dilute aqueous solutions. In fabric detergent formulations based on synthetic surfactants, the alkalies listed above care realistically regarded as fillers rather than builders.

Phosphates : Trisodium phosphate (trisodium orthophosphate, Na_3PO_4) may be used with soaps, surfactants, or other alkalies. It precipitates many heavy-metal ions but does not sequester in the sense of forming soluble chelates. Functionally, it can be considered an alkali.

Tetrasodium pyrophosphate ($Na_4P_2O_7$) is one of the most important primary detergents and builders for fabric substrates. It has high sequestering, suspending, and cleansing action. Functionally, it is both an alkali and a true builder for synthetic surfactants, i.e., a sequestering agent.

Pentasodium triphosphate (sodium "tripolyphosphate", $Na_3P_3O_{10}$) is the most widely used builder for heavy duty fabric detergents based on synthetic surfactants. It has a somewhat stronger suspending and sequestering action than tetrasodium pyrophosphate and a somewhat lower pH.

Sodium "hexametaphosphate" vary in composition depending on the manufacturer. They exert powerful suspending and sequestering effects and are used where these effects are important. They have a low pH, about 6 or 7, and tend to hydrolyze or "revert" to pyrophosphates and orthophosphates when heated in aqueous solution.

Silicates : The sodium silicates function primarily as alkalies and have been extensively used as builders for soap in laundering formulations since well before the era of synthetic detergents. They are also widely used as primary detergent alkalies in hard surface cleaners, particularly in compositions for machine dishwashing. A minor percentage of alkali silicate is included in modern household laundering formulations, where it functions as an anticorrosive agent and prevents deterioration of the washing machine. In these formulations, it has little effect on soil removal.

Neutral soluble salts : Whether the neutral soluble salts, sodium sulphate and sodium chloride, should be regarded as builders or as diluents in synthetic surfactant compositions has been debated extensively. Sodium sulphate does, in fact, serve as an excellent diluent and standardizing material. It also has the effect of lowering the critical micelle concentration of organic surfactants, thereby lowering the concentration at which good washing can be achieved. To offset this effect, a corresponding increase in soil redeposition occurs so the net effect is usually inconsequential, and sodium sulphate is best regarded as a diluent.

Insoluble inorganic builders : Clays, such as kaolin, the montmorillonites and bentonites, have been advocated and used from time to time as ingredients of washing compositions and other formulations involving surface active agents. Under certain favourable conditions, particularly in soft water of low dissolved solids content, clay suspensions have a marked detersive effect on ordinary soiled fabrics. Bentonite acts as a builder in soap and synthetic detergent washing compositions, although it is not widely used because consumers dislike the muddy appearance of the bath, and because it is difficult to get free of grit. It is an excellent emulsifying and suspending agent. Sodium bentonite has some water-softening power by virtue of its ability to sorb calcium ions and has been used to a considerable extent.

Table 2.1 Commercially Important Detersive Systems

	Soil	Mechanical action	Bath ratio	Detergent
	Fabric and fibrous systems			
Textile and allied manufacturing				
raw wool scouring	liquid at operating temperature	very gentle	high	organic surfactant
Wool yarn and piece goods	liquid	gentle	moderately high	organic surfactant
Scouring gray cottons	mostly solid; waxy and strachy	vigorous	low	built surfactant
Scouring manmade fabrics	mixed; oily lubricant and sizing residues	moderate	medium	built surfactant
De-inking paper	mixed; oily and pigment	vigorous	high	heavily built surfactant
Laundering				
household	mixed and variable	moderate	high	built surfactant
commercial and industrial	mixed and variable; heavier than household soil	vigorous	high	built surfactant
Rug cleaning				
plant	heavy solid	moderate gentle	medium to low	organic surfactant, may be built
On location	heavy solid	vigorous;super-ficial brushing	very low; foam bath	organic surfactant foam

Organic builders and special purpose additives : The effect of certain nonsurface-active organic additives in increasing the detergency and other desirable properties of cleansing compositions has long been recognized. These additives are usually present in relatively minor percentages and usually serve one or more of the following specific functions : (1) decreasing the redeposition of soil from the detergent bath onto the substrate; (2) sequestering heavy metal ions, both in the concentrated detergent and in the diluted cleansing bath; (3) promoting foaming power and foam stability; (4) increasing the whiteness and/or the optical appearance of cleanliness; (5) increasing the solubility or otherwise modifying the physical form of the detergent composition; (6) inhibiting injurious effects which the detergent may have on the substrate or the washing machine.

Of these materials, the organic sequestering agents and the antiredeposition agents have a direct effect on true detergency, i.e., on soil removal. The organic sequestering agents, of which ethylenediaminetetraacetic acid is most widely used, serve the same purpose as the sequestering phosphates. They are used where the less expensive phosphates are, for one reason or another, not applicable. Antiredeposition agents are indispensable in laundering compositions based on nonsoap surfactants. By far the most widely used antiredeposition agent is sodium carboxymethylcellulose, NaCMC. The detergent grade of NaCMC is a low viscosity material containing about 0.7 CH_2COONa groups per glucose unit in the chain.

Bleaching agents : Usually sodium perborate an percarbonates are used. These chemicals bleach by oxidation of colouring matter in dirt attached to the fabrics and yarns.

Whitening and optical brightening agents : These are used to overcome the yellowing of the substrate. Ultramarine blue are used. Blue complements the yellow colour and makes the substrate appear, white. Optical brighters are various organic compounds which absorb the incoming light rays and gives out fluorescence radiation. This makes the substrate appear white. Stilbene dyes like Tinopal, Broncophor etc. are such compounds.

3

Surfactants

The word **surfactant** is a condensation of the descriptive phrase surface active agent. The phrase "surface-active agent" was awkward to use repetitively and was too extensive in its meaning. The new word overcame these disadvantages. Six fundamental characteristics of surfactants, representative of current usage, are taken as the basis for calling a chemical as surfactant.

1. **Solubility** : A substance must be soluble in at least one phase of a liquid system in order to be classified as a surfactant. Bentonitic clays, for example, were excluded by this constraint even though they exhibit some of the fundamental properties of surfactants.
2. **Amphipathic structure** : Surfactant molecules are composed of groups with opposing solubility tendencies.
3. **Orientation at interfaces** : Surfactant molecules or ions form oriented mono-layers at phase interfaces.
4. **Adsorption at interfaces** : The equilibrium concentration of a surfactant solute at a phase interface is greater than its concentration in the bulk of the solution. Consequently, surfactants cause a greater lowering of the surface tension than would be expected from their gross concentration.
5. **Micelle formation** : Surfactants from aggregates of molecules or ions called micelles when the concentration of the solute in the bulk of the solution exceeds a limiting value that is a fundamental characteristic of each solute — solvent system.
6. **Functional properties** : Solutions of surfactants exhibit some combination of the following functional properties: detergency, foaming, wetting, emulsifying, solubilizing, dispersing.

Surfactant phenomenology deals with di-, tri-, or polyphase systems of which at least one phase is a surfactant solution. In many practical applications the role of the surfactant may simply be to enhance the performance of a "pure" liquid.

7. **Hydrophile - lipophile balance** : A surfactant is an organic compound that encompasses in the same molecule two dissimilar structural groups, e.g. a water-soluble and a water insoluble moiety. The composition, solubility properties, location and relative sizes of these dissimilar groups in relation to the overall molecular configuration determine the surface activity of a compound.

A variety of pairs of names have been used to designate and describe the opposing tendencies of the moieties or groups that make up a surfactant molecule, viz., hydrophobic, water disliking; hydrophilic, water liking, lipophobic, fat disliking; lipophilic, fat liking; oleophobic, fat disliking, oleophilic, fat liking. The terms polar and non-polar can also be used to refer to the groups that are soluble or insoluble, respectively, in water.

The hydrophile and lipophile groups orient themselves in different manner in diffluent media as shown in fig. 3.1.

Classification : Surfactants are classified on the basis of their hydrophilic or "solubilizing groups" into four categories: anionics, nonionics, cationics and amphoterics, The anionic solubilizing groups are carboxylates, sulphonates, sulphates and phosphates. Nonionics are solubilized by hydroxyl groups and polyoxyethylene chains. Primary, secondary and tertiary amines and quaternary ammonium groups are the cationic solubilizers. Amphoteric surfactants are solubilized by some combination of anionic and cationic moieties; nonionic solubilizing groups may also be part of amphoteric molecules. In addition to the primary solubilizing groups, other structural units contribute to the hydrophilic tendencies of molecules, e.g. ester linkages and amide linkages. The hydrophobic, i.e. lipophilic, moieties are almost invariably hydrocarbon or halogen-substituted hydrocarbon groups. Olefin linkages are less hydrophobic than carbon-to-carbon single bonds. Products based on silicon-containing hydrophobes are just beginning to be offered in commercial quantities.

Anionic surfactants : By far the largest class of surfactants in general use today are the anionics (including soaps). For thousands of years in the history of the application of surface activity to the needs of mankind, the soaps, derived from natural animal and vegetable fats and oils, dominated the field. The major historical and economical advantage of

Orientation in water

Orientation in
non polar solvent

Orientation at air/
water interface

Orientation at air/
oil interface

Orientation of water/
oil interface

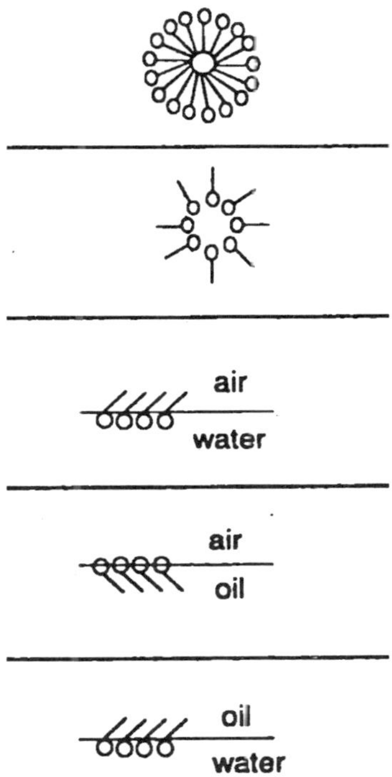

O Hydrophile group — Lipophile group

Fig. 3.1 : Orientation of surfactant in several system.

the fatty acid soaps has always been the ready availability of the raw materials from natural, renewable sources. The weakness of the classical soaps, due to the sensitivity of the carboxylate salts which mainly constitute them, in many processes requiring surfactant action, led to the development of synthetic surfactants. Classically, anionic surfactants are divided into four basic categories namely;

(a) Carboxylates, of which common soap is the most important.

(b) Sulphonates, of which linear alkyl benzene sulphate (LABS) is the most significant and is the largest used synthetic surfactant worldwide.

(c) Sulphuric acid esters such as alcohol sulphates or sulphated oils, the earliest of synthetic surfactants.

(d) Others, which category includes the nitrogen bearing taurates and sarcosinates, phosphorus bearing chemicals such as the phosphate esters and others, and industrial surfactants of the alkylnaphthalene from aldehyde condensate type.

Carboxylates:Soaps and a small volume of aminocarboxy-lates are the only commercial product types in the carboxylate class of surfactants. Soap has the general composition (RCOO) $(M)^+$ where R is an alkyl group, usually in the C_9 to C_{21} range and M is a metallic or amine ion. Although most soaps have surfactant properties, the term actually denotes the chemical composition rather than the use, and an appreciable volume of these products, particularly salts of polyvalent metals, go to nonsurfactant uses such as paint driers and gelling agents for kerosene. The surfactant properties of soaps are excellent in soft water, but the heavy metal and polyvalent metal salts of soap, e.g. Mg^{2+}, Ca^{2+}, Ba^{2+}, Fe^{2+} and Al^{2+}, are insoluble in water and form "curds" or "lime-soap" precipitates that reduce the effective concentration and adversely affect performance.

Sulphonates : The most effective structure for an anionic surfactant is a sulphonate of the general formula RSO_3Na where R is a biodegradable hydrocarbon group in the surfactant molecular weight range. The R group can be alkyl or alkylarylene and the product can be a random mixture of isomers as long as it does not contain chain branching that interferes with biodegradability. The surface activity of the SO_3" group is not oversensitive to variations in the pH or to heavy metal ions and the C-S linkage is not susceptible to hydrolysis or oxidation under normal conditions of use. The minimum cost for satisfactory performance determines the composition of the principal surfactant ingredient in household laundry detergents, the largest single use of surfactants. Other surfactant users adapt their products or processes to the large volume product because of its cost advantage. Linear alkylbenzenesulphonates replaced the branched alkylbenzene-sulphonates which had displaced soap from many uses.

Linear alkylbenezenesulphonates rank next to soaps in total usage. The sodium salt of linear alkylbensulphonate is commonly referred to as "LAS". Linear alkylbenzenesulphonic acid is called LAS acid, and salts other than sodium are named in an analogous manner, e.g. LAS ammonium salt. Commercial alkylbenzenesul-phonic acid is a light-coloured, viscous liquid that is used almost entirely as an intermediate for the manufacture of alkali metal, alkaline earth metal, and amine salts. LAS is marketed as a light-coloured flake, granule, or bead at 90+% assay and as a viscous liquid, paste, or slurry at lower concentrations. The other salts of LAS acid are usually offered as viscous liquids or pastes at 40-90 wt % active ingredient.

Sodium di(2-ethylhexyl) sulphosuccinate is widely used as speciality surfactant. These sulphosuccinate esters are available as the sodium salt from several manufacturers. They are offered as white, waxy, odourless solids or as concentrated colourless solutions. The di-C_8 esters have the optimum solubility balance for use in tap water or aqueous solutions with a low inorganic salt content; lower alkyl esters are more effective in saline solutions. Sodium dialkyl sulphosuccinates are highly surface active but the susceptibility of the ester linkage to acidic or alkaline hydrolysis limits their usefulness, The products have strong wetting, rewetting, penetration and solubilization properties.

Naphthalenesulphonates : Four series of specialty surfactants make up the widely used but relatively low volume group of naphthalenesulphonate products, viz. salts of alkylnaphthalene sulphonates; salts of sulphonated formaldehyde-naphthalene condensates; salts of naphthalene.sulphonates; and salts of tetrahydronaphthalenesulphonates.

In the concentrated dry form, most of the salts are almost odourless light-gray solids. They are readily and highly soluble in water.

The naphthalenesulphonates are used in many different applications as wetting and dispersing agents. Several members of the series are effective as stabilizing and suspending agents in disperse systems.

N-Acyl-N-alkyltaurates (taurine is $H_2NCH_2CH_3SO_3H$, 2-aminoethanesulphonic acid), is expensive and are used as speciality category surfactants. The taurates are interesting as the only class of anionic surfactants with the combination of advantages (1) They are stable against, hydrolysis by acidic or alkaline media at use concentrations; (2) they show no loss of performance in hard water; (3) they have soaplike biodegradability and residual feel on washed fabrics; and (4) they have a molecular structure capable of yielding either strong wetting or strong detergent configurations. The products RCON(R') $CH_2CH_2SO_3Na$ are strong detergents when $R = C_{11} - C_{17}$ and $R' = CH_3$ or C_2H_3, but are strong wetters when $R = R' = C_6 - C_9$.

Sodium N-oleoyl-N-methyltaurate is available as a light yellow solid at about 70% assay or at lower concentrations in water as a light coloured slurry, solution, or gel. The products are principally used in detergent applications without builders. Foaming of the N-methyl derivatives is only moderate and is not readily improved by the usual foam builders.

2-Sulphoethyl esters of fatty acids known commercially as B-sulphoesters, resemble closely in properties the fatty acids from which they are derived, but they have the advantage that hard water does not impair their performance. Only the sensitivity of the ester linkage to hydrolysis has prevented their widespread usage in consumer detergents. Hydrolysis is not a problem with detergents for personal use and the sodium salt of the 2-sulphoethyl esters of lauric acid, or the similar coconut acid mixture, has found acceptance as the foaming and cleansing ingredient in synthetic detergent bars. The oleic acid analog is less foaming but is a good detergent with speciality uses in neutral or mildly alkaline systems.

The esters can be produced commercially from sodium isoethionate (obtained by the reaction of ethylene oxide with a concentrated solution of sodium bisulphite) and the fatty acid or acyl chloride.

Olefin sulphonates : The increasing availability low cost linear 1-olefins in the C_{14} to C_{18} range has spurred research and commercial development of their sulphonate derivatives. Sulphonation of a C_{15-18} l-olefin is a complex reaction that leads to a mixture of sulphonates, of which the main components after hydrolysis of the intermediate suftones are $R'CH:CH(CH_2)_xSO_3Na$ where x has any value from 0 to 11, plus $RCH_2CHOHCH_2CH_2SO_3Na$ and $RCHOHCH_2CH_2SO_3Na$. The 3- and 4-hydroxysulphonates which may amount to as much as half of the yield of sulphonated products are not very water-soluble but they are solubilized in the presence of the more soluble olefin sulphonate. The sulphonation mixture which is referred to as a-olefin sulphonate or AOS has detergency and foaming properties similar to C_{11-14} LAS. It is superior in performance to similar products made from internal straight-chain olefins. Biodegradability of the AOS is slightly better than LAS; toxicity and skin irritation are slightly less.

Sulphates and sulphated products : The hydrophilic group, $-OSO_2-$ of the half sulphate ester surfactants is $-SO_2-$ attached through an oxygen atom to a carbon atom in the hydrophobic moiety. The additional oxygen makes the sulphate a stronger solubilizing group than the sulphonate but the C-O-S linkage of the sulphates is more easily hydrolysed than the C-S linkage of the sulphonates. The susceptibility to hydrolysis, especially in acidic media, limits the utility of the sulphates. Solubilization of hydrophobes through the combination of ethoxylation and sulphation is frequently used to obtain the optimum solubility balance and also to utilize less expensive raw materials that cannot be solubilized sufficiently by sulphation alone, e.g. derived from tallow alcohols. The shift of the detergent industry to more biodegradable products started a trend, away from ethoxylated and sulphated alkylphenols and toward ethoxylated and sulphated alcohol.

The stability of the alkyl sulphates to hard water is excellent. In fact, magnesium lauryl sulphate forms voluminous foams with a low water content that are useful in rug shampoos where the soil is removed by vacuum pickup of the foam that is generated by vigorous brushing with a minimum volume of detergent solution. Sensitivity to hydrolysis in hot alkaline or acidic media is one of the principal disadvantages of the alkyl sulphates.

A typical sulphated alkanolamides is the sodium salt of the half sulphate ester of lauric ethanolamide, i.e. $C_{11}H_{23}CONHCH, CH, OSO_3Na$. Variations in the product type include mono- and diethanolamides of all of the fatty acids in the range C_{12} to C_{18}. The degree of sulphation is adjusted to obtain the desired solubility in water. The alkanolamide sulphates are somewhat more stable toward hydrolysis at high temperatures, in alkaline or acidic media, and in hard water than the sulphates of fatty acid esters or glycerides. The products are effective detergents with good foaming and lathering properties. They add viscosity or "body" to aqueous solutions and are widely used in the formulation of janitorial cleaners and textile auxiliaries.

Oleic acid and ricinoleic acid esterified with low molecular weight alcohols and then sulphated yield useful surfactants. A typical product of this type would be $CH_3(CH_2)_7CH_2CH\ (OSO_3Na)CH_2(CH_2)_5CH_2COOR$ from the sulphation of an oleic acid ester in which the R represents an ethyl, propyl, butyl, or amyl group. Products of this type are marketed as clear yellow to brown viscous solutions with an active ingredient content as high as 85 wt %. The balance is water and sometimes as much as 10% of pine oil or terpineol. The sulphated esters have strong wetting and rewetting power combined with a lubricant effect on textile fibres. They also have good foaming, emulsifying and detergent properties. The products are stable enough in hot solutions of dilute caustic soda for use as wetting agents in kier boiling and continuous bleaching processes.

Sulphated polyoxyethylene alkylphenols are widely used in retail and industrial detergent products. The sulphated polyoxytheylene alkylphenols are marketed as colourless, odourless, aqueous solutions at concentrations from 30 to 60 wt % of active ingredient. The more concentrated products often contain 12 - 15% of ethanol to reduce the viscosity and facilitate handling. These surfactants are high-foaming detergents, strong wetters, and efficient emulsifiers and dispersants that perform effectively in hard as well as soft water. They are mild to the skin, particularly in well-formulated retail detergent products.

The alkylpolyoxyethylene sulphates have been on the market about as long as the analogous alkylphenoxypolyoxyethylene sulphates. The advantages of the ethoxylated and sulphated alcohols over the plain sulphated alcohols are (1) improved foaming, particularly in hard water, (2) decreased irritation of eyes and skin, (3) increased solubility in water, and (4) lower raw material cost as long as ethylene oxide is cheaper than the alcohols used for sulphation. The polyoxyethylene content is adjusted to obtain optimum performance for the intended use but usually its variation is within the range of 10-40% of the molecular weight calculated as the sodium salt. The polyoxyethylene alkyl sulphates are offered as essentially colourless, odourless liquids at concentrations from approx 25 to 60 wt % of active ingredient. The viscosity of the solutions increases with the concentration unless alcohol is used as diluent. The products are stable and compatible with builders in liquid and solid alkaline formulations. The sulphated polyoxyethylene alcohols are high foaming detergents, emulsifiers, dispersants, and wetting agents. They are widely used in shampoos.

Nonionic surfactants : A nonionic surfactant, as the name implies, bears essentially no charge when dissolved or dispersed in aqueous media. The hydrophilic tendency in a nonionic is due primarily to oxygen in the molecule which hydrates by hydrogen bonding to water molecules. The strongest hydrophilic moieties in nonionics are ether linkages and hydroxyl groups, but ester and amide linkages, which are also hydrophilic, are present in many nonionics. The contribution of each oxygen to solubilization is weak and nonionic molecules must contain a multiplicity of them in order to be water soluble. Nearly all of the unmodified polyol surfactants are lipophilic and they are frequently used as coemulsifiers in combinations with more hydrophilic surfactants. One advantage of the nonionics is that they are compatible with ionic and amphoteric surfactants. Polyoxyethylene solubilization is the key to the substantial and continuing growth of the nonionics. Since the polyoxyethylene group can be introduced into almost any organic compound that has a reactive hydrogen, a wide range of organic substances can be solubilized by ethoxylation.

Ethoxylated aliphatic alcohols : The alkylpoly (ethyleneoxy) ethanols were introduced in place of alkyl phenoxy compound for switching over to more biodegradable products. The hydrophobes are generally mixtures of straight-chain alcohols in the range from C_{12} to C_{18} and that the mole ratios of combined ethylene oxide to hydrophobe vary from 1 to 50. The undiluted products vary in physical form from liquids to waxy solids.

Cationic surfactants : The hydrophilic moieties in cationic surfactants are amino or quaternary nitrogens. As the name implies, these hydrophobic moieties bear a positive charge when dissolved in aqueous media. The hydrophilic tendency of one amino nitrogen is approximately strong enough to solubilize a lipophilic group in the surfactant molecular weight range in dilute acidic solution e.g. lauryl amine is soluble in dilute hydrochloric acid. To increase the water solubility, additional primary, secondary, or tertiary amino groups can be introduced or the amino group can be quaternized with a low molecular weight alkyl group, e.g. CH_3- or $HOCH_2CH_2$—. Quaternary nitrogen compounds are strong bases that form essentially neutral salts with hydrochloric and sulphuric acid. Most quaternary surfactants are soluble even in alkaline aqueous solutions. Polyoxyethylated cationics behave like nonionics in alkaline solutions and like cationics in acidic solutions.

Cationic surfactants are rarely used in detergents and are widely used in acidic aqueous and nonaqueous systems as dispersants, emulsifiers, wetting agents, sanitizers, dye fixing agents, textile lubricants, textile softeners, foam stabilizers and corrosion inhibitors.

4

Builders

The builders in a detergent formulation performs many functions like buffering of the pH, soil dispersion and soil antiredeposition. The builders can be classified as—

1. Phosphates
2. Silicates
3. Carbonates
4. Oxygen releasing materials
5. Sundry builders.

Phosphates

The phosphate builders are of two types viz. orthophosphates and condensed phosphates. The orthophosphates used in the detergent formulations are trisodium phosphate and disodium phosphate—anhydrous and hydrated. Trisodium phosphate softens water by precipitating metallic ions present in the water as gelatinous precipitate. It also helps dispersing the soil and dissolve fatty acids by saponification.

The condensed phosphates include tetra sodium pyrophos-phate, sodium tripolyphosphate sodium hexametaphosphate. They all have the power of water softening by sequestering the polyvalent metal ion present in water.

In addition, they have the power of redissolving the insoluble salts of these polyvalent metals. These phosphates synergistically aid the detergent.

Silicates

Silicates play important role in detergent formulation. Both the metal ion and the silicate portion enhance the cleaning process. The alkali radical contributes to the alkanity, buffers the medium to 9.5 pH, saponifies the acidic soils and emulsifies the oils in the soil. The silicate radical causes deflocculation of soils, prevents redeposition, softens water, inhibits corrosion, acts as plasticisers for extension of syndet bars. Sodium silicate can be used as neutralising agent for acid slurry and fatty acids. A portion of the alkalis neutralizes the slurry or acid, the balance remains with the silicate. It also has synergistic action on the phosphate and surfactants.

Zeolites

They are also known as molecular sieves. These are used as water softeners, as they contain exchangeable cations. Type A zeolites are hydrated sodium aluminium silicates. The structure of the crystalline material is a three dimensional lattice. The lattice structure results in a pore at the centre of the three dimensional crystal. The associated cation is found at the opening of the pore and this cation gives the zeolite its peculiar properties. Type 4A zeolites have sodium ion partially blocking the pore to give an opening of 4°A. Type 3 A zeolites have potassium ion and the opening is 3°A. Type 5A zeolites are calcium ion zeolites, resulting in pore size of 5°A. Zeolites are used as builders replacing phosphates. Phosphate usage are progressively being restricted because of pollution problem. Phosphate in water enhances growth of algae.

Soda ash

Besides being a cheap source of alkali in detergents, it is also used in preparation of dry products by processes other than by spray drying. Soda ash particularly in light form absorbs large quantity of liquid materials on its surface and still can remain dry and free flowing. It can also be used for neutralization of acid slurry to produce the sodium salt.

Oxygen releasing compounds

Sodium perborate in solution acts like hydrogen peroxide. It produces nascent oxygen at elevated temperature which bleaches, but does not harm vegetable, animal and synthetic fibres. Sodium perborate also add alkalinity to the detergents and act as buffering agent. It is thus a builder on its own right.

Sodium chloride

Sodium chloride is produced during sulphonation of the LAB when the same is carried out by chlorosulphonic acid. Sodium chloride is a cost effective viscosity increasing agent for anionic detergent solutions. It is widely used for this purpose.

Sodium carboxy methyl cellulose

It is an antiredepositing agent. It is also used as a thickening agent in detergents. Usually one twelfth of the active detergent material is the amount of sodium CMC added. Addition of large quantity like 10% causes gel formation and CMC can be thrown out from solution because inorganic salt in solution decreases CMC solubility in water. Other materials like hydroxy propyl methyl cellulose, methyl cellulose, hydroxy ethyl cellulose are also antiredepositing agent. However, the sodium CMC is the most economic one.

Chelating agents

EDTA (Ethylene diamine tetra acetic acid) in the form of its sodium salt and NTA (nitrilo triacetic acid) sodium salt are used in detergent formulations as chelating agents. These chemicals forms complexes with metallic ions, particularly the polyvalent ones. If the washing water contains small quantity of Fe ions, the EDTA or NTA makes it ineffective and harmless from washing and laundering form of view. They are usually added 0.5 to 1%.

5

Raw Materials

SOAP

The raw materials for soap manufacture cover a wide range of substances which may mainly be classified under the following classes:—

(1) Fat and oils
(2) Alkalies
(3) Rosin
(4) Salt
(5) Filling agents such as soap stone, sodium silicate, starch, etc.
(6) Soap colours
(7) Soap perfumes
(8) Water

As success in manufacture would depend upon the selection of the raw materials, a discussion of the raw materials and their chemical properties from the soapmakers' point of view will be useful. These properties are to be kept in view if a particular type of soap fulfilling special conditions is to be manufactured.

Fats and oils : Oils from soap makers point of view are glyceryl esters of long chain fatty acids. Their major sources are plants and animals. Mineral oil or petroleum can not be used for soap making as they are mixture of hydrocarbons. This class of oil is not considered and discussed.

India is the fourth largest producer of oil seeds in the world. In 1995 the country produced 7.2 million tonnes of various vegetable oils. However, still the country needed to import about 1.5 million tonnes of oil. In the beginning of next century the import is expected to cross 2.2 million, the cost of which is estimated to be a few thousand crores. India produces large number of seeds, fruits, plants which produce oils. Table 5.1 gives the various oil seeds available for exploitation in India.

Table 5.1 Oil-Bearing Materials of India

	Common names	Botanical nomenclature
Group A. Historical oil-bearing materials		
Al.	Sesame	Sesamum indicum
A2.	Cottonseed	Gossypium spp.
A3.	Rape-mustard	Brassicaspp.
A4.	Coconut	Cocos nucifera
A5.	Linseed	Linum usitatissimum
A6.	Castor	Ricinus communis
A7.	Niger	Guizotia absyssinica
A8.	Safflower	Carthamus tinctorius
Group B. Newer oil-bearing materials		
B1.	Groundnut	Arachis hypogaea
B2.	Soyabean	Glycine max
B3.	Sunflower	Halianthus annuus
B4.	Oil palm	Elaeis guineensis
Group C. Oil-bearing materials derived as byproducts of cultivated crops		
Cl.	Ricebran	Oryza sativa
C2.	Tapioca seed	Manihot esculenta
C3.	Maize germ	Zea mays
C4.	Tobacco seed	Nicotiana spp.
C5.	Rubber seeds	Hevea brasiliensis
C6.	Tung seeds	Aleurites spp.
C7.	Jute seeds	Corchorus spp.
C8.	Spent coffee grounds	Coffea spp.
C9.	Tea seeds	Camellia spp.
Group D. Oilseeds with unusual lipid associates		
Dl.	Neem	Melia indica
D2.	Karanja	Pongamia pinnata
D3.	Kusum	Schleichera oleosa
D4.	Nahor	Mesua ferrea
D5.	Undi	Calophyllum mophyllum
D6.	Rayana	Amoora rohituka

(Contd.)

	Common names	Botanical nomenclature
Group E. Oilseeds carrying vegetable hard fats		
EI.	Mahua	Madhuca indica
E2.	Sal	Shorea robusta
E3.	Dhupa	Vateria indica
E4.	Kokum	Garcinia indica
E5.	Tamal	Garcinia morella
E6.	Pulwara	Diploknema butyracea
Group F. Oilseeds carrying soap-making oils		
FI.	Khankan-Pilu	Salvadora spp.
F2.	Pisa	Actinodaphne hookeri
F3.	Chirandi	Litsea glutinosa
Group G. Oilseeds with oil of unusual nature		
GI.	Maroti	Hydnocarpus laurifolia
G2.	Kamala	Mallotus philippinensis
G3.	Pinari	Sterculia foetida
G4.	Malkanguni	Celastrus paniculatus
Group H. Oilseeds from shrubs		
HI.	Ratanjyoti	Jatropha curcas
H2.	Gokhru	Xanthium strumarium
H3.	Hurthur	Cleome icosandra
H4.	Somraji	Vernonia anthelmintica
H5.	Argemone	Argemone mexicana
Group I. Oilseeds from trees that yield other commercial products		
11.	Akra	Calotropis spp.
12.	Simul	Bombax ceiba
13.	Kapok	Ceiba pentandra
14.	Baheda	Terminalia belerica
15.	Palas	Butea monosperma
16.	Teak	Tectona grandis
17.	Tamarind	Tamarindus indica
Group J. Oilseeds from fruits		
JI.	Mango kernel	Mangifera indica
J2.	Thumba	Citrullus colocynthis
J3.	Water melon	Citrullus vulgaris
J4.	Musk melon	Cucumis melo

(Contd.)

	Common names	Botanical nomenclature
J5.	Lime	Citrus aurantifolia
J6.	Sweet orange	Citrus sinensis
J7.	Papaya	Carica papaya
J8.	Sitaphal	Annona squamosa
J9.	Sapota	Manilkara achras
J10.	Grape	Vitis vinifera
JII.	Kapittha	Limonia acidissima
Group K. Oil from vegetables		
KI.	Ambadi	Hibiscus cannabinus
K2.	Okra	Abelmoschus esculentus
K3.	Tomato	Lycopersicon lycopersicum
K4.	Chilli	Capasicum annuum

Animal fats like tallow lard etc. are not produced in India. Because of religious sentiment animal fat import is banned.

Tallow is procured chiefly from the fat of cows, bullocks, buffaloes, sheep, goats and similar animals. It is separated by fusion from the membranes and fatty matter by rendering, a process involving the use of heat and steam.

Tallow as available in the market is very variable in quality and colour. The tallow obtained from the thick fatty deposits surrounding the abdomen is considered to be of the highest quality and is much used for edible purpose. Inferior qualities of tallow are obtained from hollow bones of animals and are commonly known as bone grease, bone fat, bone tallow, marrow tallow, etc. An oil separates out when melted tallow is allowed to crystallise out. This is known as tallow oil and is also employed in soap making to some extent. The genuineness of tallow can be tested by its specific gravity (0.943 to 0.942) and melting point (42° to 46°C).

Tallow contains about 24% of C_{18} and 25% of C_{16} saturated fatty acids. It also contains 42% C_{16} unsaturated single and double bond acid.

The fatty acids which are mainly present in naturally occurring oils and fats are lauric (C_{12}), myristic (C_{14}), palmitic (C_{16}), stearic (C_{18}) and behenic (C_{22}) saturated acids, palmitoleic (C_{16}), oleic (C_{18}), crucic (C_{22}) unsaturated with one double bond, linoleic (C_{18}) unsaturated acid with two double bond and linolenic (C_{18}) unsaturated acid with three double bonds. Castor oil is the only oil which contains a hydroxy acid ricinoleic acid i.e. 12 hydroxy oleic acid.

The figures in bracket indicates the number of carbon atoms in the fatty acids. Naturally occurring fatty acids are all even number carbon atom acid. Odd number carbon atom acids do not occur in nature.

Rice bran oil which is a major oil available to soap industry contains C_{16} and C_{18} unsaturated fatty acids with one double bond. It also contains about 12% lauric acid. Hydrogenated rice bran oil will contain lauric, palmitic and stearic acids in the same proportion.

Soyabean oil contains 11% myristic acid 51% C_{18} unsaturated fatty acid with one double bond and 25% C_{16} fatty acid with one double bond.

Palm oil contains 48% myristic acid and 38% oleic acid. Palm oil is distilled to stearin and olein. Palmstearin is very suitable for soap making,

Coconut oil contains 48% lauric acid and is the richest source of lauric acid for soap making.

Most of the common vegetable edible oils in India are far expensive to be used for soap making. Castor oil, because of its content of about 80% ricinoleic acid has high value for oleochemicals, which are used for paints, varnishes etc. It is also used in textile processing after sulphonation.

Coconut oil has a pleasant odour, characteristic of its own. Its specific gravity is 0.93 at 15°C and 0.87 at 100°C. It melts at 20° to 25°C and remains in the liquid state for the greater part of the year. It is saponified readily, taking a stronger alkali (20° to 22° Tw) than any other fat at the ordinary temperature with the evolution of much heat. It lends itself to the cold process of soap making with the greatest facility. But one great draw-back which the oil suffers from is that it goes rancid on keeping and gives out of offensive smell. The oil consists of stearic, palmitic, oleic, myristic and lauric acids as triglycerides and contains small quantities of lower acids, butyric, caproic, etc.

The oil requires 18.2 to 18.6 per cent of caustic soda and 25.5 to 26 per cent of caustic potash for complete neutralisation. With weak lyes the saponification is retarded till the lye gets concentrated to 20° to 22° Tw as against 10° Tw in the case of tallow. The oil foams considerably and special precautions are to be taken to prevent boiling over. During graining the oil requires twice as much salt as tallow or any other oil.

Coconut oil yields a good white soap, lathering freely in both fresh and salt water. The lather, however, is of thin body and lacks permanency, which is a feature of lard soap. The oil is therefore made the chief basis in the manufacture of marine and hard water soaps. It is capable of taking up a very large percentage of water and filling agents which would go to cheapen the cost of production. It is also used in making toilet soaps but the product is rather harsh to delicate skin unless blended with other oils.

The soap from coconut oil is fairly hard in consistency but is rubbed off easily. It is often used in admixture with tallow to give the soap a greater lathering property. This admixture will also prevent cracking of the tallow soap when dried up. The yield of glycerine from coconut oil is also great being 12 per cent of the soap. The soap, however, does not keep well long and is likely to go rancid on long keeping.

Palm oil is obtained from the fleshy portion of the fruit of the oil palm (Elacis Guineensis). The oil varies from a light yellow to a dark red colour and is sometimes of a buttery or tallow like consistency. The fatty acids contained in the oil are chiefly palmitic and oleic.

From the soap manufacturers' point of view palm oil makes an excellent soap stock yielding a pale soap of a firm texture and compact body. It can be treated by the cold process also. For those having objections to the employment of tallow in the soap stock, palm oil will form a good substitute. The oil also constitutes a good ingredients in toilet soaps, but they are liable to lose their scent readily. Like tallow it can be used with coconut oil.

The oil melts at 27° to 30°C and solidifies at 30° to 40°C according to the age and origin of the oil. The oil requires 14.0 to 14.7 per cent of caustic soda for complete saponification. The percentage of caustic potash for the same purpose comes up to 19.7 to 20.3.

Cotton seed oil is available in the cotton bearing tracts and can be used as a soap stock. The soap made from crude cotton seed oil is good but the colour is rather dirty. The refined oil is a clean bright oil of a pale yellow colour and produces a white soap but this is liable to be soon discoloured and does not also keep well. The oil, however, may be used in admixture with other fats and oils is suitable proportions.

Cotton seed oil has a specific gravity of 0.916 to 0.930 at 15.5°C. The flash point of the oil is 475°F and it solidifies at 0°C to 1°C. It requires 19.2 to 20.0 per cent of caustic potash and 13.71 to 14.3 per cent of caustic soda for complete neutralisation. The process of saponification in the case of cotton seed oil is rather difficult, the lye remaining in the body of the soap. The soap is therefore hard to obtain in a neutral condition. Saponification is best begun with caustic lye at 15°Be; addition of soap scraps or admixture with easily saponifiable fats accelerates the operation.

The soap also is not so easily grained as tallow soap. Cotton seed oil yields a soap of thin body which can be hardened by mixing soda ash and sodium silicate. It is darker than the tallow soap and comparatively easily soluble in water. It is more soluble in water than tallow soap and comparatively easily soluble in water. It is more soluble in water than tallow soaps and therefore lathers in water than tallow soaps and therefore lathers freely but the lather does not last as long as the soap made from tallow and other fats. An addition of tallow hence improves the washing property of the soap.

The soap made from cotton seed oil has a pale reddish tinge and a high detergent property but often gets rancid on long storage. The oil consists chiefly of the glycerides of palmitic, oleic, linolic, myristic and stearic acids.

Mahua is found in West Bengal, Bihar and the greater part of Central India. Mahua oil has come into large use among the soap makers. It is cheap and gives a soft body to the soap. It is used along with other oils to give a balanced soap stock.

The oil is much used in laundry and cheap toilet soaps on account of its low price. The oil has a pale yellow colour but oil of light yellow colour is also met with. It is used in conjunction with coconut oil ricebran and other oil. It is often substituted for animal fat.

The soap from the mahua oil has a rather soft consistency. It gives thin but ample lather. When wheat flour is used in the soap as a filler it can absorb much water.

The oil requires 13.6 per cent of its weight of caustic soda and 18.7 to 19 per cent of caustic potash. The soap solidifies after graining at 57°C.

Margosa oil, commonly known as Neem oil, is the oil obtained from the seed of *Melia Azadirachta,* a large evergreen tree growing wild throughout the greater part of the Indian Peninsula. Certain medical properties are attributed to the oil which has accordingly some application, a nominal quantity only being used by a few soap makers to make medicinal soaps possessing the odour of the original oil. The oil contains oleic palmitic and stearic acids with smaller quantities of linoleic, arachidic and lignocerie acids.

Neem oil is a stock capable of producing a fairly hard soap, and as such, should be highly valued, since most of cheap soap stocks available from vegetable source in India are of the soft kind. The soap from Neem oil is almost as hard as the mahua soap.

The oil has a specific gravity of 0.9143 at 30°C and requires 19.62 per cent of caustic potash and 14.01 per cent of caustic soda for complete neutralisation. The oil is, therefore, quite suitable for the making of grained soap, moulded or stamped. Unsaponifiable matter is present to the extent of 2.3 per cent, in the oil while the acid value is 5.7.

Neem oil saponifies readily and the soap produces profuse lather which is slightly greasy. But the oil gives a perfect washing soap in judicious mixture with other harder and softer stocks.

Karanja or Pongam oil is obtained from the seed of Pongamia Glabra. The oil is used for the manufacture of settled soap. The oil has a specific gravity of 0.9297 at 31°C and a saponification value of 185.3, i.e., it requires 18.53 per cent of its own weight of caustic potash for saponification.

The oil contains a compound substance having a disagreeable smell which is passed on to the soap unless removed before hand by bringing about its decomposition. The latter is brought about by protracted boiling with caustic soda in course of saponification. The oil cannot therefore be use by itself or in combination with other oils and fats for making soap by the cold process free from objectionable odour. Karanja oil saponifies fairly easily to form a soap of a soft consistency and having good cleansing properties. It lathers freely and has a thick greasy feel, the latter due to the presence in the oil of some resinous matter which is converted into soap. The stock has been found to be suitable for the making of moulded and settled soaps still possessing good lathering and cleansing properties.

Since Karanja oil is a comparatively soft stock, moulded soap of the proper degree of hardness cannot be made of a mixture of oils and fats containing more than 25 per cent, of this oil. Having regard to the other requirements of the soap it will be found convenient to use the oil in proportion lower than the maximum stated above, for ensuring good body and high cleansing property to the soap. Soaps made from mixtures containing higher proportions of Karanja oil than 25 per cent, will dissolve too quickly. Such soaps will have a tendency to turn slightly brownish on long storage. In a moulded soap, however, a brownish colour is not generally considered so much a disqualification.

The soap made entirely from Karanja oil can be grained and moulded, but it develops a dirty brown colour on prolonged storage. The soap grained over brine has a solidification point of 39°C as against 66.5°C for tallow, 57°C for mahua oil, 54°C for punnal oil, 52°C for rayna oil and 54°C for groundnut oil.

Chaulmoogra oil is extracted from the seeds of Taraktogenous Kurzii, a tree found in Assam and West Bengal. The oil is known for its high optical rotation. The average specific rotation at 15°C is about 50. The importance of the oil lies in its use as medicine. It has been used for many years in the treatment of leprosy and other skin diseases. The oil has a specific gravity a 30°C of 0.945 to 0.952. The oil requires for complete saponification 19.8 to 20.83 per cent, of caustic potash and 14.4 to 14.8 per cent, of caustic soda.

Majority of the vegetable and animal oils and fats can be used for soap making. What determines their use is their availability and price.

India's large population consumes majority of the vegetable oils, except non edible oils, for edible purpose. The price of oil is high and is uncompetitive for soap production compared to synthetic detergents.

Caustic soda: One of the most important ingredients in soap making is the caustic soda. Caustic soda of reliable quality now is readily available at affordable price.

Caustic soda comes into commerce in four forms :

(1) Solid

(2) Flakes

(3) As 50% and 30% lye

Commercial caustic soda is a creamy or white mass, having a slightly fibrous structure. It is very hygroscopic, readily absorbing water from the air and passes into a highly caustic liquor. It also readily absorbs carbonic acid from the air, passing into carbonate so that it is not desirable that caustic soda should be exposed too much to the air. Usually the lye is used after dilution for soap making.

Caustic potash : Caustic potash possesses chemical properties very similar to those of caustic soda. Only it is much stronger in chemical action than the latter in every respect. But from the manufacturers' point of view there is an essential difference between the soaps produced with caustic soda and caustic potash. Soaps made with caustic potash are generally softer in consistency and more soluble in water than those made with caustic soda. Hence when soft soaps are to be manufactured caustic potash is required but it is rarely used in making ordinary domestic soaps. In making toilet soaps sometimes a fraction of the total alkali consists of caustic potash. It is used for making shaving soap.

Caustic potash dissolves readily in water forming a lye with considerable evolution of heat. It is hygroscopic and readily absorb carbon dioxide from the air and is converted into potassium carbonate. Hence it is of the utmost moment to the manufacturers that the caustic lye should be as little exposed to the air as possible.

Caustic potash, neutralises fatty acids to soap. But generally the percentage of the potash is rather higher than in the case of caustic soda. Usually 18.5 to 20 p.c. of pure caustic potash is required for saponification as against 13 to 14 per cent of pure caustic soda. As a matter of fact the quantity of caustic potash required to neutralise a sample of oil is exactly 1.4 times the quantity of caustic soda required for the same purpose.

The soaps made with caustic potash are soft and dissolve readily in water. The soaps therefore lather more freely.

Soda ash is consumed by the soaps and detergent industry as builder material. Soda ash is marketed in two varieties dense soda ash and light soda. Light soda ash is used in soap and detergents as in this form soda ash has large capacity to absorb moisture and drying of the product becomes easier. It is also useful in neutralising the acid lye while making the formulation.

Sodium silicate is brittle, breaking with a conchoidal fracture and resembles glass. Liquid sodium silicate is a viscous liquid (50°Be, sp. gr. 1.50 - 1.54). Generally it is of an alkaline character and possesses good detergent properties. Neutral silicates containing smaller proportion of soda are often used.

Usually 5 per cent is the quantity employed in making pale soaps and such a quantity will harden a soap. The proportion of the silicate is sometimes increased to 25 per cent in soaps and detergents. Larger excess makes the soap pasty. The presence of silicate of soda increases the alkalinity of the soap.

The detergent properties of the soap do not suffer by such addition though the soap is liable to get more caustic.

Another filling agent is **starch.** This has got the property of combining with water in the presence of alkalies into a gelatinous mass soluble in water. Hence this is added to make the soap of proper texture when it has got thin without dispensing with its large water. The use of starch does not produce any alteration in the appearance of the soap but the detergent property of course deteriorates. 2 per cent is, however, a fair quantity to use.

Glauber's salt is another filling agent which has got the property of rendering soap hard. But its use is accompanied by a very undesirable deposition of saline efflorescence on the soap. It is used in detergents freely.

Soap stone, otherwise known as French chalk or talc, is often incorporated to the extent of 5 to 10 per cent as a filling agent. It lacks the detergent properties of silicate or soda crystal and the binding power of starch.

Borax has often been suggested as a filling agent especially because it has got a good detergent property. But it is rather expensive to be so employed and can hardly go to cheapen the cost of production.

Some manufacturers make use of a small percentage of borax in their soap and detergent preparations. The addition is stated to improve the cleansing power of the product owing to the feebly alkaline nature of the soap and imparts to it a slight bleaching property.

Borax is chemically known as borate of sodium and occurs in fine, rather efflorescent crystals. Borax is soluble in half its weight of boiling water and about 12 parts of cold water.

Perfumes : Soaps made from animal fats and oils are often attended with an unpleasant, if not offensive, smell. This has to be masked if the products are to find a ready market. Detergents are also perfumed so as to have a consumer appeal. With this object in view the manufacturers employ a wide range of cheap scents, natural or synthetic to distinguish the odour of the soap. Again toilet and medicated soaps have to be delicately scented. For this purpose essential oils of the high qualities are mixed. To make the fragrance lasting the use of some fixative agents such as tincture of musk, ambergris, tolu balsam, benzoin civet oils, Peru balsam, sandal wood, patchouli, cloves, aniseed, benzyl benzoate, etc., is recommended.

In selecting perfumes for soap care should be taken that the perfumes have neither deleterious effect on the colour of the soap nor disturb the composition of the soap. Again suitable blending of perfumes is very much necessary as two unsuitable perfumes may by mutual reaction cancel each other's effect.

Clove oil, cassia oil, heliotropin, vanillin when added to the soaps cause them to be discoloured or to darken in keeping. Delicate perfumes such as bergamot oils, etc., should not be added to soaps with free alkalies.

Natural perfumes : A knowledge of the principal natural perfumes used in soap manufacture is necessary for soap makers. A list follows:—

Anise oil—Colourless, or at most faintly yellow oil when fresh. Has a pleasant odour and an aromatic sweet taste.

Bergamot oil—Has a light yellow colour but is often met with having a greenish tint. Has a strong agreeable odour. Is largely used in scenting toilet soap. Should be kept out of contract with air. Is often replaced by lemon oil for cheapness.

Carraway oil — Has a light yellow colour, an aromatic odour **and** burning taste. Is largely employed in the scenting of soaps **both alone** and in combination with other essential oils.

Cassia oil — Has a yellow colour but turns dark brown on standing. Has a pleasant odour not unlike that of cinnamon but not so pleasant. Gives the characteristic odour to brown. Windsor soap and is useful for sweetening coal-tar medicated soaps. Causes darkening.

Cinnamon oil — Viscid, golden yellow or golden brown **according** to age and has a burning but sweet taste. Much used in soaps.

Citronella oil — It has a pale yellow colour and a peculiar pleasant odour. Much used by soap makers

Clove oil — Colourless but soon becomes yellowish to brown and has a pleasant spicy odour and strong burning taste. Is largely used in soap making and indispensable in carnations.

Coriander oil — Pale yellow colour, pleasant odour, sharp aromatic taste. Very largely used in scenting soaps.

Eucalyptus oil — Is colourless, possesses characteristic odour, and is chiefly used in medicated soaps.

Geranium oil — Used largely in making rose and bouquet soaps. Particularly suitable for use in high class soaps. Has an odour like rose.

Lavender oil — Light yellow colour and a sharp burning taste. Only used in high class soap. The oil undergoes decomposition in the presence of air. It is scarcely used alone, oakmoss, rosemary, thyme and borneol being usually blended with it to modify and round off the scent.

Lemon grass oil—A colourless oil, possessing the scent of roses or rose geranium. It is much used in scenting soaps and forms the basis of all verbenas.

Mirbane oil—Has a strong lasting odour. Its use is not recommended.

Neroli oil — Has an odour like orange, and bitter taste. It is a cheap scent and is much used.

Orange oil—Has a golden yellow colour and yields the characteristic odour of orange.

Rosemary oil— Is good and stable, imparts freshness, useful in many compounds, specially lavender.

Sandal wood oil — This has got the characteristic smell of sandal wood and is yellowish in colour. It is much used in toilet soaps.

Vetivert oil — Gives persistent odours, good for violets.

Thyme oil — Excellent for imparting freshness to all kinds of soap compounds and has got good antiseptic value.

Besides these, other oils are used by the soap manufacturers, e.g., palmarosa oil, oil of sassafras, wintergreen oil, oil of peppermint, oil of nutmeg, oil of citron, spike oil, ylang oil, patchouli oil.

Synthetic perfumes : Synthetic perfumes are, however, being employed to a great extent by the soap manufacturers. The more important of them are benzyl butyrate, citral, citronellol, coumarine, eugenol, geraniol, heliotropin, ionone, linalol, rhodinol, safrol, santalol, skatol, terpeneol, etc. These are not generally used alone but are blended two or more together, to reproduce the odour of some well known flowers. Modifiers are also included to impart a sweet floral touch to the body perfume. For example, oil of lavender is modified by coumarine and benzylacetate; jasmine by indol and linalylacetate; lily by bois de rose femelle and linalol; narcissus by paracresol methyl ether and jasmilone; rose by geraniol and phenylethyl alcohol' and so on.

The following basic bodies, amongst others, will bring about a distinct natural tone if suitably blended :-

Lilac—Terpeneol, heliotropin, etc.

Violet— Ionone, irison, viodoron, irisoil.

Sandalwood oil— Santalresinoid, geraniol, phenylethyl-alcohol.

Jasmine — Benzyl acetate, indol, lenalylacetate, etc.

Orange — Yara yara (beta-naphtholethyl ether), bromelia (beta-naphthol-ethyl ether), etc.

Rose—Geraniol, rhodinol, geranilacetate, hydroxicetronellol, linalol, citronellol, phenylethyl alcohol, reuniol, etc.

Musk — Musk xylol, musk ambrette, benzylbenzoate, etc.

Clove — Eugenol, isoeugenol

Goldlack — Iris recinoid, neroline, etc.

Mayflower — Linalol terpeneol, etc.

Almond — Benzaldehydes, etc.

Geranium — Diphenylmethane, diphenylether, etc.

Trefle — Amylsalreylate, heliotropin etc.

Hay — Coumarine, liquid storax, etc.

Fixatives : There are various gums and resins which have got the property of fixing the scent of the perfumes added. Chief of them are Peru Balsam, Tolu Balsam, Gum Benzoin, Myrrh, Storax, etc., etc. When these are added in the soap they make the scent lasting and do not allow them to pass off too quickly. Various tinctures and infusions are also employed for the same purpose. The most popular of them are infusion ambrette, infusion musk, tincture civet, tincture iris, etc., etc.

Colours : In selecting colours for the soaps and detergents care should be taken that they are not acted upon by alkalies which may be present in the free state in them. This precludes the use of prussian blue, chrome yellow, alkali blue, magenta, etc. Organic dyes which are soluble in soap and detergent solutions can be readily mixed and pioduce every imaginable shade. The colour also should not have any deleterious action on the perfumes and should resemble so far as possible the colour of the flower whose odour is sought to be reproduced. Dyestuffs are generally preferred to pigments.

A list of the more important colours follows:—

White — Zinc oxide, titanium dioxide.

Yellow — Fluoresceine yellow, soap yellow, quinoline yellow (water soluble or spirit soluble), metanil yellow, cadmium yellow, ochres, napthol yellow, tartrazine, uramine opal.

Red — Cardinal red B, ponceau 2 R, rhodamine, saffranine, crocein scarlet.

Rose — Ponceau, scarlet, vermilion.

***Bright** rose* — Brilliant roses, rhodamine B.

Deep pink — Erythrosine B, eosine

Bluish pink — Bluish pink N., saffranine, rhodamine B extra-G.

Green — Fast light green, Ultramarine green chrome green, alizarine or naphol compounds.

Orange — Brilliant orange G.

Brown — Soap browns, soudan brown, caramel, umbers, burnt sienna, bismark brown.

Blue — Methylene blue, ultramarine, cyanole blue FF.

Violet — Formyl violet S4B, methyl violet.

A variety of other shades may be obtained by mixing these different colours, e.g., a mixture of red and blue will produce violet and lilac tints; blue and yellow greens of various tones; red and yellow scarlet rose, etc.

The colours require careful testing before use. They must be perfectly soluble in hot water, not cause spottiness in the soap, be stable, when exposed to light and the froth caused by the coloured soap should be white.

Detergents

Linear alkyl benzene sulphonic acid (acid slurry): This is the largest amount of detergent raw material used in the industry. In the beginning Dodecyl benzene sulphonate was used. Later on it was found that the linear alkyl chain attached to benzene instead of dodecyl side chain makes the sulphonate better biodegradable. The linear chain has 12 carbon atoms to make the sulphonate best surfactant. Alpha olefin is reacted with benzene to produce linear alkyl benzene. The alpha olefin is produced from straight chain dodecane obtained from kerosene fraction. The catalyst used is HF or BF_3. The sulphonation is done by concentrated sulphuric acid or by oleum or by SO_3. In SSI sector the most popular sulphonating agent is concentrate sulphuric acid. Some people carry out sulphonation using chlorosulphonic acid.

Economic size of a batch sulphonation is 1 tonne of acid slurry per batch. 500 kg and 750 kg per batch are also prevalent. The reactor is SS316. The reactor is jacketed for cooling water circulation and is provided with a mechanical agitator. After sulphonation the acid slurry is separated in a lead lined conical vessel. Temperature during sulphonation is kept at 45 - 50°C. Time taken for sulphonation is 2-3 hours and 6-8 hours for settling. Sulphuric acid and alkylate are charged into the vessel at the ratio of 1:1.5.

Long chain fatty alcohol sulphate : Fatty alcohols are produced by hydrogenation of respective fatty acid which are obtained from vegetable and animal oils. It is also produced by Ziegler process using ethylene as raw material and $A1H_3$ as catalyst. Fatty alcohols are also produced by OXO process. However, the product is a mixture of straight chain and branched chain alcohol. The sulphation is carried out by sulphuric acid.

Ethylene oxide condensate: Fatty alcohols are reacted with ethylene oxide to produce a nonionic surfactants. 10-15 moles of ethylene oxide addition per mole of fatty alcohol is optimum for detergent purpose. Ethylene oxide is also reacted with alkyl phenol, fatty acid, fatty acid amide. In all cases surfactants are produced which are used in hair care product or speciality surfactants.

6

Analysis and Testing

Oils and fats are analyzed by standard methods adoptec by the Fat Analysis Committee (F.A.C.) of the American Chemical Society or by the official methods of the American Oil Chemists Society (A.O.C.S.). The tests that follow are abridged from these official methods, with slight modification. For routine commercial analysis, they will be found quite satisfactory.

TEST FOR MOISTURE

Weigh a sample of 5 g into a shallow glass dish, 6 to 7 cm diameter and 4 cm deep, and heat it to constant weight in a vacuum over repeatedly for 1 hour at 20 - 25°C above the boiling point of water at 100 mm of mercury.

Alternately, heating in an air oven at 100 - 105°C or one half hour, until the loss in each heating period is not greater than 0.05%, is sufficiently accurate for most industrial laboratory work :

$$\frac{\text{Loss in weight} \times 100}{5} = \text{\% moisture}$$

The air-oven method applies to all oils except those of the coconut group and oxidizing oils.

TEST FOR FREE FATTY ACIDS

Dissolve a 5 g sample in hot neutral alcohol (pink to phenolphthalein) or No. 30 Special Denatured Alcohol. Titrate this with standard sodium hydroxide solution.

$$\frac{ml \text{ NaOH} \times \text{normality} \times 28.2}{5} = \text{\% Free fatty acids, as oleic}$$

An alternate method, which does not require weighing, is to heat the oil or fat to 150°F; then pipette an 8 ml sample into 50 ml cf hot neutral ethanol or isopropanol, and titrate with N/4 sodium hydroxide, using a few drops of a 1% alcoholic solution of phenolphthalein as indicator. The test can be performed in a 4-oz oil sample bottle. When pink end-point is reached, shake the bottle vigorously, until the pink remains 30 seconds.

Reading on burette = % Free fatty acids (as oleic)

TEST FOR IMPURITIES

The presence of impurities in the oil or fat under examination can usually be seen with the naked eye, when the fat is hot, as it is being removed from the oven during the test for moisture. If only a trace of dirt or fat insoluble matter is present, it may be disregarded. If the amount is considerable or when testing house grease or bone grease that may contain lime soap — soluble in hot fat — 5 g of the sample used for determining moisture is dissolved in 200 ml of petroleum ether and set away in a cool place for 1 hour. Then the oil is filtered through a Gooch crucible or weighed filter paper.

$$\% \text{ impurities} = \frac{\text{increase in weight} \times 100}{5}$$

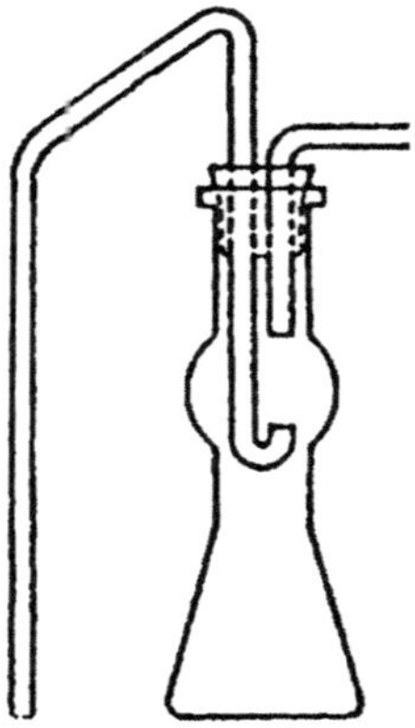

Fig. 6.1. Stokes flask

TEST FOR UNSAPONIFIABLE MATTER

Boil a sample of 5 g under reflux condenser with 30 ml of redistilled ethanol and 5 ml of 50% aqueous potassium hydroxide for 1 hour. Using ethanol transfer this to 4-oz oil bottle or Stokes flask (Fig. 6.1), add in equal volume of water, cool it, and extract it five times with 25 ml of petroleum ether, shaking the solution vigorously after each extraction. Allow the extract to come to the surface and by means of a bent glass tube, held in the cork of the Stokes flask, blow the supernatant extract, as from a wash bottle, into a 500 ml pear-shaped separatory funnel. Repeat this four times.

Wash the petroleum ether extracts twice with 50% ethanol. Filter the extract into a weighed Soxhlet flask, and distill or evaporate it. The residual petroleum ether may be evaporated by setting the flask in a hole of the steam bath for about 15 minutes and then drying in the oven for another 15 minutes. Cool the residue in a desiccator and weigh it.

$$\frac{\text{Gain in weight} \times 100}{5} = \%\ \text{unsaponifiable}$$

The sum of the moisture, impurities, and unsaponifiable matter is called MIU.

TEST FOR TITER

The titer test is the determination of the highest point in °C reached during the solidification of fatty acids of an oil or fat, under conditions explained as follows : The test will give the soapmaker an idea of the character of the soap he will obtain.

Dissolve 250 g of C.P. caustic potash in 1000 ml of C.P., or dynamite grade, glycerol to avoid foaming, do not heat over 140°C.

Heat 80 ml of the glycerol/caustic solution to 150°C, and add 50 ml of melted fat. Stir the mixture well and continue heating at 140 - 150°C until the soap becomes fairly viscous, clears and thins out again. This should require at least 15-20 minutes. Pour a bit of the soap into a test tube, add hot distilled water and stir until solution takes place. The solution should be very clear. If so, it may reasonably be assumed that the saponification is complete.

Allow the mass to cool somewhat, add hot water to dissolve the soap, heating to boil if necessary. Add cautiously, 50 ml of 30%, sulphuric acid, and boil until the clear fatty acids separate out. The aqueous solution must be acidic to break the soap completely. If insufficient acid is used, the entire soap may not be decomposed and the fatty acids will not be clear. (The whole operation may be carried out in an 8-inch evaporating dish.) Cool somewhat, syphon off the acid water, and wash the fatty acids several times with hot water.

Transfer the fatty acids to a 100 ml beaker, taking care that in decanting, no water runs into the beaker. Heat to 130°C as rapidly as possible, while stirring with the thermometer. Allow solution to cool to 2-3 degrees above the expected titer.

Transfer to a titer test tube (100 mm x 25 mm), which is set into a perforated cork of a 16-oz salt-mouth bottle, so that the test tube will be held rigidly. Suspend the standard titer-test thermometer (graduated in 0.2°C), so that the bulb reaches the center of the fat in the test tube. Stir with the thermometer rapidly, while the mercury drops, then remains stationary, and begins to rise gradually. Stop the stirring and observe the highest point to which the mercury rises.

This figure is recorded as the titer.

TESTS FOR COLOUR

There are several systems by which colour of oils and fats is measured. For vegetable oils, fairly light in colour, the American Oil Chemists' Society's official method CC13 b-45 has been adopted. The colour is determined by matching a column of oil 133.35 mm (5.25 in.) high, in a tintometer, using red and yellow standard Lovibond color glasses for comparison.

The standards for red glass are determined by the National Bureau of Standards, in terms of the Priest-Gibson N colour scale. The yellow glasses are not standardized because there is little visual difference between the glasses produced by the different manufacturers. The Wesson tintometer is equipped with 31 Lovibond glasses.

For refined bleached oil, the ratio of yellow to red is :

Oil	Yellow		Red
Cottonseed, peanut, corn	10	to	1—3.5
	35	for	3.5 and up
Coconut, palm kernel	6	to	1—3.9
	10	to	1 for 3.9 and up
Soyabean	10	to	1—3.5
	70	to	3.5 or above
Tallows, greases, fatty acids	10	to	1—3.5
	35	for	3.5—5 inclusive
	70	for	Above 5

For refined oil : Use only 1 yellow glass, 35 yellow for refined cottonseed oil and refined peanut oil; 70 yellow for refined soybean oil. Use not more than two red glasses up to and including 13 red, and not more than 3.red glasses above 13 red.

The colour of dark oils may be read by using a column of oil, 25.4 mm (1.25 in.) high and matching with yellow and red glasses, making note that the reading was taken on a column of 25.4 mm. Specifications covering grades of crude and refined oils are published by the National Cottonseed Products Association.

The test for colour used by soapmakers, and also the official method of the American Oil Chemists' Society, applicable to animal fats and all fats and oils too dark to be read by the Wesson Tintometer, is as follows :

Fat analysis committee colour test : In the A.O.C.S. Methods of Analysis (Revised, 1964), the fat to be tested is heated to about 10°C above the melting point. It is then poured into a small test tube and matched with the LaPine Colour Standards. The latter consists of a 3-Aperture Colour Grading Comparator, with four discs of the F.A.C. colour scale. Discs are also supplied for Gardner Colour Standards, for evaluating color of varnishes, oils, lacquers and reins. The paint industry has adopted the Gardner standards.

Tubes of the same size as the standards, filled with the oil to be graded, are matched to the nearest colour standard.

Other systems : The National Petroleum Association uses a colour system which corresponds numerically to the system of the ASTM and Union colorimeter.

The Hardy recording spectrophotometer permits exact measurement of colour and thus eliminates possibility of visual error. However, the instrument is expensive and colours cannot be expressed in single figures as yellow and red.

IODINE NUMBER (WIJS METHOD)

The iodine number or iodine value of an oil is expressed as the number of centigrams of iodine absorbed by 1-g sample (% iodine absorbed). It is also a measure of the unsaturation of an oil or fat. The higher the iodine number, the more unsaturated is the oil, i.e., the more readily will it oxidize and vice versa.

Preparation of reagents : *Wijs iodine solution*

The Wijs method calls for the solution of 13 g resumblined iodine in 1 litre of glacial acetic acid. Dried chlorine gas is added to the solution until the original titration is not quite doubled.

N/10 sodium thiosulphate

Dissolve 24.8 g sodium thiosulphate ($Na_2S_2O_3.5H_2O$) and dilute it to 1 liter at the temperature at which the titrations are to be made.

Starch paste

Boil 1 g of starch in 200 ml of distilled water for 10 minutes and cool to room temperature.

Potassium iodide solution

Dissolve 150 g of potassium iodide in distilled water and make up to 1 litre.

Potassium dichromate solution

Dissolve 0.9658 g of potassium dichromate in distilled water and make up to 250 ml. This solution is equivalent to 0.01 g iodine/ml. In laboratories where the iodine number is determined frequently, one may make up a litre at a time, using four times the quantity of potassium dichromate.

All the reagents should be chemically pure and of a standard recommended by the American Chemical Society (A.C.S. Grade).

Standardization of sodium thiosulphate solution : With a pipette, place 25 ml of potassium dichromate solution in an Erlenmeyer flask. Add 10 ml of potassium iodide solution and 5 ml of hydrochloric acid. Dilute with 100 ml of distilled water and titrate with the sodium thiosulphate until the solution turns straw yellow. Add a few drops of starch paste and continue the titration until the blue colour disappears. Note the number of ml. required to discharge the colour.

Determination iodine value : Weigh into a dry 250 ml iodine flask (or an 8-oz glass stoppered bottle) containing 20 ml of re-distilled carbon tetrachloride, 0.1 to 0.5 g of oil or melted fat, using the lower quantity for oils with high iodine values. Add 25 ml of Wijs solution by means of a pipette, allowing it to drain for a definite time. The excess iodine should be 50 - 60% of the amount added; that is, 100 - 150% of the amount absorbed. Moisten the stopper with 15% potassium iodide solution to prevent loss of iodine or chlorine, but guard against an amount sufficient to run down inside the flask. Stopper the flask and set it in a dark place. Prepare two blanks identical with the sample, but without the fat or oil. Let the flasks stand in the dark for 30 minutes at room temperature.

Remove the flasks from storage and add 20 ml of potassium iodide solution and 100 ml of distilled water. Titrate with sodium thiosulphate solution — which is added gradually with constant rotary motion of the flask — until the yellow colour has almost disappeared. Toward the end of the titration, stopper the flask and shake it vigorously, so that any iodine that may still be dissolved in the carbon tetrachloride may be taken up by the potassium iodide solution. Finish this titration, adding a few drops of starch paste. Discharge any blue colour still remaining. Then titrate the blanks.

Variations in temperature appreciably affect that titer of the iodine solution, as acetic acid has a high coefficient of expansion. It is therefore essential that the blanks and the determination on the sample be run at the same time. The number of ml of standard thiosulphate solution required by the blanks, less the amount used in the determination, gives the thiosulphate equivalent of the iodine absorbed by the sample. Calculate to centigrams of iodine absorbed by 1 g sample (% iodine absorbed).

Example : Sample, 0.2264 g of olive oil

	$Na_2S_2O_3$ ml
The blank requires	27.65
Back titration on sample	17.45
The difference is	10.20

Therefore, $\frac{10.2}{0.2264}$ = of thiosulphate for a gram of olive oil.

The 25 ml of potassium dichromate, equivalent to 0.25 g of iodine, requires 13.8 ml of thiosulphate for titration. Consequently, 1 g of iodine will require four times 13.8 ml, or 55.2 ml of thiosulphate. Therefore

$$\frac{\frac{10.2}{0.2264}}{55.2} \times 100 = 81.6\%$$ of iodine absorbed, which is designated iodine value or iodine number.

SAPONIFICATION NUMBER

The saponification number of Koettsdorfer Number, of an oil or fat is the number of milligrams of potassium hydroxide required to saponify 1 g of the sample.

The saponification equivalent corresponds approximately to the molecular weight, in case of fatty acids or esters of monohydric alcohols. For glycerides, the saponification equivalent multiplied by 3 corresponds to the molecular weight.

$$\text{Saponification equivalent} = \frac{56{,}100}{\text{Saponification Number}}$$

Preparation of reagents : ***N/2 Hydrochloric acid*** : Carefully standardized.

Alcoholic potash : Prepare the alcohol (S.D. 30 or 34) by boiling 1500 ml with 10 g of potassium hydroxide, under a reflux condenser, on a steam bath, for one hour and distil off 1 litre. Dissolve 27 g of potassium hydroxide in 1 litre of distilled alcohol, without heating. The solution should be clear.

Alcoholic phenolphthalein : Prepare a 1% solution of phenolphthalein in alcohol.

Determination of saponification number: Weigh accurately about 5 g of the filtered sample into a 150 ml Erlenmeyer flask. Pipette 50 ml of alcoholic potash into the flask, allowing it to drain a definite time. Connect the flask with an air condenser and boil gently for 30 minutes. Cool and titrate with N/2 hydrochloric acid, using phenolphthalein as indicator. Run a blank simultaneously.

Calculate saponification number as follows :

$$\frac{\text{(Titration of blank-Titration of sample) } 28.05}{5} = \text{Saponification number}$$

This holds when exactly 5 g are taken for the determination otherwise, use the weight of the sample as the divisor.

MELTING POINT OF FATS

There are several methods for determining the melting point of natural fats. Where two chemists are checking each other, there should be a mutual agreement previously, on the method to be employed. Fats and oils are not pure organic chemicals and therefore, their melting points are not well defined. In melting, they go through an opalescent stage and finally turn clear.

Capillary method : the fat to be tested should be clean and absolutely dry. The hot fat may be run through a filter paper. The capillary tubes, 1 mm in diameter and 80 mm long, are immersed in the hot fat to a distance of 10 mm. The tubes are then sealed at the bottom, by holding them in a bunsen flame, taking care not to burn the fat. Three capillary tubes are set in the refrigerator at 40°C overnight. The tubes are then attached to the titer thermometer, by means of rubber bands, so that the bottom of each tube is flush with that of the thermometer bulb.

The bulb and tubes are suspended in a 600 ml beaker of distilled water to a depth of 30 mm. The water is heated with a bunsen flame so that the temperature will rise 1° a minute. When the fat turns clear, the thermometer is read and the average of the three melting points taken. This should be within 0.5°.

ACID NUMBER

The acid number of an oil or fat is expressed as milligrams of potassium hydroxide required to neutralize 1 g of the sample.

Weigh 5 - 20 g of the sample into a 4-oz oil bottle, add 50 ml of hot ethanol, previously neutralized with N/10 sodium or potassium hydroxide, using phenolphthalein as indicator. Titrate until the pink colour persists for half minute. Calculate milligrams of potassium hydroxide required.

$$\frac{\text{ml x normality x 0.056 x 1000}}{\text{Weight of sample}} = \text{Acid number}$$

Ester value = Saponification Number minus Acid Number

The ester value indicates the approximate amount of glycerides present.

ACETYL VALUE

The acetyl value is the number of milligrams of potassium hydroxide required to neutralize the acetic acid obtained on saponification of 1 g of acetylated fat.

The determination is based on the principle that glycerides that contain hydroxylated fatty acids assimilate, on heating with acetic anhydride, one or more acetyl groups, according to whether the fatty acids contain one or more hydroxyl groups. In this reaction, the hydrogen atom of the alcoholic hydroxyl group or groups is replaced by the acetic acid radical.

Determination of acetyl number : Boil 10 - 50 g of a sample with an equal volume of acetic anhydride, in an acetylation flask, for two hours. Then pour the mixture into a large beaker containing 500 ml of water and boil this for 30 minutes. To prevent bumping, pass a slow current of carbon dioxide through a finely drawn out tube that reaches the bottom.

Allow the mixture to separate into two layers. Syphon off the water, and boil the only layer with fresh water until it is no longer acid to litmus. Separate the acetylated fat from the water; dry and filter the fat while it is kept hot in the drying oven.

Saponification : Follow the method prescribed under *Saponification Number,* and calculate in the usual way the milligrams of potassium hydroxide required to saponify 1 g of sample.

The acetyl value is calculated from the following formula :

$$A = \frac{S' - A}{1 - 0.00075\ S}$$

where A is acetyl value

S' is saponification after acetylation

S is saponification number before acetylation

COLD TEST

Place 28 ml of the oil in a cold test bottle or 4-oz oil bottle. Set the bottle in a freezing mixture consisting of shaved ice and salt. Immerse a cold test thermometer in the oil and hold it in the bottle by means of a cork gasket. When the oil becomes solid, let it stand for half in hour longer. Then remove the bottle from the freezing mixture and stir it with the thermometer as soon as the oil has softened sufficiently. Grasp the top of the bottle so that the heat of the hand does not warm the oil and tip it at an angle of 45° below the horizontal.

Note the temperature at which the oil will just run from one end of the bottle to the other. This point, expressed in Fahrenheit degrees, is taken as the cold test.

The cold test of an oil is a measure of how well it will lubricate at low temperatures. Therefore, the lower the cold test, the better the lubricity at low temperature.

Emulsions utilizing neatsfoot oil of low cold test are more fluid and strike through leather more easily, e.g., in fat-liquoring.

SMOKE, FLASH, FIRE TESTS

The smoke, flash, and fire points of animal and vegetable fats and oils are determined by heating the dry oil or fat under standard conditions in the Cleveland open cap. They are expressed in Fahrenheit degrees.

Smoke test: Fill the cup to the mark with the sample to be tested, and then heat it slowly over a bunsen flame to within 75°F of the expected smoke point.

The cup, with the thermometer hanging in the center of the melted fat or oil, should be suitably shielded by means of a box, constructed of asbestos board, which supports an electric bulb on one side, at the level of the surface of the oil. When a bluish smoke appears, the temperature is noted. This is the smoke point.

Flash test: Fill the cup with the molten fat to be tested, and suspend a thermometer so that the bulb is about 6 mm from the bottom of the cup. Heat slowly, to raise the temperature to within 100°F of the expected flash point, and then regulate the heat so that the rise will be about 10°F a minute. By means of a blowpipe, light a gas flame so that it will be about 1/8 inch in diameter. As the oil is heated draw the flame of the blowpipe across the surface of the oil at intervals of one half minute.

At first, a bluish halo may appear as the flash point is approached. The real flash point is recorded when the flash gives a yellow flicker and goes out again.

Determination of fire point: After noting the flash point, continue the heating until a point is reached, when touching the surface of the oil with the first flame causes it to burn for a least five seconds.

THIOCYANOGEN VALUE

The thiocyanogen value $(SCN)_2$ is a measure of the unsaturation of fats and oils, expressed in terms of the equivalent centigrams (%) of iodine absorbed by 1 g of sample.

Thiocyanogen reacts to the same extent as iodine with oleic acid, but adds to only one bond of linoleic acid and to two bonds of linolenic acid. The method permits the determination of oleic, linoleic, and linolenic acids, provided that other unsaturated acids are not present, and that the iodine number and amount of saturated acids are known.

The method requires 24 hours to complete and is quite complicated requiring considerable analytical skill.

VOLATILE FATTY ACIDS

The volatile fatty acids are those that can be separated from hydrolyzate of a fat or oil by steam distillation. Butter fat, the lauric acid oils and a few others, containing up to twelve carbon atoms, yield volatile fatty acids.

Although no method has as yet been devised to separate all the volatile from the non-volatile fatty acids, the Reichert-Meissl method gives an approximate determination of the water soluble volatile fatty acids, and the Polenske method may be used to determine the insoluble volatile fatty acids, with reproducible results, if the methods are followed carefully.

The Reichert-Meissl value is defined as the number of ml. of N/10 potassium hydroxide solution required to neutralize the soluble fatty acids from 5 g of sample.

The Polenske number is defined as the number of ml of N/10 potassium hydroxide solution required to neutralize the insoluble fatty acids from a 5 g sample.

Determination of Reichert-Meissl value : Weigh a 5 g sample into a clean dry 300 ml flask (Fig. 6.2). Add 20 ml glycerol sodium hydroxide solution (made by adding 20 ml. of 50% sodium hydroxide to 180 ml of pure glycerol). Heat over asbestos covered wire gauze until completely saponified, shown when the mixture becomes clear. Shake the mixture by rotating the flask to keep the foam down. Add 130 ml of recently boiled cold water and add slowly 10 ml of dilute sulphuric acid (200 ml of concentrated acid diluted to 1000 ml with water). Add 1 g of powdered pumice, which has previously been strongly ignited and cooled under water until used. Distill without previously melting the separated fatty acids.

All the apparatus should be set up as in figure 6.2. The 300 ml distilling flask should rest on a piece of heavy asbestos board, provided with a 50

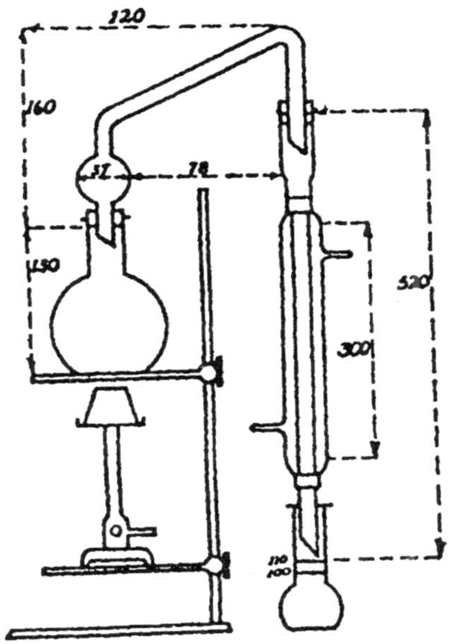

Fig. 6.2 : Apparatus for determining Reichert-Meissl and Polenske values

mm hole in the center. The flame should be so regulated that 110 ml of distillate will collect in as nearly 30 minutes as possible; and the distillate should come over at a temperature not higher than 18-20°C.

When 110 ml of the distillate has been collected, remove the flame and substitute for the receiving flask a 25 ml cylinder to catch any drops of distillate that may fall later. Mix the contents of the flask containing the distillate and immerse the flask almost completely in water 15°C for 15 minutes.

Filter the distillate through a dry 9 cm filter paper. Titrate 100 ml of the filtrate with N/10 potassium hydroxide solution, using 6 drops of 1 % alcoholic solution of phenolphthalein. The pink colour should persist for 2 minutes. Make a blank determination, using the same proportion of reagents as in the actual determination.

1.1 (Titration of sample minus titration of blank) = Reichert-Meissl value

Determination of polenske number : Remove the remainder of the soluble acids from the insoluble acids on the filter, by washing with three successive 15 ml portions of water previously passed through the condenser, the 110 ml receiving flask and the 25 ml cylinder. Dissolve the water insoluble acids with three successive 15 ml portions of neutral 95% ethanol through the filter, each portion having previously been passed through the condenser, receiver and 25 ml cylinder.

Titrate the combined alcoholic washings with N/10 potassium hydroxide, and calculate the polenske number according to the definition given previously. All determinations should be made in duplicate. All details must be followed precisely to obtain satisfactory results.

BLEACH TEST ON ANIMAL FATS

Weigh 50 g of the sample into a 100 ml tall form beaker, and heat it to 105°C until most of the moisture is driven off. Add 2 g of A.O.A.C. standard fuller's earth. Agitate with the thermometer for 15 minutes, keeping the temperature of the fat between 100 and 105°C. Filter through dry filter paper, using a hot funnel if necessary, until a sufficient quantity has been filtered, for reading colour.

SPECIFIC GRAVITY OF OILS

The specific gravity of an oil should be determined at 25°C with a pycnometer. For close approximation, the hydrometer may be used. The so-called weight per gallon pycnometer is an instrument constructed of metal, whose volume is 83.3 ml. When filled with a liquid, the net weight in grams, divided by 10, is the weight in pounds per gallon. This instrument is very useful as a laboratory tool.

The Westphal balance is also a very useful instrument in a soap and chemical specialities laboratory. The appropriate weights or riders on the beam may be used for determining the specific gravities of liquids lighter or heavier than water.

TEST FOR MARINE ANIMAL OILS IN VEGETABLE OIL

This test is applicable only in the absence of metallic salts.

Dissolve about 6 g of the sample in a test tube, in 12 ml of a mixture of equal parts of chloroform and glacial acetic acid. Maintain the solution at 20°C and add bromine, drop by drop, until a slight excess is indicated by brown colour. Let it stand 5 minutes and then place the test tube in boiling water. If only vegetable oils are present, the solution will become perfectly clear. In the presence of fish oil, the solution will be cloudy or show a precipitate, due to the presence of insoluble bromides.

There are several qualitative tests to determine the presence of certain oils in a mixture. For example, olive oil, which is an imported product and is generally higher in price than domestic oils, has at times been found to be adulterated with less expensive oil.

HALPHEN TEST FOR COTTONSEED OIL

Although the Halphen test is supposed to detect the presence of cottonseed oil in admixture with other oils and fats, there are many exceptions in which the test becomes inoperative.

Kapok oil reacts with equal if not greater intensity than cottonseed oil and fats from animals which have been fed with cottonseed meal often respond to this test.

Hydrogenated cottonseed oil, or even oil heated to 250°C, interferes with the reaction so as to make it indefinite.

For carrying out this test, mix carbon disulphide (containing 1% of sulphur in solution) with an equal volume of amyl alcohol. In a large test tube, mix 10 ml of the sample with an equal volume of the reagent. Set the test tube in a steam bath to boil off the carbon disulphide and then immerse it in a bath of boiling brine for one to two hours. A red colour indicates the presence of cottonseed oil. The greater the quantity of cottonseed oil present, the sooner will the red colour appear.

BAUDOIN'S TEST FOR SESAME OIL

To 10 ml of oil in a test tube, add 2 drops of a 2% alcoholic solution of furfural and 10 ml of concentrated hydrochloric acid. Shake well. In the presence of sesame oil, the aqueous liquid will become crimson in colour. This test is sensitive to 1% of sesame oil.

The colour reaction is due to the presence of sesamin and sesamoline in the unsaponifiable portion of the oil.

BELLIER'S TEST FOR GROUNDNUT OIL

Preparation of reagents : ***Alcoholic potash*** : Dissolve 8.5 g potassium hydroxide in 70% alcohol and make up volume to 100 ml.

Acetic acid: Dilute 120 ml of 36% acetic acid to 150 ml. 1.5 ml of this solution should completely neutralize 5 ml of the alcoholic potash.

Procedure : Weigh 1 g of sample into a dry test tube, add 5 ml of alcoholic potash; and boil gently over a small flame, holding the tube with a holder until the oil is completely saponified, avoiding evaporation as far as possible. The requires about 2 minutes.

Add 1 ml of acetic acid, mix well, and cool for 30 minutes in tap water, shaking the tube occasionally. Then add 50 ml of 70% alcohol, containing 1% by volume of hydrochloric acid (sp. gr. 1.16). Shake well and again place the tube in water for an hour.

If no peanut oil is present, a clear opalescent liquid is formed; if more than 10% is present, a flocculent crystalline precipitate remains. Even with 5%, a distinct precipitate remains and separates out on standing.

FITELSON TEST FOR TEASEED OIL

Of all the oils that resemble olive oil, none matches it so well in chemical and physical constants, as teaseed oil. It is for this reason, that olive oil has been occasionally adulterated with it, or it has been substituted for olive oil.

Qualitative test : Measure into a test tube (approximately 18x150 mm) exactly 0.8 ml of acetic anhydride, 1.5 ml of chloroform, and 0.2 ml of concentrated sulphuric acid. Mix and cool in water to 5°C. Add 7 drops of oil. (For this, ordinary glass tubing, 4 mm outside diameter and 2 mm inside diameter, is used). These 7 drops will weigh approximately 0.22 gram.

If the solution of the oil and reagent is cloudy, add acetic anhydride, drop by drop, shaking after each addition until the turbidity disappears. Maintain at 5°C for five minutes. Add 10 ml of cold ether, cork the tube, and invert it. Place it in ice water and observe the colour.

Pure teaseed oil gives an intense red colour within a minute and then fades. The depth of colour is proportional to the amount of teaseed oil present. By making up known mixtures of olive oil and teaseed oil and subjecting them to the same reaction if the sample contains at least 10% of teaseed oil, a fair estimate of the amount of teaseed oil present in a suspected sample can be made.

Dark olive oil or industrial oils sometimes mask the colour. In the latter case, 5 g of the sample, mixed with 5 g white mineral oil, is saponified by boiling for 10 minutes with 5 ml of 50% potassium hydroxide in about 30 ml of ethanol. This is poured into a separatory funnel. An equal volume of water is added and the mixture is shaken. When the layers separate, the aqueous portion is drawn off and the oily portion is washed several times with water. The oil is then dried with anhydrous sodium sulphate, filtered through dry filter paper, and the test for teaseed oil is made, as indicated before.

KREIS TEST FOR RANCIDITY

Pour 5 ml of the oil and 5 ml hydrochloric acid (free from nitrosyl chloride) in a test tube. Stopper and shake well for 30 seconds. Add 5 ml of 0.1 % solution of phloroglucinol in ether. Shake mixture again for 30 seconds and allow it to stand for 10 minutes. A good pink colour, appearing in the lower acid layer, indicates rancidity. Pale orange, yellow or slight pink should be disregarded. If the acid layer becomes pink, make a mixture of 1 part of the sample with 9 parts of liquid petroleum and another mixture of 1 part of the sample and 19 parts of liquid petroleum. Test both mixtures as before.

TEST FOR HARDNESS IN WATER

Hardness of water is determined by titration of a measured amount of water, with a standard soap solution. The point at which a good lather is maintained for five minutes is noted on the burette and the hardness is calculated from that.

The actual procedure is as follows :

The reagent used, is the Standard Soap Solution, prescribed by the American Public Health Association, one ml of soap solution is equivalent to 1 mg of $CaCO_3$.

This value is based upon the test of a 50 ml samples of standard CaCl, solution titrated at 72°F to a permanent foam end point. Permanent Foam is defined as a lather persisting for five minutes, with unbroken surface, the bottle lying on its side.

Test: Transfer 50 ml sample to an 8-oz round bottle. Add standard soap solution from a burette (0.3 - 0.3 ml), at a time and shake vigorously after each addition. Lay bottle on its side and observe the time required for a break to foam on the surface. Continue additions until a lather persists, unbroken for five minutes. Multiply the result by 20. That represents parts per million of $CaCO_3$ or hardness. To read grains per gallon, use 58.3 ml sample. Deduct lather factor from burette reading. The corrected burette reading is directly equal to grains $CaCO_3$ per gallon. That is, each ml soap solution equals 1 gr. per gal. hardness.

ANALYSIS OF SOAP AND SOAP PRODUCTS

Sampling and Preparation of Sample

This method of sampling is applicable to bar soap, soap powders, cleansers, flakes, paste and liquid soaps.

Product is sampled as convenient, taking a sample of 1 % of the packages from lots of one thousand; or, of bar soap, one bar from each ten cases. The samples are placed in airtight containers. Liquids are sampled with a glass tube one half inch in diameter, which is long enough to reach the bottom of the drum or barrel. Pastes are sampled with a trier, which is a half round metal tube, long enough to reach the bottom of the package. For bar soap, a portion of each bar is ground through a meat chopper and a composite sample is made up in two Mason jars. One is for analysis and the other for future reference; or for shipment to a referee chemist.

TEST FOR MOISTURE

The following method is applicable to soap and soap products, except those that contain water-m scible, volatile substances. The soap is distilled

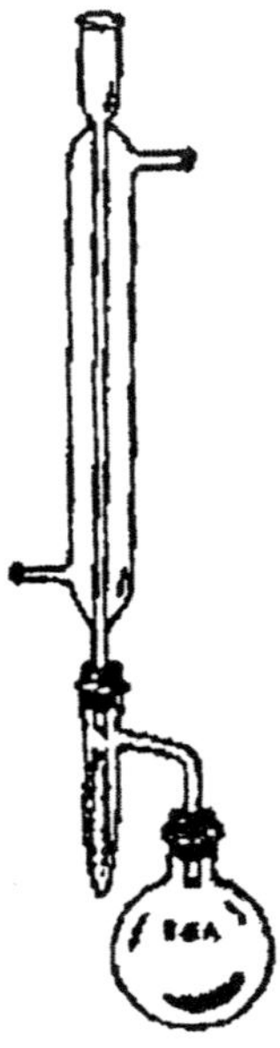

Fig. 6.3 : Stark and Dean distillation unit

from a flask with xylene or toluene, using a Stark and Dean distillation trap and a reflux condenser (Fig. 6.3).

For soaps containing 5 - 25% of moisture, use a 20 g sample. For products containing over 25% moisture, use a 10 g sample.

Weigh the sample into a flask, add 50 ml of toluene and 10 g of anhydrous sodium acetate, or 20 g of rosin, to prevent frothing. Also, add a few glass beads or small pebbles.

Distill until no more water drops into the distillation trap. Then allow it to boil for ten minutes more. A spiral copper wire is used to push down the last drop of water that may remain in the condenser, and it is washed down with a few ml of toluene, when cool.

$$\frac{\text{Volume of water x 100}}{\text{Weight of sample}} = \text{Moisture \%}$$

Moisture by air-oven method : When soap and other products do not contain large amounts of silicate or over 1% glycerol, or for soaps not produced from linseed oil, which do not oxidize readily, the following method may be used. Otherwise the distillation method is employed.

Weigh accurately, a sample of about 3 grams in a crystallizing dish and place it in the oven at 105°C for four hours, until the weight is practically constant. Cool in desiccator and reweigh.

$$\frac{\text{Loss in weight x 100}}{\text{Weight of sample}} = \text{Moisture and volatile \%}$$

TEST FOR FREE CAUSTIC ALKALI

Weigh a 5 g sample into a 300 ml tall form beaker. Dissolve it in 150 ml of neutral ethanol, using phenolphthalein as indicator. Filter with suction and titrate the filtrate with N/10 sulphuric acid.

ml N/10 H_2S0_4x 0.004x20 = %NaOH

ml N/10 H_2SO_4 x 0.00561 x 20 = % KOH

TEST FOR CARBONATE

The residue on the filter, from the previous determination, is dissolved with hot water and when cool, titrated with N/10 sulphuric acid, using methyl orange as indicator.

ml N/10 H_2SO_4 x 0.0053x20 = % Na_2CO_3

ml N/10 H_2SO_4 x 0,0069x20 = % K_2CO_3

If the soap contains no fillers or builders, sodium and potassium carbonate are the only free alkalies that will ordinarily be found. It fillers and builders are suspected, it is always best to make a qualitative test for sodium silicate and other alcohol-insoluble matter. When the free caustic is being determined and insoluble matter is detected in the alcoholic solution of the soap, this insoluble residue must be analyzed.

TESTS FOR SODIUM SILICATE

Qualitative test: Dissolve about 1 g of the sample in 25 ml of hot distilled water. Heavily silicated soaps may show turbidity because some of the silicate has been dehydrated to such an extent that it no longer dissolves. Especially is this true of soap chips and some of the spray-dried powders. There may also be present insoluble fillers such as silex, starch, etc. In the absence of starch or dextrine, take 10 ml of the clear solution and pour it into a test tube containing 10 ml of acetone and 1 ml of a solution prepared by dissolving 10 g of pure sodium aluminate and 2 g of sodium chloride in 1 litre of distilled water. A flocculent precipitate indicates sodium silicate.

In the case of small amounts of silicate, such as may be present in white floating soap or toilet soap, the test tube containing the sample and reagent may be heated in a steam bath for a minute. If silicate is present, a light precipitate appears. This is a very ingenious test.

Quantitative determination : Ash 1 g of soap in a platinum crucible. Dissolve the ash in hot distilled water and transfer the solution to a 300 ml beaker. Acidify with concentrated hydrochloric acid and a few drops of concentrated nitric acid. Evaporate to dryness and heat on a hot plate around 130°C for an hour. Pick up the silica residue with hot water, again acidify as before, and wash down anything that may have spattered on the sides of the beaker using a policeman.

Evaporate and heat as before. Add a little water and a few drops of hydrochloric acid and filter through ashless filter paper. Incinerate in a platinum crucible. Heat over a bunsen flame until all traces of carbon have disappeared and the silicon dioxide is perfectly white. Cool in a desiccator and weigh.

g SiO_2 x 1.2571 x 100 = % sodium silicate ($Na_2Si_4O_9$)

TESTS FOR BORAX

Qualitative test: To a 1 g sample in a test tube, add 10 ml of dilute hydrochloric acid. Boil until the fatty acid separate out. Cool and filter through paper that has previously been wetted with water.

Immerse a strip of turmeric paper in the aqueous filtrate and allow the paper to dry. It will be coloured a deep red if borax is present. If a few drops of ammonia are placed on the test paper, a blue colour confirms the presence of borax. The test is sensitive to 0.05% of borax.

Quantitative determination : To 10 g of soap (5 g if soap contains more than *5%* of borax) in a platinum evaporating dish, add 2.15 g of a fusion mixture consisting of 200 g of sodium carbonate and 15 g of silicon dioxide, finely powdered. Add 15 ml of 95% alcohol and mix with a glass stirring rod. After washing off the rod with a few ml of alcohol, evaporate the mass to dryness on a water bath. Ignite gently until all the combustible matter is destroyed, cover the dish with platinum foil and fuse.

Completely disintegrate the fused mass by boiling with water and transfer the solution to a 250 ml round bottom flask. Acidify with 20 ml dilute hydrochloric acid (1:1). Heat nearly to boiling and add a moderate excess of dry precipitated chalk. Connect with a reflux condenser and boil vigorously. Filter the precipitate through a folded filter and wash with hot water keeping the total volume of liquid below 100 ml. Return the solution to the flask, add a little chalk and again boil under the reflux. Remove the flame and connect the top of the condenser with a suction; pump until the boiling has ceased.

Add 50 ml of glyceol and titrate with N/10 sodium hydroxide, using phenolphthalein as indicator. When the end point is reached, add 10 ml of neutral glycerol and titrate once more, Repeat this until the addition of glycerol does not affect the end point.

$$\frac{\text{ml N/10 x 0.00955x100}}{\text{Weight of sample}} = \text{\% Borax } (Na_2B_4O_7\ 10\ H_2O)$$

This method is described in *J. Ind. Eng. Chem.,* 5 : 645 (1913).

TEST FOR TOTAL ALKALI AND TOTAL FAT

Dissolve 5 g of soap in hot water. Add 25 ml of N/H_2SO_4 and set the solution on the steam bath until the clear fatty acids float on the surface of the water. Cool and transfer to a pear-shaped separatory funnel with

U.S.P. ether. Allow liquids to settle and run the aqueous portion into another separatory funnel. Wash the ether in the first funnel once with water and when settled, combine the washings and shake out with ether. Then filter the ether extracts from both funnels into a Soxhlet flask and distill off the ether. Dry the fatty acids on the steam bath, cool in a desiccator, and weigh.

Fatty extract x 20 = % Total fatty acids and unsaponifible matter

The combined aqueous solutions are titrated with N/NaOH using methyl orange as indicator.

25 ml - NaOH titration x 0.031 x 20 = % Total $Na_2 0$

The total Na_2O includes the alkalinity due to free caustic, carbonate silicate, if any and all alkaline builders, which must be subtracted to find the percentage of sodium oxide combined as soap.

Conversion factors :

Multiply		by		to find
Sodium silicate	x	0.20448	=	Na_2O
Sodium carbonate	x	0.5849	=	Na_2O
Sodium hydroxide	x	0.775	=	Na_2O

TEST FOR SODIUM CHLORIDE

To the aqueous solution of the preceding determination of total alkali, add a few drops of 10% potassium chromate and titrate with N/10 silver nitrate.

ml $AgNO_3$ x 0.00585 x 20 = % NaCl

TEST FOR UNSAPONIFIABLE AND/OR UNSAPONIFIED FAT

Dissolve 5 g of soap in 50 ml of hot water, cool and add 50 ml of ethanol. Transfer the solution to a separatory funnel and shake it with 50 ml of petroleum ether. Allow liquids to settle and draw off the alcoholic layer into a second separatory funnel. Wash the extract with 25 ml of 50% ethanol. Draw off the washings into the second separatory funnel and shake with 25 ml of petroleum ether. Draw off the alcohol and wash the extract as before, and filter both extracts into a 150 ml Soxhlet flask. Distill off the petroleum ether. Dry the residue on the steam bath, cool it in a desiccator, and weight it.

Wt extract x 20 = % unsaponifiable, unsaponified fat

TEST FOR STABILITY OF SOAP

There are several methods for testing the effectiveness of an antioxidant in soap. In the Swift test for stability, the soap is aerated in an oven at 97.7°C. Other methods employ higher or lower temperatures.

A method suggested by Monsanto Chemical Co., is as follows:

5 mg Sopanox is added to, and uniformly mixed with, 5 g of soap. The treated soap is then placed in a 250 ml Erlenmeyer flask with a ground glass stopper. A 7 cm filter paper is cut into small pieces, saturated with a ml of distilled water, and added to the mixture in the flask. The flask is well shaken to mix the soap and paper and then placed in an oven, maintained at 50°C. Each day the stopper is removed from the flask and the odour of the sample under test is noted. A blank test of the soap without Sopanox is run in parallel with the test indicated.

For determining the effect of discolouration by sunlight, the test is conducted by mixing thoroughly 20 g of freshly prepared soap with 0.1% by weight of Sopanox; 5 g of water is stirred into the soap and the mixture is pressed into a hard cake in a 2 inch crystallizing dish. It is then exposed to direct sunlight in a glass case and the discolouration observed, in comparison with soap containing no antioxidant.

EXAMINATION OF FATTY ACIDS

Dissolve 4 oz soap in water in 800 ml beaker; add slowly 50 ml 50% sulphuric acid. Heat on the steam bath until the clear fatty acids float on the surface, keeping the beaker covered with a watch glass. Syphon off the acid water, wash the fatty acids twice with hot water and decant them into a 100 ml beaker on top of the hot oven, to settle traces of water.

Place a beaker with funnel and filter paper in the oven, and when hot, filter the fatty acids. Determinations, such as titer, saponification and iodine numbers, qualitative and quantitative tests for rosin, etc., may now be made on the fatty acids.

QUALITATIVE TEST FOR ROSIN

Liebermann-Storch reaction : Dissolve several drops of fat in acetic anhydride, in a porcelain evaporating dish or on a dropping plate. Add a few drops a sulphuric acid of 1.53 specific gravity (17 ml of concentrated sulphuric acid is added to 19 ml of water). In the presence of rosin acids, a fleeting reddish-violet colour appears. The test is very sensitive. Cholesterol, however and some other substances give a similar reaction.

QUANTITATIVE TESTS FOR ROSIN

Wolff method : The American Oil Chemists' Society's Official Method, Da 12 - 42, known as the McNicoll method, is somewhat more accurate than the Wolff method, but it requires a special reagent. For commercial work, the Wolff method is sufficiently accurate.

If the presence of rosin has been determined by the Liebermann-Storch reaction, dissolve 3g of fatty acids, in 20 ml of absolute ethanol. Add 10 ml of a solution of 1 volume concentrated sulphuric acid in 4 volumes of absolute alcohol, and boil for about four minutes under reflux condenser. Add to the liquid about five times its volume of a 7 - 10% solution of sodium chloride, and extract with ether. Shake out the aqueous portion two or three times with ether. Unite the ether solutions and wash with sodium chloride solution until the washings are neutral. Titrate the rosin acids with standard alcoholic sodium hydroxide solution. (1 ml N/ alkali = 0.346 g rosin). Calculate the percentage of rosin.

McNicoll method : *Apparatus:* A glass flask connected, preferably by a ground glass joint, to a reflux condenser; a 150 ml flask of either the round bottom or Erlenmeyer type, for carrying out the esterification; any suitable water-cooled reflux condenser.

Reagent: An approximately N/5 solution of potassium hydroxide in neutral ethanol; naphthalene-B-sulphonic acid solution, made by dissolving 40 g Eastman grade or equivalent reagent in a liter of C.P. absolute methanol; phenolphthalein indicator; 0.5% solution in neutral redistilled alcohol.

Procedure : Dissolve 5 g sample in 100 ml of hot water in a 250 ml Erlenmeyer flask. When solution is complete, add dilute sulphuric acid (1:1) in slight excess, using methyl orange as indicator. Insert a small funnel in the neck of the flask and heat to cause the fatty and rosin acids to separate as a clear layer. Cool to room temperature (20 - 25°C) and transfer to a separator/ funnel, using small portions of ethyl ether to wash the flask. Draw off the acid layer into a second separatory funnel and shake the acid aqueous liquid with two 20 ml portions of ethyl ether. Dissolve the fatty acids in the ether used for washing the aqueous liquid, and shake with 10 ml portions of water until it is no longer acid to methyl orange. Unite the water portions used for washing and shake with 20 ml of ether. Wash the ether until the water is neutral to methyl orange.

Unite the ether solutions, filter through anhydrous sodium sulphate on a filter paper and wash thoroughly with ether into the tared esterification flask. Evaporate the ether and finally heat the flask at 105°C for 15 minutes. When cool, weigh and calculate the percentage of fatty and rosin acids.

Pour 25 ml of naphthalene-B-sulphonic acid solution into the esterification flask. Add a few glass beads to ensure smooth boiling, attach the reflux condenser and boil for 30 minutes; also run a blank test using 25 ml of reagent. At the end of the boiling period, cool the contents of the flask, add 0.5 ml of phenolphthalein indicator, and titrate immediately with standard alcoholic potassium hydroxide.

Calculations

$$\% \text{ Uncorrected rosm, original sample} = \frac{(S—B) \times N \times 34.6}{\text{Wt. of sample}} = (R)$$

$$\% \text{ Corrected rosin, original samples} = R—0.01\ F \quad (R_1)$$

$$\text{Rosin soda soap } \% = R_1 \times 1.064$$

In these calculations:

S: Titration of esterified fatty acids

B: Titration of blank

N: Normally of standard KOH solution

F: Percentage of total fatty acids in soap.

If the true fatty acid soap is desired, subtract the rosin soap from the total anhydrous soap.

Where the rosin content is found to be less than 5%, the actual presence or absence of rosin should be checked qualitatively, by the Liebermann-Storch test.

Comparative studies have shown that the McNicoll method gives results approximately 1% higher than the amount of rosin present. Consequently 1% should be deducted from the percentage of rosin found in the fatty acids, or 0.01F from the percentage found in the original soap.

ANALYSIS OF POTASH SOAP

With the exception of the determination of potash itself the methods used here are similar to those employed in the analysis of soda soap.

Although a gel soap may appear to be made of potash, it is not always true it is therefore essential to make a qualitative test for potash before going further.

Qualitative test for potash : Incinerate 1 g of soap, leach the ash with 10 ml of hot water, neutralize with acetic or hydrochloric acid, and add a few ml of 10% solution of sodium cobaltinitrate. A yellow precipitate on slight warming indicates potash.

Quantitative determination of potash : The least expensive and easiest method for determining potash is with perchlorate, which is in use for many years and found satisfactory for all practical purposes.

Incinerate 3 g of soap in a platinum crucible. Dissolve the ash in hot water, filter if necessary, and titrate with N/HCl, using methyl orange as indicator. Evaporate to dryness in a tall 300 ml beaker, on a hot plate. Dissolve the residue in hot water and add 5 ml of perchloric acid (20% solution). Evaporate again, to dense fumes. To ensure that all salts have been converted to perchlorates, dissolve as before, add 5 ml of perchloric acid and evaporate once more to dense fumes.

To the perchlorates, add 25 ml of absolute ethanol, saturated with potassium perchlorate and 0.2% perchloric acid. Break up the crystals or dried solids with a stirring rod, allow to stand for one half hour to ensure solution of all perchlorates, expect potassium perchlorate. (This determination depends on the insolubility of $KClO_4$ in absolute alcohol). Filter through a prepared Gooch crucible, washing the precipitate four times by decantation, with 25ml of the alcoholic mixture. Transfer the precipitate to the crucible and wash it twice with 10 ml portion of ethanol solution and ether, 1:1. Dry for one hour in the oven at 120° - 130°C. Cool in a desiccator and weigh. Dissolve the potassium perchlorate on the crucible with hot water, dry and weigh the crucible as before. The loss in weight represents the amount of potassium perchlorate.

$$\frac{KClO_4 \times 100}{3} = \%\ \text{potassium perchlorate}$$

If a test of the soap shows the presence of sulphates, these must be precipitated with barium chloride and filtered off, before determining the potash.

Conversion factors :

Multiply		by to find		
Potassium perchlorate	x	0.3399	=	K_2O
Potassium hydroxide	x	0.8294	=	K_2O
Potassium carbonate	x	0.6816	=	K_2O
Potassium chloride	x	0.6313	=	K_2O

Calculation of soap analysis

Total fat minus unsaponifiable x 0.97 = Fatty anhydrides

Fatty anhydrides plus combined Na_20 = Anhydrous soap

In heavy silicated soaps, the carbonate should be determined by evolution of gas and absorption in potash bulb or similar device. When carbonate, silicate and free caustic are subtracted from the total Na_2O, even in the absence of other alkalies, there may be more Na_2O left, than is necessary for the saponification of the fatty acids. This may be due to caustic soda, which is sometimes added to the soap in the crutcher to prevent the silicate from dropping out while the soap is cooling.

The true combined alkali may be determined by distilling off the alcoholic filtrate from the determination of free caustic, then decomposing the soap with normal sulphuric acid, and titrating the aqueous portion after removal of the fatty acids.

If the K_2O found gravimetrically, minus K_2O represented by chlorides, is equal to K_2O found by filtration, the soap is made entirely with potash. If it is less, subtract from the total K_2O found by titration, the K_2O determined gravimetrically minus the K_2O as chlorides. The difference is recalculated to Na_2O. There are some soaps which are made partly with potash and partly with soda; e.g., shaving soap.

ANALYSIS OF SOAP POWDERS

The analysis of soap powders follows the scheme outlined for soap. Soap powders, however, may contain several additional chemicals or builders not ordinarily found in soap. The better class powders contain, besides sodium carbonate and silicate, also trisodium phosphate and other phosphates. The latter are found especially in the household detergents. It is therefore essential to make qualitative and quantitative tests for the various compounds.

Tetrasodium pyrophosphate : ***Qualitative test:*** The reagent used is a solution of 5 g of zinc acetate and 20 ml of concentrated acetic acid in 100 ml of water.

Treat a 5 g sample of soap powder with 50 ml of hot 95% ethanol and filter. Wash the residue with hot ethanol and dissolve in hot water.

Add concentrated acetic acid to the aqueous solution of the residue, until the pH drops to 3.8.

The pH may be determined in several ways. Using bromphenol blue — La Motte colour standard 3 to 4; or if this is not available universal pH paper serves as a sufficiently close guide. The best, of course, is a pH metre. Add 25 ml of zinc acetate slowly, with stirring. A white precipitate of zinc pyrophosphate indicates the presence of sodium pyrophosphate.

Sodium carbonate, bicarbonate, orthophosphate, borate and silicate do not interfere.

Quantitative determination

1. Reagents

1.1 Neutral ethyl alcohol (95%). Freshly boiled ethyl alcohol 95% or higher and neutral in phenolphthalein.

1.2 Hydrochloric acid (approximately 0.5 N).

1.3 Sulphuric acid (approximately 0.1 N).

1.4 Zinc sulphate solution (7%). Dissolve 125 g of reagent grade zinc sulphate ($ZnSO_4.7H_2O$) in water and dilute to 1 litre, filter and adjust the pH to exactly 3.8 with a glass electrode titration assembly using 0.1 N sulphuric acid.

1.5 Sodium hydroxide (approximately 0.5 N). Standardize the sodium hydroxide solution against reagent tetrasodium pyrophosphate ($Na_4P_2O_7$) prepared by recrystallizing the technical product three times from water, and igniting at 400°C to constant weight.

2. Procedure

2.1 Accurately weigh a sample containing an equivalent of approximately 1 g of tetrasodium pyrophosphate, and digest it on a steam bath with 200 ml of hot, freshly boiled, neutral alcohol. Filter through a filter paper or Gooch crucible with suction, and wash with hot alcohol until free from soap. Change receivers, placing a 400 ml beaker under the funnel, and wash the alcohol insoluble portion remaining on the filter with hot water, until the washings are neutral to phenolphthalein. Cool and add sufficient distilled water, so that the resulting solution will just cover the electrodes of a glass-electrode titration assembly. Adjust the pH of the solution to exactly 3.8 with 0. 1N sulphuric acid. Add 50 ml of zinc sulphate solution (7%), and allow 5 minutes for the reaction to become complete, as shown by the pH becoming constant. Titrate the liberated acid with 0.5N sodium hydroxide until apH of 3.8 is again reached. This titration is a measure of the pyrophosphate content.

3. Calculation

3.1 Calculate the percentage of tetrasodium pyrophosphate in the soap powder as follows :

$$\frac{\text{ml sodium hydroxide x F x 100}}{\text{Wt. of sample}}$$

$$= \% \text{ tetrasodium pyrophosphate } (Na_4P_2O_7)$$

where F equals g of tetrasodium pyrophosphate equivalent to 1 ml of the sodium hydroxide solution used for the titration, as calculated by standardization against reagent tetrasodium pyrophosphate.

As alternate quantitative method for tetrasodium pyrophosphate: Treat 5 g of soap with 100 ml of hot 95% ethanol and filter. Wash the residue with hot ethanol to remove all traces of soap, and then dissolve it in hot water. Transfer an aliquot, containing about 0.1 g of tetrasodium pyrophosphate, to a 300 ml tall beaker and add concentrated acetic acid until the pH is 3.5. Adjust the volume to 75-100 ml and add excess of 0.2 M zinc acetate solution, drop by drop, with constant stirring. Filter the precipitated zinc pyrophosphate and wash with zinc acetate reagent, diluted ten times with water. Ignite the filter and precipitate in a porcelain crucible, cool in a desiccator, and weigh.

As a choice of treatment, the precipitate may be dissolved in nitric acid, and after conversion to the orthophosphate by boiling the content of P_2O_5 may be determined in the usual way.

$$Zn_2P_20_7 \times 0.8734 = Na_4P_2O_7$$

Trisodium phosphate : ***Qualitative test:*** Prepare reagent as follows:

Dissolve 100 g of molybdic acid in 144 ml of concentrated ammonium hydroxide and 271 ml of water. Adding slowly with constant stirring, pour the solution so obtained into 489 ml of nitric acid and 1148 ml of water. Keep the mixture warm for several days and decant the clear solution.

Treat the sample with hot alcohol, as before, to free it from all traces of soap (and usually of any synthetic organic surfactant, if present). Filter and dissolve the residue in water. To a few ml in a test tube, add 3 ml of ammonium hydroxide and acidify with nitric acid. Heat to 65°C and add 10 ml of ammonium molybdate solution. Shake or stir the contents; a yellow precipitate indicates trisodium phosphate.

Quantitative determination : Treat 5 g of the product to be tested as in the previous determination, to free it of all traces of soap. Dissolve the alcohol insoluble matter with water and filter into a 250 ml volumetric flask. Transfer a 10 ml aliquot to a 300 ml beaker and adjust the volume to 75 ml. Add 5 ml of ammonium hydroxide and 7 ml of concentrated nitric acid. The solution should be acidic at this point. Heat to 65°C and add 25 ml of ammonium molybdate slowly, with stirring until the precipitate forms.

After an hour, when the ammonium phosphomolybdate in the sample under test has settled, it is filtered and the precipitate is washed with ice water until two fillings of the filter paper require only 1 drop of normal alkali to produce pink colour with phenolphthalein.

The filter and precipitate are transferred to a beaker, the yellow precipitate is slowly dissolved by flowing N/sodium hydroxide from a burette. The filter paper may be broken up so as to allow the precipitate to dissolve. Water is added and when no more yellow particles are visible, the excess sodium hydroxide is titrated back with N/sulphuric acid, using phenolphthalein as indicator.

$$\frac{\text{ml N/NaoH - ml N/}H_2SO_4 \times 0.007124 \times 100}{\text{Wt. of sample}} = \%\ (Na_3PO_4)$$

Total phosphate

1.1 If a qualitative test has shown the presence of phosphates and their determination is desired, the matter insoluble in alcohol or the ash from the incineration of an original samples may be used.

2. Reagents

2.1 Molybdate solution is the same as that used for determining trisodium phosphate.

2.2 Ammonium nitrate solution. Dissolve 100 g of phosphate free ammonium nitrate in distilled water, and dilute to 1 litre.

2.3 Magnesia mixture. Dissolve 55 g of crystallized magnesium chloride ($MgCl_2$- $6H_2O$) in water, add 140 g of ammonium chloride, make slightly ammoniacal to phenolphthalein, allow to stand overnight and filter. Acidify the filtrate with hydrochloric acid, add 5 ml of the acid in excess and dilute to 1 litre.

2.4 Dilute ammonium hydroxide for washing. Dilute 100 ml of ammonium hydroxide (sp. gr. 0.90) to 1 litre.

3. Procedure

3.1 Weigh out a 2 g sample of the alcohol insoluble or ash, and proceed to remove the silica, if any, just as in the quantitative determination of sodium silicate, using nitric acid instead of hydrochloric. Boil the covered solution 30 minutes to convert other phosphates that may be present to orthophosphate, wash off and remove cover glass, and evaporate as described. Save the filtrate. Make up to 250 ml, concentrating if necessary. Pipette an aliquot corresponding to 0.5 or 1 gram of the original material, into a 250 ml beaker; add ammonium hydroxide in slight excess; and barely dissolve the precipitate formed with a few drops of nitric acid, stirring vigorously. Add about 15 g of dry ammonium nitrate or a solution containing that amount. Heat to about 60°C and add 70 ml of the molybdate solution for every decigram of phosphoric anhydride (P_2O_5) present.

3.2 Digest at about 65°C for an hour, and determine if the phosphates have been completely precipitated, by adding more molybdate solution to the clear supernatant liquid. Filter and wash with ammonium nitrate solution. Dissolve the precipitate on the filter with ammonium hydroxide (1:1), and wash with hot water into a beaker, keeping the volume under 100 ml. Neutralize with hydrochloric acid, using litmus paper or bromthymol blue as an indicator, cool in ice and from a pipette add slowly (about 1 drop per second), stirring vigorously, 15 ml of magnesia mixture for each decigram of P_2O_5 present. After 15 minutes, add 15 ml of ammonium hydroxide (sp. gr. 0.90) slowly while stirring. Let stand till the supernatant liquid is clear (2 hours is usually enough), filter, wash the precipitate with dilute ammonium hydroxide until the washings are practically free from chlorides, dry, burn first at a low heat (platinum should not be used), and then ignite to constant weight, preferably in an electric furnace, a 1050° to 1100°C, cool in a desiccator, and weigh as magnesium pyrophosphate ($Mg_2P_2O_7$).

Calculate and report the result as percentage of phosphoric anhydride (P_2O_5).

$$\frac{\text{Weight } Mg_2P_2O_7 \times 63.77}{\text{Weight of original sample}} = \text{\% phosphoric anhydride } (P_2O_5)$$

When the highest accuracy is not required, the molybdate precipitate and paper, after being thoroughly washed free from acid, may be transferred to a beaker, dissolved in a measured volume of standard sodium hydroxide solution and the excess titrated with standard acid solution using phenolphthalein as the indicator.

$$\frac{(\text{ml.of NaOHxN})}{\text{Wt. of original sample}} - (\text{ml of HCl x N}) \times 0.31$$

$$= \text{\% phosphoric anhydride}$$

SYNTHETIC DETERGENTS

Presence of synthetic detergent

Qualitative test

1.1 The presence of synthetic detergent shall be determined by dissolving approximately 5 g of the sample in 100 ml of warm distilled water. Add 25 ml of magnesium nitrate solution (20%). Stir and filter, collecting 50 ml of the filtrate in a 250 ml glass-stoppered graduated cylinder. Stopper and shake the cylinder vigorously for 10 seconds. A foam greater in volume than 10 ml and which persists for more than 1 minute, indicates the presence of synthetic detergent. Note. The absence of foam does not necessarily indicate the absence of synthetic detergent.

Another qualitative method is that of L.F. Hoyt.

Small amounts of anionic, cationic and nonionic surface active agents can be detected by their solubilizing action on dilute aqueous suspensions of National Brilliant Oil Blue BMA.

If soap is resent, the sample should be acidulated and the fatty acids filtered off, before testing the neutralized filtrate.

A 10 g sample is ground and digested with 50 ml of hot 50% ethanol and filtered. The extract is evaporated to dryness, digested with 3 ml of distilled water and the solution is filtered.

As a reagent, 2 g of National Brilliant Oil Blue BMA is ground with 98 g of salt.

To the filtered aqueous solution of the extracted sample, 0.02 g of reagent is added. The solution is shaken and set aside for one hour. The presence of surface active agents is shown by the formation of blue solution.

To differentiate types of surfactants : It is often necessary to know whether a surfactant is anionic, or nonionic. In one portions of an acidified test solution, the reaction of a surfactant with methyl yellow, shows a change from red to yellow or orange colour only with nonionic and cationic surfactants.

In a second portion, the reaction of benzidine and meta vanadate gives a dark green colour only with nonionics; with cationics and sulphonated anionics, a purple. Then methyl yellow is added, which yields an orange colour if a cationic surfactant is present.

Calculation of anhydrous salt free materials : In order to accomplish that **(Method 6501), Method 5701** (Alcohol soluble matter), **Method 5601** (anhydrous salt free, soda soap) and **Method 6201** for chlorides must be employed. These methods follow :

Alcohol soluble and alcohol insoluble matter : (Alcohol soluble matter includes all the anhydrous soap, synthetic detergents, and some inorganic salts. Most of the sodium chloride will be included). Applicable to soap and soap products including those containing synthetic detergents.

1. *Reagents*

1.1 Neutral ethyl alcohol (95%) freshly boiled ethyl alcohol, 95% or higher and neutral to phenolphthalein.

2. *Procedure*

2.1 Weigh 2 grams of the sample into a 250 ml beaker. Add 100 ml of neutral alcohol (95%), cover the beaker and heat on the steam bath with frequent stirring until completely disintegrated. Let settle and filter the supernatant liquid through a counterpoised filter paper or a tared Gooch crucible with suction, into a 300 ml Erlenmeyer flask, retaining as much of the residue as possible, in the beaker. Repeat this extraction three times with 25 ml portions of hot neutral alcohol, each time retaining as much of the residue as possible in the beaker. Finally evaporate any remitting alcohol and dissolve the residue in the smallest possible quantity of hot distilled water (5 ml is sufficient). Re-precipitate the alcohol insoluble matter by slowly adding, while stirring vigorously, 50 ml of neutral (absolute) ethanol.

Note 1 : Solution and reprecipitation of alcohol insoluble matter is necessary for complete separation from alcohol soluble matter.

2.2 Heat the solution to boiling on the steam bath, filter and transfer the precipitate quantitatively to the Gooch crucible or filter paper, washing several times with neutral ethyl alcohol (95%). Combine the alcohol filtrate and washings in a tared 250 ml beaker, evaporate on the steam bath, and then dry to constant weight at 105°C ± 2°. Calculate total alcohol soluble matter.

2.3 Reserve the beaker and contents for the determination of free fatty matter **(Method 6101).** Reserve the paper or the Gooch crucible and contents, without drying for the determination of matter insoluble in water **(Method 5801)** and total alkalinity of matter insoluble in alcohol (alkaline salts) **(Method 5901).**

Anhydrous, salt-free, soda soaps

Apparatus

1.1 Separatory funnel, 250 ml capacity.

1.2 Separatory funnel, 500 ml capacity.

2. Reagents

2.1 Neutral ethyl alcohol (95%) as previously described.

2.2 Methyl orange indicator : prepare a 0.1% solution in water.

2.3 Hydrochloric acid (approximately 0.5N).

2.4 Hydrochloric acid (1:1) : Slowly add 1 part of HCL (sp. gr. 1.19) to 1 part of distilled water.

2.5 Petroleum ether.

2.6 Sodium sulphate, anhydrous, reagent grade.

2.7 Phenolphthalein indicator 1% as previously described.

2.8 Standard sodium hydroxide (approximately 0.1 N, accurately standardized.

2.9 Sodium chloride solution. Saturated solution in distilled water.

3. Procedure

3.1 Weigh a sample (sufficient to yield 1 to 5 g of fatty acids, into a tared 250 ml beaker. Add 25 ml of water and 25 ml of neutral 95% ethanol, and warm on the steam bath until solution is complete. Cool, add 5 drops of methyl orange indicator and titrate with approximately 0.5 N hydrochloric acid to a pink colour. Add 5 ml of HC1 (1:1) in excess.

3.2 Transfer the contents of the beaker to a 250 ml separatory funnel. Wash the beaker alternately with equal parts of hot distilled water and hot ethanol 95% adding the washings to the separatory funnel. Add sufficient sodium chloride solution to make 160 ml in the funnel. Add 50 ml of petroleum ether and allow to stand for one half hour without shaking. Remove the greater part of the fatty acids by drawing off the petroleum ether layer as closely as possible into a 500 ml separatory funnel. Repeat the extraction five more times with petroleum ether, using 50 ml portions and shaking thoroughly each time.

Note 1 : If an emulsion appears at this point, it may be broken by the addition of about 10 g of anhydrous sodium sulphate.

3.3 Combine the petroleum ether extracts and wash with small portions of distilled water until the water washings are no longer acid to methyl orange indicator. Dry the combined, washed petroleum ether extracts with anhydrous sodium sulphate, and filter through paper into the original tared 250 ml beaker. Wash the separatory funnel with two small portions of petroleum ether, filtering and adding the washings to the beaker.

3.4 Evaporate the petroleum ether extract on the steam bath until the odour of petroleum ether is no longer perceptible. Then place the beaker in an oven at 100° to 105°C for five minutes to ensure complete removal of the solvent. Cool and weigh as fatty acids plus fatty matter.

3.5 Dissolve the fatty acids and fatty matter in 50 ml of neutral alcohol (95%) with warming. Add phenolph-thalein indicator and titrate with standard sodium hydroxide solution to a pink end point. Evaporate off the alcohol, dry to constant weighty and calculate to obtain soda soap plus fatty matter (G). Make a blank test on the sodium hydroxide solution for neutral salts and correct the result accordingly.

4. Calculation

4.1 Calculate the percentage of anhydrous, salt free, soda soap as follows :

$$A = G - F$$

G may be calculated as follows :

$$G = \frac{(VN \times 0.022) + E \times 100}{W}$$

Where A = % anhydrous, salt-free soda soap

G = % soda soap plus fatty matter or calculated

F = % fatty matter **(See Method 6101)**

V = ml, sodium hydroxide solution used in titration

N = normality, sodium hydroxide solution

E = grams of extract

W = grams of sample

Fatty matter : The alcohol soluble matter is dissolved in a mixture of 25 ml of ethanol and 25 ml of water, warming if necessary. The solution is transferred to a separatory funnel and shaken out with petroleum ether. The combined petroleum ether extracts are washed four times with 10 ml portions of N/5 sodium hydroxide. The petroleum ether extracts are evaporated on the steam bath, dried at 100 - 105°C for half hour, cooled in a desiccator and weighed. The percentage of fatty matter is calculated.

Chlorides : The alcoholic solution from the determination of fatty matter is saved for **Method 6201.1** Chlorides.

To this solution is added 25 ml of 20% magnesium nitrate, warmed to precipitate and coagulate soaps. If the solution is alkaline it must be neutralized with N/sulphuric acid. It is then titrated with N/10 silver nitrate, using potassium chromate as indicator. A blank, using the same volume of water and magnesium nitrate as in the test, is titrated with silver nitrate.

Calculate the percentage of chloride (NaCl) in alcohol soluble matter as follows :

$$C = \frac{(V_1 - V_2)N \times 5.85}{W}$$

where C = % NaCl in alcohol soluble matter

C_1 = % KCl (if any) in alcohol soluble matter

V_1 = ml $AgNO_3$ required for titration of sample
V_2 = ml $AgNO_3$ required for titration of blank
N = Normality of $AgNO_3$
W = Weight of sample

Having made all of these determinations, the synthetic detergent calculated according to Method 6501 is

1. Determination by difference

1.1 Calculate the percentage of anhydrous, salt free synthetic detergent as follows :

$$D = A—(W + F + C)$$

where D = % anhydrous, salt-free, synthetic detergent
A = % alcohol soluble matter **(Method 5701)**
W = % anhydrous, salt free soda soap **(Method 5601)**
F = % fatty matter **(Method 6101)**
C = % chloride as (NaCl) in alcohol soluble matter **(Method 6201)**

TESTS FOR BIODEGRADABILITY

Though foam from the faucet and suds in the stream, post definite problems, which are not attributable entirely to the presence of conventional surfactants, the change over to linear alkylates is calculated to mitigate the effect insofar as detergents can be blamed.

Researchers on detergents employ several analytical approaches to determine the degree of biodegradation for syndets. In Industry's three most widely used tests, the straight chain surfactants, show practically complete degradability in minimum time.

Quoted from Conoco's literature, the following is a brief and concise description of the three tests :

Activated sludge method : Laboratory activated sludge simulates conditions in large scale sewage disposal operations. Both continuous (dynamic) and batch (static) methods utilize sludge from waste disposal plants as the bacterial culture. The batch procedure, sometimes termed semi continuous, or fill and draw, has gained wide acceptance, because it requires only simple and inexpensive equipment even through it offers limited throughput and does not accurately duplicate conditions in a sewage plant.

In this test, the sample of detergent is added to water containing a synthetic nutrient medium and activated sludge, in a vertical cylindrical chamber. Air bubbling through the liquid, agitates the mixture. After a 23 hour testing period, the air is turned off to allow the sludge to settle. The supernatant liquid is then sampled and analyzed. This company further states that Conoco's biodegradable detergents average 95 - 100% degradation over a weekly series of these one-day tests. These results complete with data on biodegradability from the unique, continuous activated sludge system in Conoco's Ponca City, Oklahoma, research centre. This dynamic laboratory unit closely simulates conditions found in full scale sewage disposal plants.

River die-away method : River water is added to a sample of detergent solution in a clean glass jar. Covered with a loose top, the liquid incubates at rest in the dark. Activating a magnetic stirrer for one minute gives adequate mixing before period sampling. Conoco normally runs this test 20 to 30 days to determine the degree of biodegradability of various surfactant materials. In general, soft detergents achieve essentially complete degradation in 5 to 20 days under these conditions.

Shake flask method : After surfactant solution is measured into a shake flask, the sample is sterilized in an autoclave, cooled and inoculated with an adapted mixed microbial culture 72 hours old. Loosely capped after addition of environmental medium, the liquid incubates at 25°C during continuous agitation on a rotary shaker. Biodegradable detergents generally take two to five days to degrade in this test.

MOISTURE TESTS ON SOME POPULAR LIQUID DETERGENTS

Vel dishwashing compound	67.0%	H_2O
Chiffon dishwashing compound	57.0	
Ivory liquid	42.0	
Joy for dishes	44.0	pH 6
Wisk	54.0	USP2 859 182
P&G pink lotion dishwashing compound		USP 2 618 608
Mr. Clean	65.0	pH 10
Lux pink lotion dishwashing compound	53.28	
Top job	69.67	pH 9

Analysis of residual surfactants lends itself to either manual or automated analytical procedures. The best of today's automated analytical systems provides high accuracy and prodigious throughput as well. The trace quantities of active detergent components present in treated samples (20 ppm down to 0.5 ppm) have required the development of sensitive and reproducible techniques. Conoco's chemists and microbiologists used standard methylene-blue colorimetry for determining anionic compounds. For nonionics, a special cobaltothiocyanate colorimetric procedure yields uniformly accurate results. Upon request, Conoco will gladly furnish detailed information on its tests and analytical techniques for determining detergent biodegradability.

ANALYSIS OF GLYCEROL

Dichromate method : Weigh 20 g of bar soap or 15 g of flakes or powdered soap. Dissolve in 100 ml of water and add sufficient sulphuric acid (1:1) to separate the fatty acids. Heat on a steam bath until the fatty acids are clear, keeping the beaker covered with a watch glass. Cool and filter into a 250 ml volumetric flask. Neutralize the filtrate with 10% sodium hydroxide solution and add basic lead acetate (dry powder), rotating the flask after each addition, until no further precipitate forms. Fill to mark, shake, filter and transfer 25 ml aliquot into a 300 ml Erlenmeyer flask. Add a few ml of dilute sulphuric acid to precipitate the lead salts.

Weigh out in a small evaporating dish exactly 2 g of C.P. potassium dichromate crystals and wash this into the Erlenmeyer flask. When the dichromate has dissolved, add 50 ml of sulphuric acid (1:1), cover with a small beaker, and keep in a steam bath for two hours. Cool and titrate with a standard solution of ferrous ammonium sulphate, running a blank with 2 g of dichromate and 50 ml of sulphuric acid 1:1 and placing this in the steam bath with the Erlenmeyer flask that contains the sample.

Where such determinations are made infrequently, powdered ferrous ammonium sulphate may be used. It is added from a weighing bottle, directly into the cooled Erlenmeyer flask, a little at a time, to slight excess, titrating back with a 1% solution of potassium dichromate. A little skill must be developed in recognizing the change in colour of. the dichromate, which will be a muddy green or even dark brown after boiling, depending on the amount of glycerol present. Upon adding excess ferrous ammonium sulphate, the solution turns bluish green. A freshly prepared 0.1% solution of potassium ferricyanide is used as indicator, on a dropping plate. Excess of iron salt is indicated by a deep blue colour (Turnbull's blue) when dropped over a drop of potassium ferricyanide. The end point is indicated by a light green colour.

Titrate a blank containing 2 g of potassium dichromate by adding ferrous ammonium sulphate from a weighing bottle, making sure that all the crystals are dissolved after each addition, until a drop on the plate with potassium ferricyanide turns blue. If the end point is approached cautiously, one may obtain a slight green colour and then, the 1% dichromate need not be used to titrate back any excess. We find that exactly 16.12 g of ferrous ammonium sulphate is required. Dividing 2.00 by 16.12 = 0.1241 g dichromate, which is equivalent to 1 g of ferrous ammonium sulphate.

On titrating the sample, we find that 11.597 g of ferrous ammonium sulphate and 2 ml of 1% dichromate are required to bring back the excess to a light green end point. Consequently, we have used 2.02 g of dichromate :

$$11.597 \times 0.1241 = 1.439 \text{ g potassium dichromate}$$

$$2.02 - 1.439 = 0.581 \text{ g dichromate}$$

actually used to oxidize the glycerol in 2 g of soap.

As 1 g of dichromate oxidizes 0.133411 g of glycerol,

$$\frac{0.581 \times 0.13411 \times 100}{2} = 3.85\% \text{ glycerol}$$

This analysis was made on a half-boiled potash soap, which contained about 35% of vegetable oils. The result is very close to the theoretical.

Acetin method for crude glycerol : It has been found that in the analysis of pure glycerol either by the dichromate method or by the acetin method, the results are identical. In the analysis of crude glycerol, however, the dichromate method gives higher results. Consequently, by agreement, between committees of American, British, French and German chemists, it has been decided that for crude glycerol, which contains not in excess of 60% of water, the acetin method gives the truer result.

The highest grade of acetic anhydride should be employed. Chemically pure sodium acetate should be fused again carefully, without charring, in a platinum or silica dish, quickly ground up, and kept in a stoppered bottle in the desiccator. Other reagents used in this analysis are normal sodium hydroxide, free from carbonate; normal sulphuric acid, carefully standardized; 0.5 g of phenolphthalein dissolved in 50 ml of alcohol and neutralized.

Into a thoroughly cleaned and dry narrow-mouth round bottom flask, weigh rapidly 1.25 to 1.50 g of glycerol. A Grethan or Lunge weighing bottle will be found useful. Add 3 g of fused sodium acetate and 7.5 ml of acetic anhydride. Connect the flask with an upright Liebig condenser, the inner tube of which should not be over 50 cm long. The flask may be connected to the condenser by either a ground glass joint or a rubber stopper, which has had a preliminary treatment with hot vapours of acetic anhydride. Heat for one hour, taking precautions to keep the salts from drying on the sides of the flask during boiling.

Allow the flask to cool and add 50 ml of distilled water at 80°C through the tube of the condenser. By giving the flask and condenser a rotary motion, the salts may be brought into solution. Caution must be observed so as not to loosen the stopper until the flask is quite cool. When cool, wash down the inside of the condenser tube with water, loosen the stopper and wash it down, then filter the contents of the flask, though an ashless filter paper into a litre flask. Wash thoroughly with cold distilled water free from carbon dioxide. Add 2 ml phenolphthalein solution and add normal sodium hydroxide from a burette, until the solution in the flask has been neutralized to a faint, pinkish yellow throughout.

The neutralization must be done very carefully while the solution in the flask is being swirled. Now add 50 ml of normal sodium hydroxide. Boil gently for 15 minutes with an air condenser. Then cool the flask and titrate with normal acid until the pinkish yellow colour previously chosen for the end point is reached. From the volume of normal sodium hydroxide consumed, the percentage of glycerol, including acetylizable impurities, may be calculated, after making correction for the following blank test. One ml of normal sodium hydroxide is equivalent to 0.03069 g glycerol.

Blank test : The acetic anhydride and sodium acetate may contain impurities that affect the result. A blank determination, is therefore, run exactly as for the glycerol, except that no glycerol is added. It is not necessary to filter the solution of the melt, but sufficient time must be allowed for the hydrolysis of the acetic anhydride before neutralization.

When the solution has been neutralized to a pinkish-yellow, 10 ml of normal sodium hydroxide is added and the solution is boiled 15 minutes, as in the test for glycerol. When cool, the excess is titrated with normal acid. The amount of sodium hydroxide absorbed may be calculated to glycerol equivalent and then deducted from the percentage found in the first test.

Glycerol value of acetylizable impurities : The residue at 160°C is found by dissolving 10 g of sample in distilled water, in a 100 ml volumetric flask. The solution is made alkaline to 0.2% sodium oxide, with sodium carbonate, or reduced with hydrochloric acid, if too strongly alkaline. It is made up to the 100 ml mark and thoroughly mixed.

From this solution, 10 ml is transferred to a Petri dish and evaporated to dryness on the steam bath. The Petri dish is then placed in the oven, at 140°C until most of the glycerol has volatilized. The residue is taken up with water, evaporated slowly, and then placed in the oven at 160°C, where it remains for an hour. The solution of the residue is evaporated and heating at 160° is repeated. Finally it is cooled in a desiccator and weighed. The process is repeated until the loss in the oven is 1 to 1.5 mg an hour.

The residue is taken up with a few ml of water and transferred to the acetylating flask. It is dried in an oven and acetylated and its glycerol equivalent determined.

Calculation of actual glycerol content : Determine the apparent glycerol in the sample; that is, the first test minus the value of the blank test. Determine the total residue at 160°C, then determine the acetyl value of the residue in terms of glycerol and deduct this from the apparent glycerol content.

7

Manufacture of Acid Slurry

Acid slurry is sulphonic acid of LAB (Linear alkyl benzene). LAB is sulphonated by sulphuric acid, oleum or sulphur trioxide by batch or continuous process. For small scale sector batch sulphonation with sulphuric acid or oleum will be the chosen one. This chapter discusses sulphonation of LAB.

Sulphonation with sulphuric acid and oleum

Batch sulphonation : Out of the various sulphonation process available, selection of a particular process is depended upon a number of factors such as :

(a) Size of the plant

(b) Location of the plant and easy availability of sulphonating agent

(c) Process control limitations and

(d) Processing time required

In the case of batch sulphonation plants, the plant size is relatively small. They are normally centred in areas near to the consumption point and in locations where basic raw materials like sulphur may not be easily available. Being small in size these plants are not in a position to make large investments for the manufacture of SO_3 and implement all the necessary pollution control measures imperative in such cases. Due to these reasons in batch sulphonation plant SO_3 sulphonation process is normally not employed.

Oleum is directly used for sulphonation. Due to this oleum sulphonation is less capital intensive and feasible in a batch plant. Due to this number of small units employing batch process use 20 - 22% oleum as the sulphonating agent. However, here the reaction is very fast and proper temperature control by offering cooling on the reacting material is very essential. Improper cooling can lead to charring and polymerisation of alkyl benzene producing undesirable products like sulphones, disulphonic acid and sulphonic anhydrides. This will lead to a product

Table 7.1 Storage and Handling Equipment for Various Strengths of Sulphuric Acid and Oleum

Products	Storage tank materials	Pipe and fittings	Valves	Gaskets	Pumps	Pump packing
Sulphuric acid 54 - 60°Be 66°Be-100%	Heavy steel	Steel, Sch 80 pipe welding fittings and 150 lb welding flanges Cast-iron pipe, with cast-iron flanged 250 lb fittings	FA-20 Alloy with TFE plastic packing and 150 flanges. Plug type FA-20 Alloy, TFE plastic sleeve and 150 lb flanges	TFE plastic CFE plastic compressed asbestos Blue African asbestos	Centrifugal FA-20 Alloy All iron with FA-20 Alloy impeller High-silicon cast-iron	Packless or mechanical seals TFE plastic CFE plastic Graphited lubricated blue African asbestos
Sulphuric acid electrolyte and other grades up to 60°Be	Steel or wood with chemical lead lining	Chemical lead pipe, 0.25° minimum wall thickness, with 6% antimony lead 125 lb flanges or lap joint flanges. High silicon cast-iron pipe and fittings. Rigid, unplasticised, normal impact polyvinyl chloride (PVC) Sch. 80 pipe and fittings	FA-20 Alloy or high-silicon cast-iron with TFE plastic packing and 150 lb flanges 6% antimony lead with TFE plastic packing and 125 lb flanges. Plug type, FA-20 Alloy, TFE plastic sleeve and 160 lb flanges	TFE plastic CFE plastic compressed asbestos Blue African asbestos	Centrifugal type FA-20 Alloy High-silicon cast-iron -	Packless or mechanical seals TFE plastic CFE plastic Graphited lubricated blue
Sulphuric acid electrolyte and 66°Be	Steel or wood with chemical lead lining Steel with baked phenolic lining such as Heresite P-403	Chemical lead pipe, 0.25" minimum wall thickness, with 6% antimony lead 125 lb flanges or lap joint flanges High-silicon cast-iron pipe and fittings	FA-20 Alloy or high-silicon cast iron with TFE plastic packing and 150 lb flanges 6% antimony lead with TFE plastic packing and 125 lb flanges. Plug type, FA-20 Alloy, TFE plastic sleeve and 150 lb flanges	TFE plastic CFE plastic Compressed asbestos Blue African asbestos	Centrifugal type FA-20 Alloy High-silicon cast iron	Packless or mechanical seats TFE plastic CFE plastic Graphited lubricated blue African asbestos

(Contd.)

Products	Storage tank materials	Pipe and fittings	Valves	Gaskets	Pumps	Pump packing
Sulphuric acid chemically pure (reagent ACS — 95.5-96.5%	Glass-lined steel	Pyrex glass TFE plastic-lined house	Porcelain 'Y' valves with TFE plastic discs and 150lb flanges	TFE plastic envelope type	Centrifugal type glass lined Diaphragm type with TFE or diaphragm	TFE plastic CFE plastic
Oleum all strengths	Heavy steel	Steel, Sch. 80 pipe, welding fittings and 150 lb welding flanges	FA-20 Alloy with TFE plastic packing and 150lb flanges Plug type, FA-20 Alloy TFE plastic sleeve and 150 lb flanges	TFE plastic CFE plastic Compressed asbestos Blue African asbestos	Centrifugal type FA-20 Alloy Mechanite CB-3	Packless or mechanical seals TFE Plastic CFE plastic TFE impregnated blue African asbestos
Sulfan (stabilised sulphuric anhydride)	Heavy steel	Steel, Sch. 80 pipe, welding fitting and 150 lb welding flanges	FA-20 Alloy with TFE plastic packing and 150 lb flanges Plug type, FA-20 Alloy TFE plastic sleeve and 150lb flanges	TFE plastic CFE plastic	Centrifugal type FA-20 Alloy Mechanite CB-3	Packless TFE plastic CFE plastic CFE plastic TFE impregnated blue African asbestos

TFE — Polytetrafluoroethylene - Representative trade names - Teflon
CFE — Polychlorotrifluoroethylene - Representative trade names - Halon, *Kel-F and Flour othene
FA-20 Alloy - Representative trade names - Durimet 20. Aioyco 20, Carpenter 20
Cast iron and high silicon cast iron on must not be used for Oleum
Trademark of Allied Chemical Corporation

with lower active matter content as well as dark in colour unacceptable to the market.

Sulphonation can also be effected by using 98% sulphuric acid alone. In this case, the reaction is slower and as such duration of sulphonation is more and require initial heating of the mixture. This normally causes high percentage of free oil (unreacted alkyl benzene) in the product. This will also result in darkening of the product due to prolonged contact of it with spent acid. However, in this process cooling requirement is slower.

Due to the above reasons, the most appropriate process for the manufacture of alkyl benzene sulphonic acid (LAB SA) in batch plant is considered to be that using a mixture of 98% sulphuric acid and 20 - 22% oleum as sulphonating agent. Sulphonation using 20% oleum along as well as 98% sulphuric acid alone are also very much in practice in the industry now.

Thus, various routes of sulphonation employed in batch sulphonation plants are summarised as follows :

(a) Sulphonation with 20 - 22% oleum

(b) Sulphonation with 98% sulphuric acid and

(c) Sulphonation with a mixture of 20 - 22% oleum and 98% sulphuric acid

The plant and machinery required and the procedures of operation for all the above three routes are the same. We will therefore, discuss in detail the process based on a mixture of oleum and sulphuric acid, which in principal is applicable to a two routes also.

Manufafcturing process : Chemical reaction involved in the process is As evident from above, the formation of sulphonation acid is followed by liberation of water. Water liberated dilutes the sulphuric acid and retards or even stops the progress of reaction. This is why, addition of oleum suggested. Oleum enables to retain the acid concentration at the required

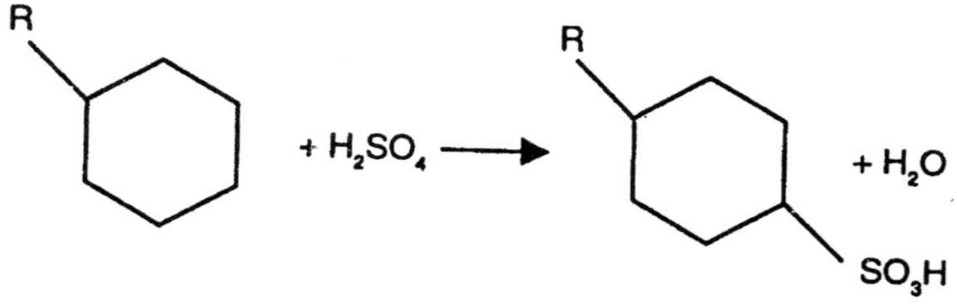

level until the reaction is over. In the absence of oleum, very large excess of sulphuric acid will be required.

Economic size of a batch sulphonation unit is 1 tonne (1000 kg) acid slurry capacity per batch, even though 500 kg and 750 kg batches are also prevalent.

Principal equipment required are :

1. Storage tanks for sulphuric acid and oleum
2. Storage tank for alkyl benzene
3. Acid dosing tank
4. Alkyl benzene dosing tank
5. Reactor
6. Separator
7. Cold water dosing tank
8. Spent acid tank
9. Pump for acid dosing
10. Pump for alkyl benzene dosing
11. Compressor/pump for reaction product and
12. A set of pipes, valves and fittings

While the storage tanks and dosing tanks are of mild steel construction, the reactor should be of stainless steel grade 316. It is jacketed externally for circulation of cooling water and is provided with an anchor type stirrer. Separation is done in a lead lined vessel with conical bottoms for easy separation of spent acid. It is also provided with a paddle type stirrer.

Requirement of raw materials per batch of a 1000 kg batch plant with 85% active matter is as follows :

Alkyl benzene	673 kg
98% sulphuric acid	846 kg
20-22% oleum	212 kg
Ice-cold water for dilution	150 litres

Process parameters to be maintained during the sulphonation are:

Temperature during sulphonation	45 - 50°C
Temperature during digestion	45 - 48°C

Temperature during d lution	60°C maximum
Time taken for sulphonating agent	addition *2½* to 3 hr.
Duration of digestion	1 hr.
Settling time	8-10 hours

Sulphuric acid and oleum of required quantities are pumped into the acid dosing vessel by means of the dosing pumps and are allowed to mix properly inside the dosing tank. Meanwhile, alkyl benzene is pumped into the alkyl benzene dosing tank by means of the alkyl benzene dosing pump to the measured level. Same is transferred to the reactor by operating the dosing valve at the bottom of the dosing vessel. Now cooling water through the reactor jacket is kept open. Mixture of sulphuric acid and oleum are now slowly added in small quantities into the reactor, carefully observing the temperature of the reaction mixture. Prior to the addition of the acid mixture, reactor stirrer should be kept on Speed of the reactor stirrer is designed in such a way that peripheral velocity at the tip is around 500 - 600 m/ min. corresponding to a Reynolds number of 20000 to ensure necessary turbulence and proper mixing. The addition of the acid mixture is done at intervals maintaining the temperature of the reaction mass below 50°C all the time. Control of reaction temperature as well as acid strength is extremely important in obtaining product of acceptable quality and colour.

Following table gives the guidelines to understand the relationship between acid concentration reaction temperature and digestion time required for the process. Thus it is necessary to maintain high acid concentration as well as low temperature to obtain quality product.

After completing the addition of oleum sulphuric acid mixture, agitation of the sulphonation mass is continued for *2Vz* to 3 hours, maintaining the temperature level. After some time cooling can be stopped, as by that time evolution of heat decreases considerably as the reaction will be nearing completion. The purpose of ageing the reaction mass is to reduce the unsulphonated hydrocarbon to the lowest possible level without prohibitively darkening the product because of the prolonged contact with the unused sulphuric acid. After a sufficient ageing time to achieve a maximum degree of sulphonation, the batch of sulphonic acid is ready for further processing. It is always preferable to be satisfied if the reaction is complete to the extent that residual oil is 1.2 to 1.5% of total active matter rather than achieving 100% sulphonation, as this would result in the product of poor colour and odour.

Table 7.2 Acid Sulphonation Condition

Acid strength	Ratio alkylate/acid	Reaction temperature	Digestion time
20-22% SO_3 oleum	1:1.1 (min 1:1)	30°C until half of acid addition 45° at end	2 hrs. at 40-45°C
12-14% SO_3 oleum	1:1.2 (min 1:1.1)	45° half, 55°end	2 hrs. at 50-55°C
100% H_2SO_4	1:1.5	50° half, 50° end	2 hrs. at 55-60°C
98% H_2SO_4	1:1.65 (min 1:1.55)	45° half, 55° end	2 hrs. at 50-55°C

When the digestion is complete the entire mass is transferred into the separator. This can be effected by pneumatic means using a compressor or by means of an acid slurry pump. Here the mass is stirred continuously. Ice-cold water of measured quantity is slowly added from the cold water dosing tank with continuous stirring of the mass. Instead of water, crushed ice can also be used for better temperature control. Water addition should be done carefully avoiding the temperature from rising about 60°C at any case. After completing the water addition, the mass is again stirred for another 15 minutes. Then it is allowed to settle for about 8 to 10 hours. After this, the bottom layer is detained out to the spent acid tank by opening the drain valve at the bottom of the separator. The spent acid will be approximately of 78% strength and pale greenish in colour. The upper layer which is sulphonic acid is collected in HDPE cans or carboys and stored. Separation of phase can be detected by using transparent HDPE pipe for draining the acid. Increase of the batch capacity to more than 1000 kg., external cooling of the reactor mass by passing through a heat exchanger will be needed. Heat evolved during the reaction is 97.2 Kcal/kg alkylate.

Sulphonation with 98% sulphuric acid : In this case the process is carried out in the same manner as explained above except the following :

(a) Quantity of 98% sulphuric acid required to be added will be higher, around 2475 kg for 1000 kg batch.

(b) The alkylate will have to be heated to a temperature of 40°C in order to start the reaction smoothly.

(c) Reaction temperature is maintained at 55°C,.

(d) Amount of water to be added for separation spent acid will be higher.

Sulphonation with oleum : Here also the procedure and process is the same as explained under mixed acid sulphonation except the following :

(a) Ratio of alkylate to acid is 1:1.1 i.e., amount of oleum of 20% (104.5% sulphuric acid) to be added in a 1000 kg batch is 1650 kg.

(b) The temperature of reaction should be kept at 25 - 30°C and so, rapid and more effective cooling is required. For this, instead of cold water cold brine at 0°C is circulated through the reactor jacket. Otherwise, cooling should be effected by circulating the reaction mixture through the external heat exchanger.

It is observed that to reduce the capital investment some manufacturers prefer to use a single equipment for both sulphonatin and separation. This is not at all an advisable preposition. Sulphonation is achieved at an acid concentration always above 90% and in most cases above 92%. At this concentration lead reacts with sulphuric acid. Lead is suitable only upto to a maximum concentration of 85%. Therefore, using lead lined vessel for sulphonation will reduce the reactor life drastically and not advisable.

Stainless steel cannot tolerate sulphuric acid concentration below 90%. Concentration of sulphuric acid in the reacted mixture after dilution will be around 78%. Therefore, in case dilution of the mixture and separation is done in the SS reactor itself, that will lead to corrosion of the reactor and its life gets shortened.

Thus, for prolonged life of the plant and machinery it is absolutely important that separate equipments are used both for sulphonation and separation. In short,

(a) The sulphonation should be an equipment made out of SS316 material.

(b) The separator should be a mild steel vessel internally lined with lead, Stirrer should also be lead lined.

(c) Valves for handling concentrated acid should also be of SS lined contact parts.

(d) Valves below the separating vessel should with lead lined contact parts.

(e) Pipes, valves and fittings between the sulphonator and separator preferably be of SS construction.

Sulphonation product from a standard batch plant will be having the following composition.

Active matter (alkyl benzene sulphonic acid)	85 - 90%
Free oil	0.5 - 2.5%

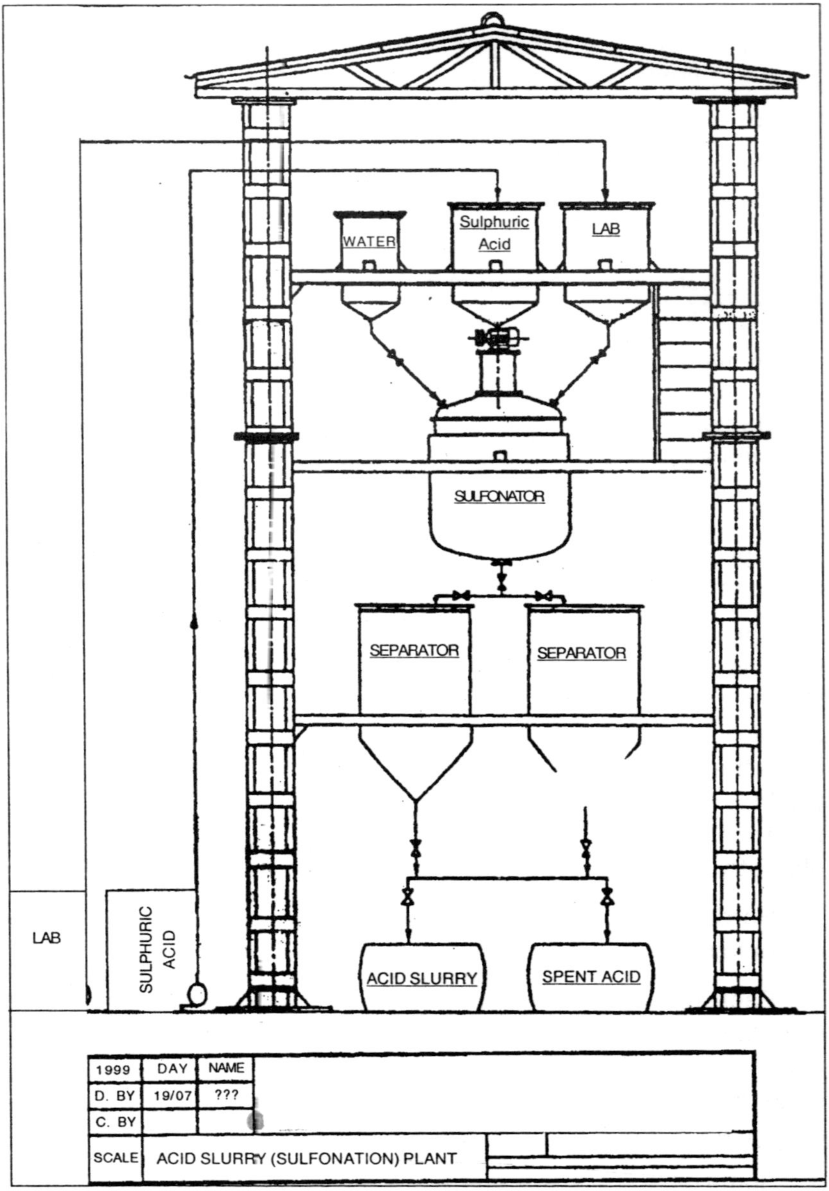

Fig. 7.1 : Acid slurry (sulfonation) plant

8

Manufacture of Soap

Soaps are sodium and potassium salt of long chain fatty acids like lauric, myristic, stearic, oleic etc. These fatty acids are present in vegetable oils and animal fats. The reaction of vegetable oils and animal fats with alkali is called saponification of oils and fats. The soap usually does not contain free fatty acid except in case of toilet soaps where particularly emollient property is desired to be induced. Free alkali is also not desired as it is harsh towards the fabric or skin. The proper pH of the soap solution desired is 12 to 12.5.

The selection of oil is important for soap making. Sodium/potassium laureate and myristate produces good foams and are well soluble in water. On the other hand sodium/potassium stearate and palmitate are less soluble in water and produce little foam. However, these two compounds holds the soap structure and do not allow the soap to be wasted during washing process. A judicial selection of oils is necessary so that the soap contains appropriate proportion of lauryl/myristil and stearic/palmitic etc. fatty acids.

Hardened oils and fats are rich in stearic and palmitic acid. Coconut oil contains high quantity of lauric acid.

Each oil requires different quantity of alkali to saponify. This is calculated from saponification value of the oil to be experimentally determined. The Sap value determination method is given in a later chapter under analytical methods. The calculation of alkali required for a batch is also given in a later chapter.

Some oils are well saponified with strong solution of alkali and some with weak solution of alkali. Addition of scrap soap to the batch accelerates soap forming reaction. Elevated temperature speeds up the reaction. Usually 30°Be caustic soda solution is employed for saponification. This is equivalent to about 19% NaOH solution.

Soaps are manufactured by three processes viz. (a) cold process, (b) semiboiling process and (c) by full boiling process.

Cold process : The process essentially consists of adding to melted fats just sufficient alkali that will ensure saponification and produce a neutral soap. The fats and oils which are to be used as soap stock are just heated so that the fats are melted and the oils give out a cracking sound when a few drops of water are poured over them. These are then brought in contact with caustic lye and allowed to stand for a few days. The saponification goes on and the heat generated during the process accelerates the subsequent action.

The crux of the problem is the proportion of soda to be added to complete the, process of saponification. If the oils and fats were primary substances consisting simply of olein or stearin or palmitin or laurin, the matter would have been much simplified. In that case chemical equations would give us the exact proportions between the glyceride and caustic soda on the one hand and the soap and glycerine produced on the other. But as a matter of fact the oils used are a most heterogeneous mixture of a large number of glycerides and the proportions between them even in the same oil vary considerably according to the source, quality and age of the substance.

Hence the best way to arrive at a correct percentage between the fat and the oil is to make an independent chemical analysis before treatment of each batch of oil.

The coconut oil is best adapted for treatment by cold process but other fats like hardened rice bran oil can also be so treated. In all cases, however, it is the practice to incorporate a certain percentage of coconut oil in the batch, the saponification of which is thereby accelerated. Castor and mahua oils also may be made into soap by this process. Vegetable oils are expensive, thus economical and appropriate oil should be the cheapest oil available in the market. Soap stock is an economical raw material. It is the waste product obtained during edible vegetable oil purification. It is an emulsion of soap, oil and water. Addition of soap stock makes the soap making cheap. The soap stock is available from edible oil refinery and vanaspati (hydrogenated edible oil) manufacturing units.

Tallow and other animal fats are cheap and suitable for soap making. However, they are not available in India and their import is banned.

In making the soap put the fat or oil in a pan provided with an agitator. The fat or oil is then just heated to 25 - 30°C. This is the ambient temperature during most of the year in India. When melted, run in the lye at the ambient temperature into the pan and stir constantly. The mass will thicken. Now run into low and broad frames holding 80-100 kg of the mass.

The fat or oil should be at the correct temperature, If it is too cold, it will set on the addition of the lye. If too hot, the saponification proceeds too quickly resulting in curdy or grainy soaps. Strength of the alkali is a decisive factor. The alkali should be of suitable grade so that the impurities do not get into the soap during saponification and spoil the appearance by causing efflorescence.

Semi-boiling process : According to the semi-boiling process of soap manufacture fatty acids are made to combine direct with alkalies which are taken in proportions so that complete reaction of the fatty acids may be ensured.

First of all it is necessary to find out the percentage of alkali required to saponify an oil. Coconut oil requires 17.48 to 19.05 per cent of its own weight of caustic soda for complete neutralisation. The above fact will give us a fair idea about the quantity of alkali to be taken to saponify a given amount of oil. The alkali is made into lyes of appropriate strengths. The fats or oils are brought to a boil and the alkali is stirred in slowly little by little. Boiling is continued with alkalies of greater and greater strength until all the alkali has been absorbed. Water is added from time to time to keep the mass thin and homogeneous. Finally pour in frame and allow it to cool.

During saponification the oil swells up considerably. Precautionary measures maybe taken to prevent entrainment. The use of an agitator is recommended for the purpose; the addition of the oils in small portions at a time is helpful.

Boiling process : The oils and fats are placed in a large pan or reactor and is melted by heating. Caustic soda lye is then gradually added into the mass kept in a state of ebullition by agitation and boiling. The strength of the caustic solution and the quantity added from time to time is determined by the nature of the oil. At the outset weak lyes must be added slowly until saponification is well under way. This is indicated by the formation of an emulsion. When the saponification has once begun, continue boiling and go on adding caustic soda lye of greater strength in small quantities as long as it is being absorbed, so that much evaporation is not needed at the end to arrive at proper consistency. But the liquor should not be allowed to become too strong, for then the soap paste is cut into curds upon which the alkali cannot satisfactorily act. Water therefore is added from time to time. The emulsion should thicken gradually as the saponification proceeds. The concentration of the lye in the kettle is ascertained by taking out of small sample and testing its pH. The strength of the alkali can be measured by pH. Add caustic soda so long the pH is not 12.5. When pH standardizes at 12 to 12.5, the fats and oils taken in the pan have been neutralised by the caustic soda lye already added.

Expert soap makers can detect completion of saponification from the changes of colour, grain, firmness and general appearance. They take out a sample of soap with a trowel and examine it. When there is no greasiness in the sample and it feels firm and dry when pressed between the fingers and thumb, the soap is considered to be properly saponified and ready for being framed.

Usually the solution, after the completion of the saponifica-tion, becomes clear and assumes a brownish colour. The completion of the saponification is also ascertained by the following test, which is called the "ring test". A quantity of the soap is taken in a trowel and a drop from it is caught on a glass pane, or a slate, or the clean floor. This drop should be watched as it cools. If, in cooling, the edge of the drop solidifies first to form a white ring, and the central portion remains transparent until it gradually solidifies, the solidification proceeding from the edge towards the centre, then the saponification is complete. If the drop in solidifying forms something like a ring in the edge, but the central portion is turbid before solidification and the solidification is irregular, then it indicates the presence of unsaponified fat or oil. If, the drop solidifies without the formation of the ring, and a watery substance separates from the solidified soap, the fact shows that the alkali is present in excess.

The completion of the saponification can also be ascertained by the "ribbon test", as it is called. A quantity of the soap is taken on a trowel and allowed to trickle down from it. If in so doing the soap forms transparent ribbons, it indicates that the saponification is almost complete. A turbid ribbon discloses the presence of unsaponified fat or oil. If again, the soap, in falling from the trowel shows a solidified but broken film, which glides down readily, the fact indicates that the alkali is in excess.

The end of the saponification should be made when a slight excess of alkali persists even after continuing the boiling.

The pan now contains saponified fat or soap, excess of alkali and glycerol mixed together. If the soap is to be of good quality, either the excess of alkali must be removed from the soap or the soap is to be separated out from the mass and the lye left after the operation may be treated for recovery of glycerol, if possible.

The separating out of the soap still in solution from the mixture is accomplished by the addition of salt. This happens because soap is insoluble in a strong saline solution.

When the saponification point has been reached and the soap is still on the boil and has assumed a thick consistency a saturated solution of common salt 40°Tw (47° Be) is added little by little, to throw out the soap. If salting is started when the soap is diluted, a large amount of salt will be required. Instead of using brine solution, salt may be spread uniformly on the surface. The boiling is continued slowly. The soap loses its smooth transparent appearance and becomes granular and opaque. This is technically known as "opening" the soap.

The amount of salt required for the operation changes with the nature of the raw materials used. When tallow is employed as a soap stock, the soap is grained easily; more salt is, however, required in the case of cotton seed oil soaps while the amount to be mixed is the greatest in the case of coconut oil soap.

Excess of salt should not be added to the mass for graining, for then the soap will become granular and enclose salt. Only a sufficient quantity of the salt for the completion of the operation is necessary. Hence the most practical way of doing this is to go on adding the salt little by little and test the grained soap from time to time. The soap becomes turbid and frothy on the addition of salt. The operation is deemed complete when the frothy soap trends to separate in clots and the soap separates at the top without enclosing much froth and air bubbles, or a sample taken out on a wooden trowel presents distinct grains of soap and a liquid portion. The boiling is then stopped and the contents of the kettle are allowed to stand.

The contents of the kettle being allowed to settle, these separate out in three distinct layers. The first consists of a thin crust floating at the top of the pan. The second layer is the actual soap which floats on the saline liquor or waste lye, which forms the lowest stratum in the pan. For ordinary purposes the soap may be ladled out carefully from above the waste lye without disturbing it or the waste lye may be withdrawn from the pan by means of a syphon or a pump provided with suitable skimmers. The waste lye may be run into tanks for the recovery of glycerine contained in it.

The grained soap is then boiled with sufficient water. The granules begin to swell up and fuse together or "close" as it is called. The soap has now a smooth appearance. If necessary the grains of the soap may be broken with a crutcher. This when cooled and framed gives the ordinary soaps of commerce.

The soap is now ready but it may still contain traces of unsaponified fat. In the case of better quality soaps and toilet soaps this cannot be allowed to remain in the condition, for it would then go rancid and spoil the perfumes added. With this object in view the boiling on strength is carried on.

The "closed" soap, as obtained after cleansing, is treated with more alkali which is run in gradually until the soap is again grained and the boiling is continued. As the lye is being absorbed, add another portion slowly till the contents refuse to absorb more and is thrown out of solution and grained. Now continue boiling so that last traces of neutral oil may be completely saponified.

The soap solution is then just "opened" with salt. At this stage it is important to adjust the quantity of salt carefully. The soap is made just to open so that the homogeneity of the mass may be lost and the separated lye visible from above. But the soap must not be allowed to be unduly grained. Heat removed from the kettle and it is allowed to rest for several hours. The half-spent lye settles at the bottom of the kettle and can be withdrawn. This can be utilized for saponifying fresh oil, the details of which follow at the end of this cheaper.

The soap has now been freed from the presence of unsaponified fat but the excess of alkali in it is now to be got rid of. This is done by fitting.

The soap is again boiled and water is added until the desired degree of closing is attained. As the water is thoroughly mixed throughout the mass, the thick paste gradually becomes reduced to a smooth thin consistence. Samples are tested from time to time; the thin layer should drop off a hot trowel held sideways in two or three flakes and leave the surface of the trowel clean and dry. If too much water has been mixed with the soap and too fine a fit is produced which would be denoted by the layer of soap not leaving the trowel, a little caustic lye or brine may be very carefully added and the whole well boiled until the desired condition is obtained. If the soap is properly fitted, all the impurities will be precipitated on standing and the settled soap containing the correct amount of water, will look clear and bright.

The fitted soap is then covered up to keep the heat and allowed to stand for 1 or 2 days according to the size of the charge. No covering is needed when the atmospheric temperature is already high. During this settling the contents of the pan separate into three layers, the top consisting of good molten soap *{neat soap),* the intermediate is a slimy soap much richer in water *(nigers)* and the excess or liquor at the bottom. The layer of neat soap has at its topmost portion much frothy substance which is skimmed off first, Neat soap is then taken up and placed, in frames to cool and solidify, The nigers are run into another pan to be further treated.

The composition of the three layers is as follows:—

The layer	Water	Anhydrous soap	Salt and free alkali
(Neat soap)	30 to 35 p.c.	63 to 68 p.c.	0.5 to 1 p.c.
Intermediate layer (Nigers)	58 to 65 p.c.	35 to 45 p.c.	2.5 to 3.0 p.c
Under layer (Liquors)	95 to 97 p.c.	nil	4.0 to 5.0 p.c.

If filling agents, colour and perfumes are to be incorporated in the soap, these are to be crutched in or mixed with agitation into the body of soap before it is put in the frame to cool. The cooled soap is then trimmed for the market.

Modified boiling process : This method of manufacturing soap is based on the German method of soap boiling. The time of boiling in this case is considerably shortened.

The process consists in the use of a considerable excess of caustic soda in a fairly strong solution, to initiate the reactions the speed of which is maintained undiminished to the last by the caustic soda which is always present in excess of the consumable quantity. A general description of the process is given below:

A strong caustic soda lye is taken in a soap boiling pan. The exact strength and volume of the lye will depend on the proportions and combining weights of the different oils and fats making up a charge. It has been found that for charges containing small proportions only of coconut oil the proportion of caustic soda should be 23 per cent, of the entire charge of oils and fats. For charges with high proportions of coconut oil the caustic strength should be raised up to 28 per cent. Heat should be applied to the kettle after the caustic soda lye has been run in and as soon as the latter commences boiling the mixture of oils and fats is added, preferably in a thin stream or a spray, so that the contents of the pan may not go off the boil. The strength of the lye has an important bearing on the speed of the reaction. The best results are obtained with a concentration in which the oils, immediately on addition, break up with much swelling into minute globules and the saponification proceeds immediately with extreme rapidity, A too strong lye causes the oil to grain out at once the grains enclosing much unsaponified oil, while with a weak lye no swelling takes place and therefore the action is less brisk. The strength of the lye should be found out for each type of soap charge with the help of the above indications. In a very short time, the charge is practically completely saponified. At the end of the boiling, the soap is separated from the lye by allowing the latter to run off through the outlet at the bottom of the kettle.

The kettle should have outlets for soap and spent liquor.

The partly spent lye withdrawn from the soap boiling pan will still contain much caustic soda of a fairly high strength to saponify a further charge of oils and fats. This part-spent caustic lye is treated with a fresh batch of oils and fats. The object being the recovery of the alkali, complete saponification is not aimed at. Oils and fats in quantities and excess of those completely saponifiable by the alkali present in this lye are added in order that the entire quantity of the alkali may be taken up. The alkali, still of a fairly high strength, attacks the oils at once and is used up in a short time. When no more free alkali is left, the partly saponified charge is separated by means of salt. This partly saponified charge is returned to the kettle towards the end of the saponification of a fresh charge of oils and fats, so that the final product may be a completely saponified soap. The operations may thus be carried on in a cycle.

Sodium silicate and soda ash are added to soap to give it firmness. This addition is done to washing soap and not toilet soap. In addition fillers like precipitated chalk, talc, fine clays are also added while soda ash and sodium silicate are builders, the others are filler materials.

Before the silicate of soda is used in the soap stock, it should be dissolved in hot water. It should be noted that the silicate is sparingly soluble in cold water and settles down in the bottom in that case. The strength of the silicate solution should not exceed 40°Be. As a general rule by mixing equal parts of water and silicate a strength equal to 40°Be is obtained. To get lesser strengths the proportion of water should be increased.

While soap is being made by cold process, it should be the practice of the manufacturers to add the silicate in solution when the oil and the lye are well mixed. Brisk agitation is essential during and mixing operation otherwise the stock is liable to set in places and to present lumps in its body which is most undesirable.

During manufacturing of soap by the boiling process, the silicate should be poured in when the saponification is completed and the stock is yet of a thin consistency. Both the soap stock and the silicate solution should be hot before they are mixed together. Vigorous stirring is to be made during mixing with wooden poles, otherwise lumps are liable to form within the mass of the soap. Sodium silicate usually requires one-fifth its weight of caustic soda of 38°Be for action. Silicate of soda may also be added to the oil in some cases before it is treated by caustic soda for saponification.

The soda ash may be added in a powdery form when the saponification is nearing completion. Light soda ash is used. It makes the soap lye hard by absorbing moisture. Soda ash is usually added to weak soap and not to a firm soap.

LAYOUT BOX DIAGRAM FOR TOILET SOAP - NOODLE ROUTE

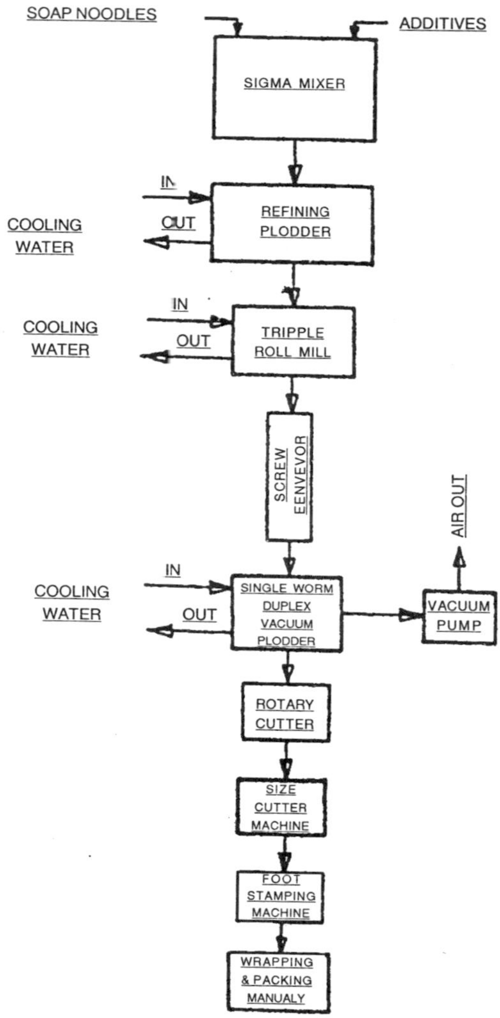

Fig. 8.1. Layout box diagram for Toilet Soap.

TOILET/LAUNDRY SOAP PLANT
TURBO REACTOR PROCESS
CAPACITY: 2500 kgs/Hr.

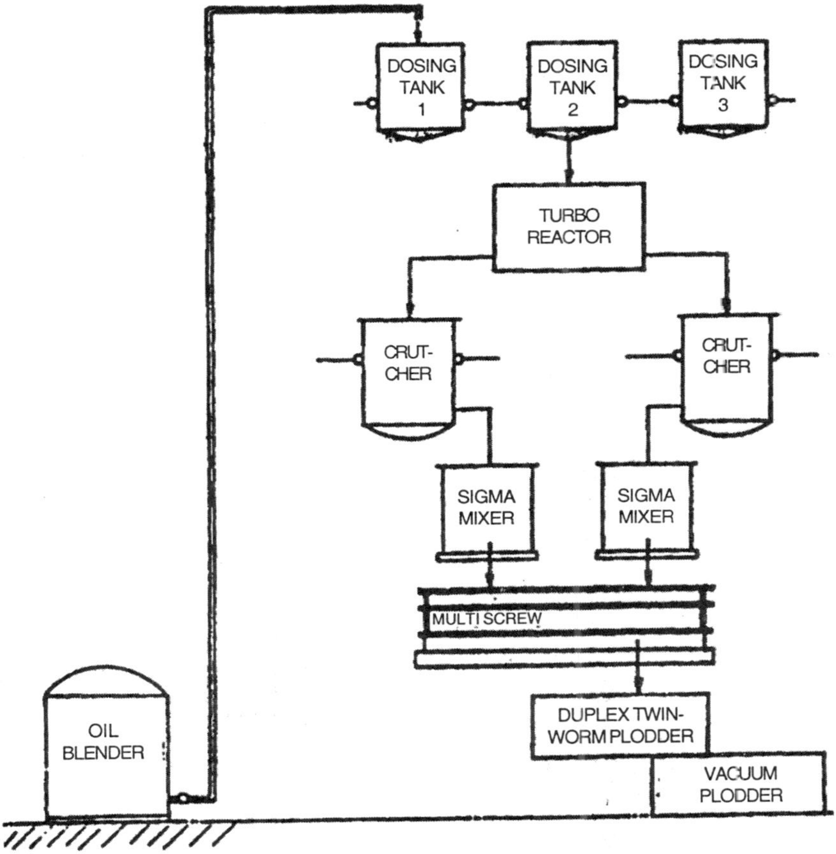

Fig. 8.2. Toilet/Laundry soap plant turbo reactor process.

LAY_OUT BOX DIAGRAM FOR LAUNDARY SOAP

STROKAGE OFFICE & LABORATORY----7. METER X METER.
HALL APPROXIMATELY-----7. METER X 12. METER.

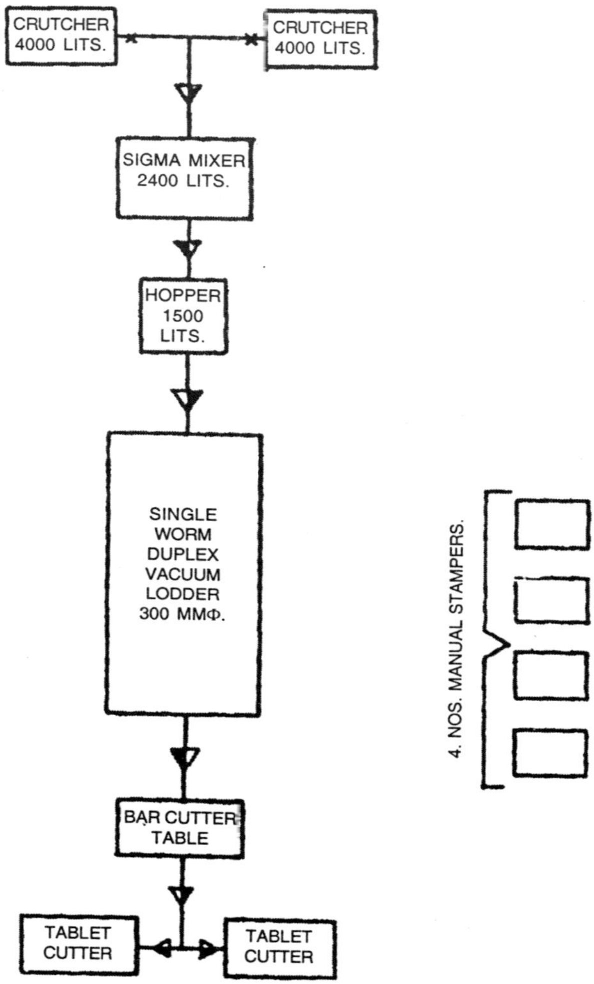

Fig. 8.3. Lay-out box diagram for laundry soap.

LAYOUT DIAGRAM FOR TOILET SOAP- OIL ROUTE
(CONVENTIONAL PROCESS)

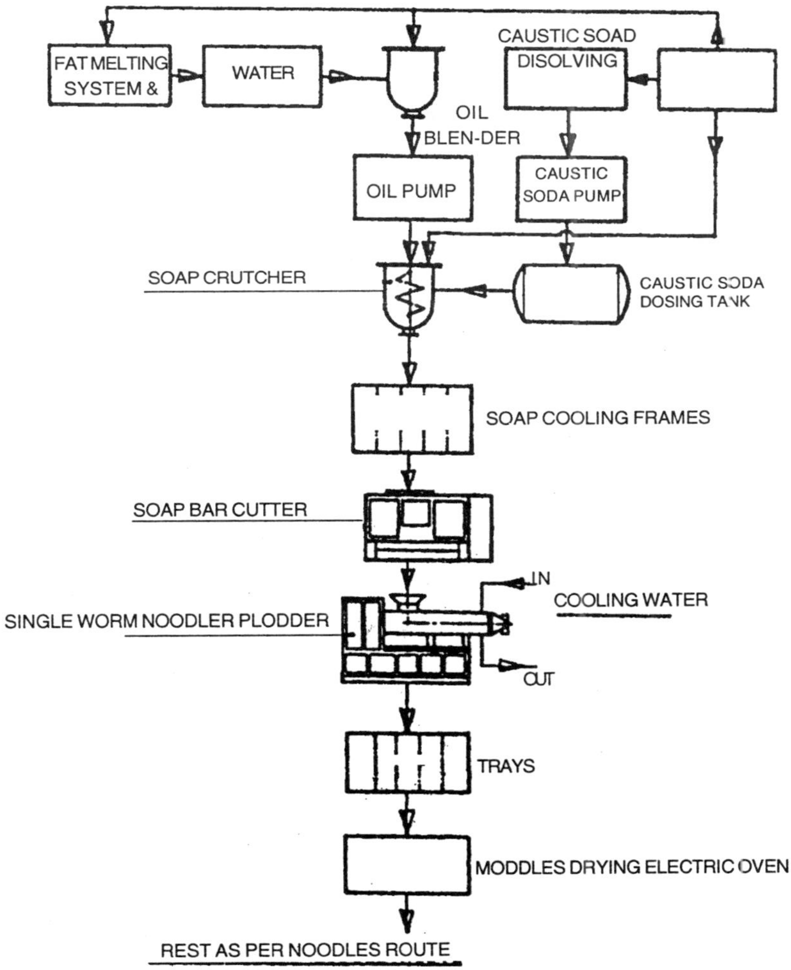

Fig. 8.4. Lay-out diagram for toilet soap-oil route.

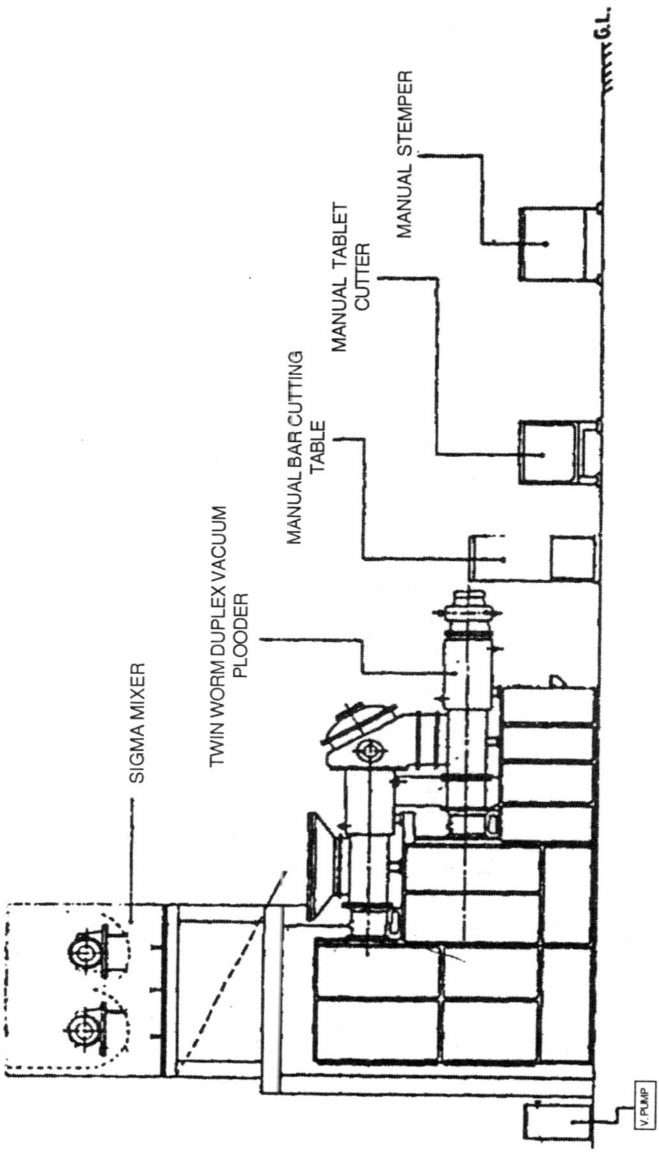

Fig. 8.5. Toilet soap finishing line

9

Technology of Surfactants

INTRODUCTION

Amongst chemical specialities, which are wide and varied, 'surfactants' are a group of materials that have evolved with the growing and ever-changing needs of society. They pervade the whole spectrum of the industrial horizon, and, as such, deserve a close look as regards their present global status and future potential. Substances containing in the same molecule groups which are strongly hydrophobic (water repellent) and hydrophilic (water loving) orient themselves in different ways when dissolved or dispersed in water or nonaqueous solvents. Such orientation, which could also be in the form of aggregates of oriented molecules, termed micelles, is known as 'Surface Activity' and materials exhibiting this are termed 'Surface Active Agents', often abbreviated as 'Surfactants'. Fig. 9.1 indicates the orientation of surfactants in several systems.

Practically almost every product in commercial use today has come in contact, at some stage or other of it's production process, with surfactants, which are classified by the nature of their hydrophilic moiety. The surfactant mosaic is made up of anionics, cationics, nonionics and amphoterics in broad classification. However, surfactants grouped together as polymeric surfactants, biosurfactants etc., depending on their end-use importance or functional aspects are gaining prominence.

The hydrophilic moiety carries a negative ionic charge in anionics, a positive ionic charge in cationics and is neutral in nonionics. The amphoterics contain, or have the potential to form, both positive and negative functional groups under specified conditions. The surfactants, in general, are governed by several criteria such as :

(a) Solubility in water, non-aqueous media and two-phase systems.

(b) Hydrophile-lipophile balance (HLB).

(c) Surface tension.

(d) Foaming characteristics.

(e) Cloud point.

(f) Orientation at interfaces.

(g) Substantivity such as adsorption on solid surfaces,

(h) Micelle formation.

(i) Functional properties such as detergency, wetting, emulsifying, solubilising and dispersing.

(j) Reactivity such as complex forming ability and antimicrobial properties.

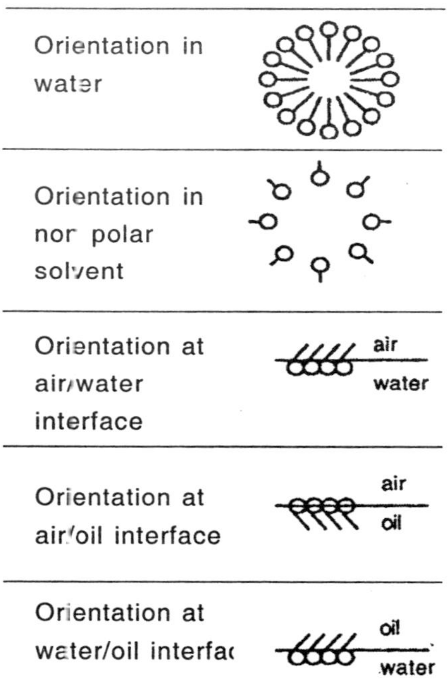

Fig. 9.1 Orientation of surfactant in several systems.

Nature has used the science of surface activity in many simple and complex ways. Surfactants have been used by man for a long time, a soap making process being recorded by Plinius as early as 70 AD. Synthetic surfactants emerged on a large scale only with the use of petroleum derived fractions in the 1950s. Over the last 50 years there has been an enormous number of new surfactants produced and many new applications. Apart from the natural and synthetic surfactants, biosurfactants have emerged on the horizon. These are a collective class of biosurface-active materials, which are basically obtained by manipulating fermentation processes with very specific microorganisms. Several biosurfactants have surface-active and emulsification properties far superior to either synthetic or natural surfactants. In addition, they have the green attributes of bio-compatibility, complete bio-degradability and superior eco-toxic characteristics. The usual picture of a surfactant as a simple rod-like hydrophobe with a hydrophilic head has changed in recent times. Many new surfactants are now being produced of more complex structure with more than one hydrophilic head. Such products form micro-emulsions more readily.

Polymeric materials, especially high molecular weight ones, have been used to give colloidal stability since almost the dawn of civilisation. In particular, naturally occurring polymeric materials, such as egg white, gum arabic and animal glues have been used to make water-based inks and paints pigmented with carbon black or metal oxide pigments. In recent years polymeric surfactants have been developed for wide applications in surface coatings. Surfactant technology thus is continuing to grow aided by a large well-established base industrial potential.

The number of surfactants available commercially today are several thousands. As a result many chemists, engineers, biologists and others, having the need to employ surfactants, feel daunted by the prospect of ploughing through the literature to find the best material for their purpose. Even if inclined to do so, they may face the investment of inordinate amounts of time and effort without guarantee of success. The breadth and complexity of the science and technology of surfactants makes it difficult to compress all the information available in a small volume. However in this chapter attempt has been made to give sufficient insight into the various classes of surfactants, major raw materials, key physico-chemical aspects, applications, present global status, market participants in the field, typical formulations, opportunities for growth and other allied matters of relevance to the surfactants industry. In analysing the surfactant markets, emphasis is laid on the household sector consuming various detergents and cleaners, industrial and institutional sectors covering important industrial segments, personal care products sector involving hair care, skin care and oral-hygience products segments and the agrosector with great demand for crop protection chemicals.

TYPES OF SURFACTANTS

Anionic Surfactants

By far the largest class of surfactants in general use today are the anionics (including soaps). For thousands of years in the history of the application of surface activity to the needs of mankind, the soaps, derived from natural animal and vegetable fats and oils, dominated the field. The major historical and economical advantage of the fatty acid soaps has always been the ready availability of the raw materials from natural, renewable sources. The weakness of the classical soaps, due to the sensitivity of the carboxylate salts which mainly constitute them, in many processes requiring surfactant action, led to the development of synthetic surfactants. Classically, anionic surfactants are divided into four basic categories, namely :

(a) Carboxylates, of which common soap is the most important.

(b) Sulphonates, of which linear alkyl benzene sulphonate (LABS) is the most significant and is the largest used synthetic surfactant worldwide.

(c) Sulphuric acid esters such as alcohol sulphates or sulphated oils, the earliest of synthetic surfactants.

(d) Other category includes the nitrogen-bearing taurates and sarcosinates, phosphorus-bearing chemicals such as the phosphate esters and others, and industrial surfactants of the alkylnaphthalene-formaldehyde condensate type.

On a global basis, the anionic surfactants usage is roughly as given in Table 9.1.

Table 9.1. Global split of anionic surfactants.

Anionic surfactant type	Percentage of the global anionics market
Alkylbenzene sulphonates	45-47
Lignin sulphonate	.23-25
Alcohol ether sulphates	13-15
Alcohol sulphates	8-10
Others	6-8

The four basic categories of anionic surfactants fall under two large classes of products—'true surfactants' and 'quasi-surfactants'. The 'true surfactants' are those which exhibit the important properties of lowering the surface tension of water and the interfacial tension between water and oils, of wetting and foaming actions, of emulsification etc. The most important of these surfactants are soap, alkylbenzene sulphonates, alcohol ether sulphates and alcohol sulphates. The 'quasi-surfactants' have feeble powers sulphates and alcohol sulphates. The 'quasi-surfactants' have feeble powers in terms of reducing the surface tension or wetting action, but are vastly superior in properties such as those of dispersion, thickening, spreading, penetrating, defoaming, demulsifying etc. Typical of these are lignin sulphonates and alkylnaphthanlene sulphonates. Most of these quasi-surfactants are used in the production of industrial commodities.

Surfactants are seldom used directly in the application sectors and are always components of formulations containing both surface-active and non-surface active chemicals. The market segments for anionic surfactants can be categorised as :

(a) The household products sector.

(b) The personal care products sector.

(c) Industrial and institutional cleaners.

(d) Other industrial applications.

In the household sector there are three important segments:

(a) Laundry detergents.

(b) Dishwashing detergents.

(c) Household cleaners.

'True' anionics are consumed to a large extent in these applications. The usage is dominated by Linear alkylbenzene sulphonate (LAS), Alcohol ethoxy sulphate (AES), Sodium alpha sulphomethyl laurate (SAS). Alkyl sulphates (AS), Alpha olefin sulphonate (AOS) new anionics such as methyl ester sulphonates and phosphate esters. In all the segments of the household sector the anionics are used alongwith other surfactant types, mainly nonionics.

The laundry detergent segment is by far the most important in terms of the volume of surfactants used and the value contribution.

Whereas in the global context the laundry detergent segment is the predominant one, in the Industrial Triad the other segments are significant contributors. The three principle types of end products in the household laundry products segment are :

(a) 'Conventional' or 'universal' powders.

(b) Liquid detergents.

(c) Superconcentrates.

Momentous changes have taken place in recent years in these products and multifunctional detergents incorporating bleach, fabric softeners etc. have landed in the market.

The personal care products sector also comprises of three segments, namely :

(a) Hair care.

(b) Skin care.

(c) Oral hygiene products.

Anionic surfactants are mainly used in these segments, but they have to compete with other types such as amphoterics and cationics. At the global level, the skin care segment dominates with consumption of large volumes of soaps. In the Industrial Triad, however, both soap and other surfactants usage in this segment is limited. The hair-care sector is dominated by shampoos, which consume large volumes of anionics such as AES, AS and soap. The oral-hygiene segment is a small user of surfactants, with the anionics as the major type.

Industrial and Institutional Cleaners are products used in :

(a) Janitorial services.

(b) Food processing and commercial dishwashing.

(c) Transportation.

(d) Commercial laundry and dry cleaning.

(e) Metals industry.

Anionics figure in large volume in these applications, LAS being the major anionic. Nonionic alcohol ethoxylates are also used in this sector.

Amongst industrial uses, anionics have substantial roles in textiles, petroleum processing, emulsion polymerisation of plastics and lattices, leather and pesticidal formulations. Other application areas include cement and concrete, paints and inks, froth flotation of ores, and laying of asphalt in road making.

Cationic Surfactants

Cationic surfactants first became important when the commercial potential of their bacteriostatic properties was recognised in early fifties. Since than a wide class of cationics with literally hundreds of molecular structures have been introduced as commercial products, although they do not approach the importance of the anionic materials in sheer quantity or value. In most of these products advantage is taken of the 'subs-tantivity' of the cation and it's semipermanent adsorption on surfaces which are normally further makes the substrate surface oleophilic.

Until the availability of straight-chain petroleum-based surfactants, the sole sources of raw materials for cationic surfactants were vegetable derivatives of fatty amines of 1, 2 or 3 alkyl chains bonded directly or indirectly to a cationic nitrogen group. The most important classes of these cationics are the amine salts, quaternary ammonium compounds and the amine oxides. The cationic nature of the fatty amines and derivatives has given rise to a wide variety of functions in many applications. These functions may be recognised as being derived from four basic functional properties, namely, (a) surface active, (b) substantive, (c) reactive and (d) antimicrobial as represented in Fig. 9.2. These properties are exploited for the following surfactant functions in various applications as indicated in Table 9.2.

Amongst the cationic surfactants there are two important categories which differ mainly in the nature of the nitrogen containing group. The first consists of the alkyl nitrogen compounds such as simple ammonium salts containing at least one long-chain alkyl group and one or more amine hydrogens, and quaternary ammonium compounds in which all amine hydrogens have been replaced by organic radical substitutions. The amine substitutions may be either long or short chain substitutions. The counterion may be a halide, sulphate, acetate etc. The second category contains heterocyclic materials typified by the pyridinium, morpholinium and imidazolinium derivatives.

Table 9.2. Basic properties of fatty amines and their derivatives and their surfactant functions in various applications.

Basic property	Surfactant functions
Surface active	Emulsifying, wetting, thickening, foaming
Substantivity	Softening, antistatic properties, lubrication, corrosion inhibition, adhesion, hydrophobation
Reactive	Flocculation, decolourisation, ion exchange
Antimicrobial	Algicidal, fungicidal, bactericidal

The economic importance of the cationic surfactants has increased greatly because of their unique properties. Their substantive property is exploited in fabric softeners, bitumen emulsions, oil-muds used in the petroleum industry, hair-care products, corrosion inhibition in oilfield and water treatment segments. The cationics are also important in the textile industry as waterproofing and dye-fixing agents. Other application areas are in flotation processing of mineral ores, lubrication, as surface modifiers in electrostatic charge control. Their biological activity seems to be characteristic of almost all-cationic surfactant species, irrespective of minor structural changes, and is utilised in killing or inhibiting the growth of many microorganisms.

Nonionic surfactants, which fit into a broader spectrum' do not carry any discrete charge when dissolved in water, unlike anionics or cationics. Some of the important advantages of this electrical neutrality are :

(a) Lower sensitivity to the presence of electrolytes in the system.

(b) A lessened effect of solution pH.

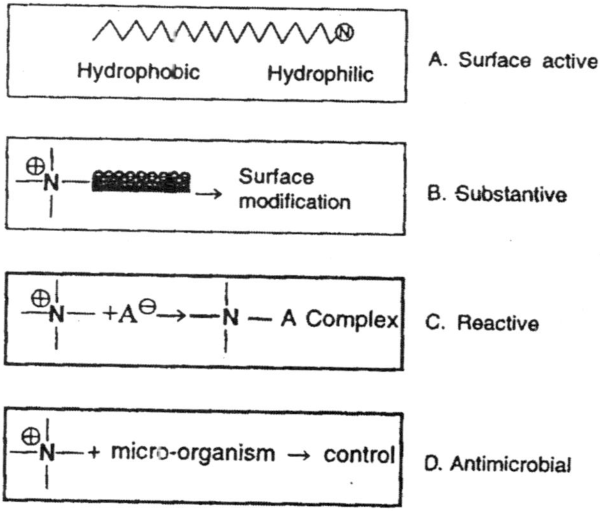

Fig. 9.2. Four basic functional properties of cationic surfactants.

(c) The synthetic flexibility of being able to design the required degree of solubility into the molecule by the careful control of the size of the hydrophilic group.

Several nonionics are currently in commercial use. The most numerous and most important technically amongst these are the polyoxyethylenes (POE) of the general formula :

$$RX\,(CH_2CH_2O)_nH$$

where R is usually a typical surfactant hydrophobic group, but may also be a polyether such as polyoxypropylene and X is O, N or another functionality capable of linking the polyoxyethylene chain to the hydrophobe. In most capable of linking the polyoxyethylene chain to the hydrophobe. In most cases the value of 'n', the average number of oxyethylene units in the hydrophilic group must be greater than 5 or 6 to impart sufficient water solubility to make the materials useful. The most common pathway to the POE surfactants is by the reaction of ethylene oxide (EO) with alcohols, acids, amides, mercaptans etc. If primary amines are used double chain surfactants of the form :

$$RN\,[(CH_2CH_2O)_nH]_2$$

can be formed with different molecular complexities. Hydrophilicity, in the case of nonionics is, provided by hydrogen bonding with water molecules. Oxygen atoms and hydroxyl groups readily form strong hydrogen bonds whereas ester and amide groups do so less readily. Hydrogen bonding provides solubilisation in neutral and alkaline media. Under highly acidic conditions oxygen atoms are protonated giving a quasi-cationic character. As each atom of oxygen can make only small contribution to water solubility, dissolution of nonionics in aqueous media necessitates the presence of several oxygen atoms in the molecule. Polyoxyethylene solubilisation has thus been the key to the substantial and growing potential of the nonionics. The compatibility of the nonionics with both ionic and amphoteric surfactants gives a boost to this class as it gives rise to synergistic systems. Nonionics like alcohol ethoxylates and alkylphenol ethoxylates serve as building blocks for deriving anionic surfactants by sulphation. A new dimension to the nonionics resulted on account of the polyoxyethylene-polyoxypropylene block copolymers, wherein the hydrophobic tendency of the propylene oxide units is taken advantage of in tailoring the products.

Apart from ethoxylated products, alkanolamides, carboxylic amides, glycerol esters, sorbitan esters, amine oxides, 'Surfynols' based or acetylenic diols, 'Silwet' surfactants comprising of siloxane back-bone with organic polyalkylene pendants, alkyl polyglucosides, fluorosurfactants, triesters of phosphoric acid and carbohydrate derived products figure in the nonionics market.

Amongst the varied applications of nonionic surfactants, emulsification, dispersion, detergency and foaming are important phenomena. Emulsions are used in a large number of applications such as foods, cosmetics, medicinals, agriculture, paints and numerous industrial processes. Their ability to control the stability of small particles is important in detergents. An important aspects of this is that the surfactant amount necessary in a composition is relatively low as compared with anionics. The nonionics serve as both foam boosters and foam inhibitors. Anionic derivatives of nonionics are particularly good high foaming detergents, whereas other derivatives serve as low foamers. Large volume uses of nonionics associated with their foaming properties is in various types of cleaners, latex paints, insecticidal and herbicidal wettable powders and emulsifiable concentrate, aerosol foam products, spray metal cleaning, foam drilling of oil and gas wells, and emulsion and suspension polymerisation. Other applications are as demulsifiers of crude oils, lubricants, antistatic agents, thickeners and emollients, dyeing assistants and pigment dispersants.

Amphoteric Surfactants

The true amphoteric surfactant carries both cationic and anionic groupings within the molecule, acting as anionic materials in alkaline pH and cationic at acid pH. This structure makes it not only possible to combine them with the other categories of surfactants without the problem of property inhibition, but also with the choice of selecting the ionic character. Although the amphoteric surfactants represent the lowest volume in the total global surfactants market, the unique properties they can impart to a formulation are improving their market position. Amphoteric surfactants have been available for many years. Early amphoterics were glycinates based on imidazoline chemistry and were the basis of many toiletry products such as mild shampoos. Betaines were also developed and used increasingly in personal care products due to their skin friendly, foaming and free rinsing properties. Although a large group of organic functionalities hold the potential for producing amphoteric surfactants, the materials mostly encountered in this category are :

(a) Imidazoline derivatives.
(b) Betaines and sulpho-betaines.
(c) Amino acid derivatives.
(d) Lecithin and related phosphatides
(e) Protein based products.
(f) Mono and dipropionates.

Most commercial y impostant imidazoline-derived amphoteric surfactants can be described as fatty acid—amino-ethylethanolamine condensates of the general structure :

$$RCONHCH_2NR'R''$$

where R is the fatty acid residue, and R' as well as R" are different functionalities. Their mildness and toxicity led to their use in shampoos and body care products. Their amphoteric nature also makes them useful in a wide range of water types, ranging from hard to soft water and high to low pH values. Such flexibility makes them useful in cleaning formulations under a variety of conditions.

Betaine surfactants can formally be considered to be special members of the ring-opened, imidazoline-derived surfactants. However, they do not exhibit many of the characteristics of other amphoterics with regard to their solubility and electrical nature in alkaline solution. They are compatible with anionics at all pH values and do not have any problems of complex formation. The carboxyl-containing betaines have been found to form external salts in very strong acids (such as hydrochlorides) while the sulphobetaines do not do so. This class is generally insensitive to the presence of electrolytes and usually perform well in hard water. The carboxyl betaines have found a number of commercial applications as levelling and wetting agents in textile processing, detergents, scrubbing compounds, antistatic agents, as fabric softeners, as lime soap dispersants and in personal care products. The sulpho-betaines are useful in special areas such as the control of static charge in photographic films.

NC_{10}-C_{12} and N C_{12}-C_{18} fatty acid amidoethyl-N-(2-hydroxy ethyl) glycinates are the types of amino acid derivatives used for the production of strongly alkaline industrial cleaning agents, baby shampoos and other mild surfactant shampoos.

Lecithins are commercially popular phosphatidyl surfactants and are high volume products. Because of their natural raw material sources, the lecithin surfactants are normally found as rather complex mixtures represented by:

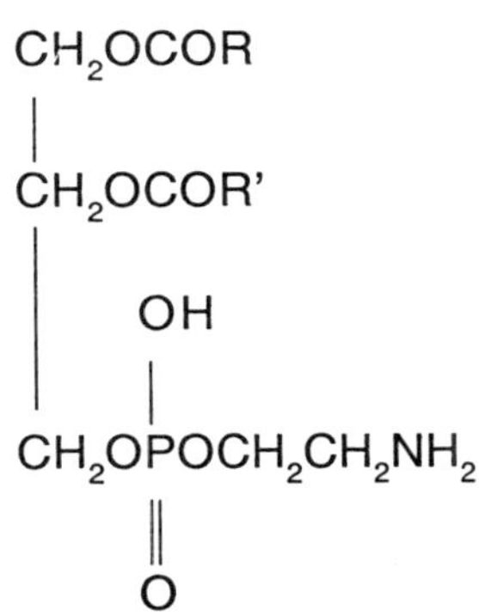

The natural lecithins have very limited solubility in water. Having good oil solubility, they have found extensive commercial application as nonaqueous emulsifiers, dispersants and wetting agents in diverse areas such as marine paints, inks, foods and cosmetics. The largest use of lecithins is in the processing of food and animal feeds and pet foods as emulsifiers or wetting agents. In the food industry they are used in baking, cake mixes, chocolates and ice creams. In cosmetics, they are used in creams, oils, soaps and hair care products. They simulate the phospholipids that are natural moisturisers in the skin and render the skin elastic. In hair care products they prevent the extraction of lipids. In soap their amphoteric nature represses the alkalinity and improves the stability of lather. Other applications of lecithins are as dispersants for dyes and pigments in the paint, ink and textile industries, in formulations of oil penetrants, in fat liquoring of leather, and as buffering agents in lubricating and other oils. Natural sources of lecithin range from egg yolks to many seed oils such as cottonseed, sunflower and soyabean. The most common source however is soyabean due to its relatively lower cost and greater availability.

Protein hydrolysed by acids and bases leads to the formation of polypeptides and amino acid residues, the proportion determined by the temperature and duration of hydrolysis. Protein sources can be vegetable protein byproducts, leather scraps and fish scales. Protein-based surfactants are produced from these hydrolysates by reaction with fatty acid chlorides, condensation with fatty acids and amines and reaction with polyamines. They find application in detergents soap and toilet bar formulations.

The need for salt-free amphoterics by industries to overcome the problems associated with high electrolyte levels and corrosion resulted in the growth of amphoteric mono- and dipropionates. Some of the many other advantages of these products are excellent dirt lifting properties, excellent hydrotropic properties, excellent free rinsing properties they impart to detergent systems, stability over a wide pH range, low toxicity, biostatic properties and lubricity. Currently, these propionate amphoterics are recommended for formulating general cleaning products, environmentally friendly vehicle cleaning systems, personal care products such as hand cleaners, shower gels, hair shampoos and foam baths, microemulsions of terpene based products and aqueous slat/chain lubricants.

Polymeric Surfactants

Colloidal stabilisation by polymeric materials in both aqueous and nonaqueous systems is described as 'Steric stabilisation'. A limited range of polymers fit this role. The polyisobutylene chain is frequently used for stabilisation in very nonpolar organic solvents like aliphatic hycrocarbons. In solvents of higher polarities such as aromatic hydrocarbons, esters and ketones, various polyesters are often used. These polyesters may be based on hydroxycarboxylic acids, with the molecular weight of the hydroxy-carboxylic acid governing the range of solvents in which the surfactant is most effective. Alternatively, a condensation polyester from a mixture of diacid, diol and a chain terminating acid or alcohol may be used. A polyethylene oxide chain may be incorporated into polyesters of this type to increase compatibility with more polar solvents. Polymethylmethacrylate is also used to provide steric stabilisation to solvents of higher polarities. The polyalkylene oxide chains can be used to give steric stabilisation in the most polar organic solvents like alcohols, glycols and glycol ethers.

Polymeric dispersants have come into prominence to solve the complex rheological problems associated with spreading, levelling, relatively capital and energy expensive dispersion processes in the ink and paint industries.

Although surface coatings are the main outlets for sophisticated polymeric surfactants, a variety of other applications have started to develop in the last few years. These include their use in oil-based drilling muds, lubricating oil additives such as ashless dispersants, processing of electroceramics, magnetic tapes and dises and inverse emulsion polymerisation processes.

Biosurfactants

Biosurfactants, derived from fermentation processes with very specific micro-organisms, depending on their nature or state typically display strong features in some respects while at the same time lacking in the versatility of conventional surfactants. Several biosurfactants have surface-active and emulsification properties far superior to either synthetic or natural surfactants. Based on their technical competence and social dictates they have the capability to penetrate all current fields of surfactant use. In particular, they have high potential for use in household detergents and cleaners and personal care products.

'Emulsan', a fully commercialised biosurface-active material is one of the best discovered emulsifiers and is classified as a 'Bioemulsifier'. 'Surfactin', another biosurfactant, has the ability to lower the surface tension of 0.1 N sodium bicarbonate solution from 72 dynes/cm to 27.9

by the addition of as little as 0.005%. Other products such as rhamnose-lipids and sophorose-lipids obtained with Torulopsis bombicola KSM35 also show excellent surfactant properties. Biological products of genetic- and protein-engineering such as Lipolase or Cellulase import restoration and repair characteristics to fabrics and are viewed as bio-detergents. In the personal care sector, biosurfactants termed biocosmetics are expected to take long strides. Sophorose- lipids are already in use in this sector as high value skin moisturisers. In the oilfield industry, microbial enhanced oil recovery (EOR), cleaning up of offshore spills, cleaning of oil tankers, pumping of crudes using bioemulsifiers, demulsification of crudes from the enriched oil recovery, extraction of bitumen from tar sands and viscosity reduction of heavy crudes are potential application areas for these surfactants. Lecithins, described earlier under amphotenics, are also bio-surface active materials used largely as food emulsifiers. Recent projections by some agencies show significant penetration of the biosurfactants into the conventional surfactant markets in the next two decades.

Widely used in consumer and industrial applications such as soaps and cleaners, laundry detergents, cosmetics and toiletries, non-consumer applications for surfactants can also be found in almost every industry. Except for cleaning uses, most of them consume minute quantities of the surfactants as processing aids. Industries where they are used include rubber, plastics, textiles, construction, petroleum-drilling, ore processing, food processing, pharmaceuticals, herbicides, machinery and metals. As new regulations and changing consumer demands arise, the surfactants industry is evolving rapidly. However, many of the surfactants initially alleged as being potential pollutants due to lot of pressure from the environmentalists are now being cleared by environmental agencies. Simultaneous with the development of new products for new or changing industrial applications, surfactants are beginning to attract attention in energy and environmental protection applications, as they are being tried out in pollution-control systems, paper processing and ultra-thin films. Main driving forces influencing changes in the surfactant industry are :

(a) The relative state of the economy.
(b) Consumer demand for 'green' products that are milder, safer and cheaper.
(c) High expenses due to regulatory compliance.
(d) Insurance and environmental costs.
(e) Technical obsolescence.

(f) Erosion of commodity/specially segment differentiation.

(g) General public perception of the chemical industry.

RAW MATERIALS OF SURFACTANTS

The surfactant industry has undergone major changes over the last few years. Surfactant companies generally have been rationa ising their product ranges in order to concentrate on their core surfactant business. Surfactant consumers are now looking for ingredients with increasing number of surfactant industry is also turning towards raw materials from renewable sources and is trying to be less dependent on petrochemical inputs. New molecules like the alkyl polyglycosides (APG) and N-alkyl glucosamide (AGA) are now being increasingly produced. Amongst the various aspects related to the surfactants industry, key factors are :

(a) Surfactant raw materials.

(b) Major surfactants.

(c) Important physico-chemical characteristics.

(d) Technologies.

There are two major materials from which the organic component of surfactant chemicals is predominantly obtained, namely :

(a) Hydrocarbons, from petroleum and gas drilling operations.

(b) Fats and oils from vegetative, animal and marine sources.

The paper industry is an ancillary source and supplies two rather important products—tall oils from which fatty acids can be obtained and lignosulphonates.

Petroleum is a unique source for benzenoid and naphthenoid surfactant chemicals such as alkylbenzene sulphonates, alkylphenols and alkylnaphthalene sulphonates. It is also the source of the most important petrochemical intermediate, ethylene and many straight chain chemical intermediates such as normal paraffins and alpha olefins from which several surfactants are derived.

Fats and oils are unique sources for straight chain, saturated and unsaturated compounds that serve as alternatives to petroleum intermediates for surfactants. An important example is that of detergent alcohols. Other intermediates derived from fats and oils are methyl esters, soaps and fatty acids. The oleochemical industry has become an important segment of the global chemical industry and particularly of the surfactants industry because of the promise of the products being natural, very biodegradable, toxicologically safe and renewable. Movements in the production and supply of fats and oils affects the economics of the surfactants industry. Traditionally petrochemical feedstocks have been cheaper alternatives but the environmental drive and causes which have led to price decline in the key oils for the surfactants industry—palm kernel oil and coconut oil—have made them preferred materials. Fig. 9.3 gives surfactants that are derived from fats and oils.

The paper industry provides two key surfactant raw materials, namely, tall oil and lignin sulphonates. Tall oil is a coproduct in the kraft pulping process for paper pulp using pine and similar woods. About 90% of all tall oil (a mixture of unesterified oleic and linoleic acids with small amounts of rosin acids and unsaponifiables) produced is fractionally distilled to get tall oil fatty acids (TOFA) used as raw material for surfactants.- Tall oil production is dependent on the growth of the paper industry.

Technically either of the two basic raw materials—hydrocarbons or fats—can be used to obtain majority of synthetic surfactants. The choice depends on the raw material availability and prices. Key surfactant intermediates worthy of attention are :

(a) Linear alkyl benzene (LAB).

(b) Detergent alcohols.

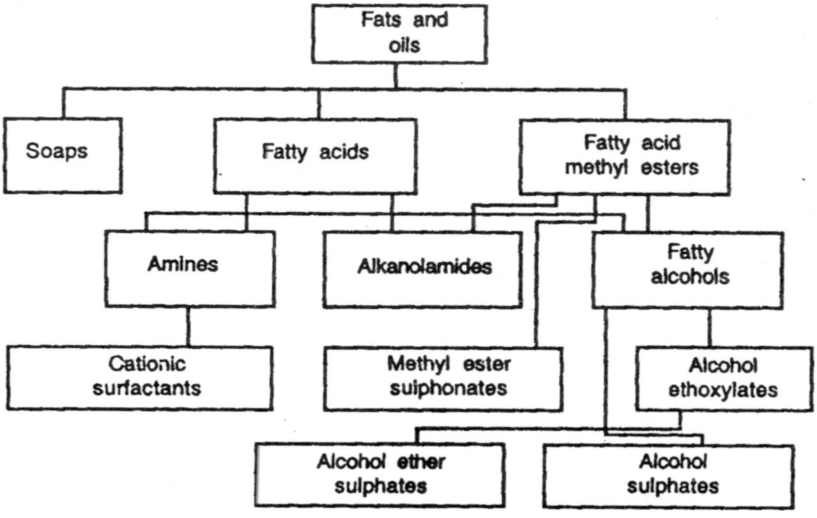

Fig. 9.3. Surfactants derived from fats and oils.

(c) Alphaolefins.
(d) Ethylene oxide/propylene oxide,
(e) Fatty amines.

Linear Alkyl Benzene (LAB)

Linear alkylbenzene is the most important industrial raw material for surfactants derived from petrochemical sources and is even otherwise the most dominant raw material of the detergent industry. Its level of consumption in any global region is an indicator of the scope for detergent products—laundry detergents, dishwashing detergents and materials used in the maintenance of buildings, offices, hospitals, schools etc. LAB is the raw material for the production of alkylbenzene sulphonic acid and alkylbenzene sulphonate (LAS). Detergent formulators use both types of these intermediates. In many formulations, a salt of LAS such as Na-LAS (sodium salt) is added directly as a formulant. In other cases, the LAS salt is formed during the formulation process through the neutralisation of the acid with the desired base—caustic soda or triethanolamine.

The structure of LAB depends on two major factors :

(a) The petroleum feedstocks used—normal paraffins and benzene in terms of range and purities.
(b) The method of manufacture of LAB.

Because of the complexities involved in the selection of LAS for a particular formulation and end use, there have been immense improvements in the methods of manufacturing LAB, the parent material for LAS. The specifications for LAB in terms of the distribution of homologues and phenyl-position isomers makes it almost a 'designer molecule'.

LAB Manufacturing Processes

Two basic routes employed for the manufacture of LAB are :

(1) The alkylation of benzene with long-chain mono-olefins using HF and other catalysts.
(2) The alkylation of monochlorinated benzene with n-paraffins using aluminium chloride catalysts.

The mono-olefins alkylation process is predominant and based on UOP technology. In the overall UOP process, internal mono-olefins obtained through the catalytic dehydrogenation of n-paraffins are used for the alkylation of benzene with HF catalyst to give LAB. UOP employs the PACOL process for producing the olefins from n-paraffins. In this process linear paraffins are dehydrogenated in the presence of selective hydrogenation catalysts, believed to be platinum, arsenic and lithium deposited on alumina. Operating temperatures in the PACOL reactor are in the range 400-600°C with dehydrogenation occurring in the presence of hydrogen. Some by-product light ends and hydrogen are separated from the reactor effluent and a part of this hydrogen-rich gas is recycled to the reactor. An equilibrium mixture of linear olefins together with unconverted n-paraffins and side reaction products like diolefins and aromatics is produced this way. If left unchanged, the diolefins will react with two moles of benzene to yield heavy diphenylalkane products or heavier polymer stocks, some of which are removed as by-product 'heavy alkylate' in the LAB refining column.

There have been several variations of the UOP process over the years. The most recent one is the DETAL process, a joint development of UOP and Petresa of Spain. The DETAL process employs a heterogeneous bed reactor with liquid feeds and utilises a solid acidic catalyst. This innovation reduces the investment of the overall plant and improves yields. Its greatest advantage is that it eliminates the use of HF and associated problems. In another of UOP's developments, the DEFINE process has the objective of increasing LAB yield and cutting down heavy alkylate production. The equilibrium mixture from the PACOL process, termed as separator liquid, is charged to the DEFINE reactor alongwith make-up hydrogen for selective conversion of diolefins to mono-olefins. A stripping column separates dissolved light hydrocarbons, and the bottoms comprising a mixture of olefins and unconverted n-paraffins are charged together with benzene to the alkylation reactor, where LAB is produced. Benzene and unconverted paraffins are fractionated from the alkylation reactor effluent and recycled. The final column fractionates LAB overhead from heavy alkylate bottoms. Reduction of dialkylates content improves the solubility of the ultimate sulphonated and neutralised product, although the presence of dialkylates contributes to improved detergency of the sodium salt.

High quality LAB with minimum isomers and side products has been obtained by varying temperature, concentration, reaction ratios, recycle points in the LAB manufacturing processes. Fig. 9.4 shows schematic flow in the UOP process.

Typical specifications for LAB from the UOP PACOL-DEFINE process are given in Table 9.3.

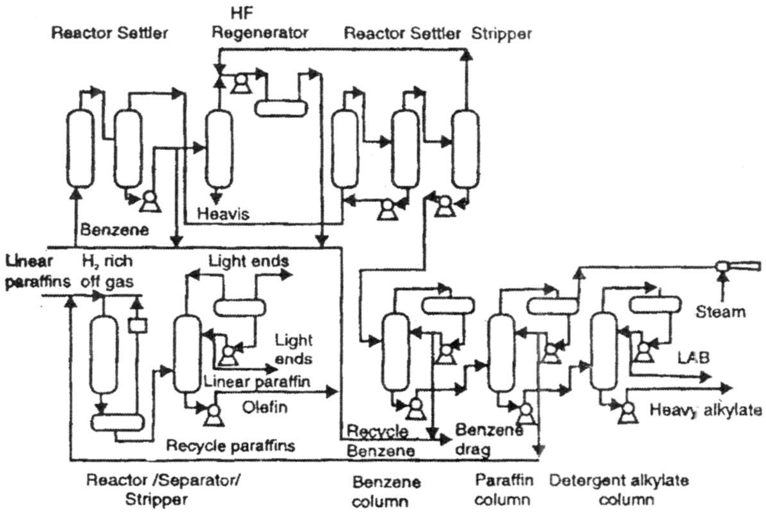

Fig. 9.4. Production of linear alkyl benzene schematic flow (UOP process).

Table 9.3. Typical specifications for LAB from UOP PACOL define process.

Bromine No.	0.02
Saybolt colour	+30
Doctor test	Negative
Water wt. %	0.01
Sulphonation wt. %	98.5
Biodegradability %	95.0
Paraffins wt. %	0.3
Indans and Tetralins	2.0
Normal LAB %	93.0
Appearance	Clear and bright

Detergent Alcohols

Detergent alcohols, as the name implies, are alcohols primarily produced for the manufacture of detergent intermediates, the most important of which are the surfactants such as alcohol ethoxylates, alcohol ether sulphates, alcohol sulphates and phosphate esters.

These alcohols are also of usage in the production of alkylpolyglucosides and have other markets in the form of free alcohols and derivatives. They are also commonly referred to as 'Fatty alcohols'. There are two basic categories of detergent alcohols, namely, the 'natural' and 'synthetic' alcohols. While both these types are interchangeably used for the manufacture of derivatives employed in several applications, the natural— oleochemical and renewable—resource alcohols are getting prominence on grounds of toxicity and environmental impact.

Derivatives of detergent alcohols are in the forefront of changes today and outpace LABS in value performance. This is due to evolutionary changes in the household laundry sector and revolutionary changes in the increased use of these products in the growing-type of detergent end-products. The evolutionary changes relate to :

(a) Their ready application in detergent formulations without phosphates.

(b) Suitability of the derivatives for detergent formulations which are effective at low washing temperatures—an aspect of importance as the washing loads are containing more and more sensitive, coloured synthetic fabrics.

(c) Their superior hardness tolerance (calcium and magnesium ions present in water) in comparison with that of LABS.

The revolutionary changes are related to four growing types of detergent end-products namely :

(a) Low temperature compact powders.

(b) High concentrated liquids.

(c) 'One packet per wash load' products combining detergent, bleach and softener.

(d) Growing concern for skin-safe low irritant products for dishwashing as well as personal care products.

These changes which vary from region to region as in United Sates, Western Europe and Japan are benefitting the derivatives manufacturers and also formulators.

Detergent alcohols are defined as alcohols containing 12 or more carbon atoms per molecule with- a carbon backbone of high linearity mainly for the manufacture of surfactant intermediates. Anionics like alcohol sulphates, alcohol ether sulphates, phosphate esters, sulpho-succinates, nonionics like alcohol ethoxylates and alkylpolyglucosides and even amines for cationic surfactants can be made from these alcohols. Highly branched alcohols, of long chain lengths, are used mainly in the manufacture of plasticisers. Alcohol structures which are slightly branched are also used in surfactants manufacture. Detergent alcohols are commercially produced from natural raw materials, principally fatty acids and methyl esters and petrochemical sources, namely, ethylene and n-paraffins. The two routes divide the alcohols into the aforementioned 'natural' and 'synthetic' alcohols.

Natural alcohols

Natural detergent alcohols, both saturated and unsaturated, are manufactured through the hydrogen reduction of fatty acids and their esters, typically by the Lurgi process, as well as the catalytic hydrolysis of methyl esters. The latter route is preferred nowadays for a variety of reasons including economy of investment. The methyl esters are, in turn, manufactured from triglyceride fats such as coconut oil, palm kernel oil, and tallow through transesterification processes. A continuous system for methyl ester production is given in Fig. 9.5 and a batch system for transesterification is shown in Fig. 9.6.

Synthetic detergent alcohols

Synthetic detergent alcohols are substantially obtained through modifications of Ziegler chemistry, often referred to as 'ethylene growth' processes. In these processes, ethylene is added to triethylaluminium to produce a mixture of alkyls which is then oxidised by air to the alkoxides and subsequently hydrolysed to the alcohols. The alcohols from Ziegler chemistry are always products with even number of carbon atoms, thus imitating the structure of the natural alcohols. Vista chemicals and ethyl corporation control most of such capacity. ALFOLS are Vista products.

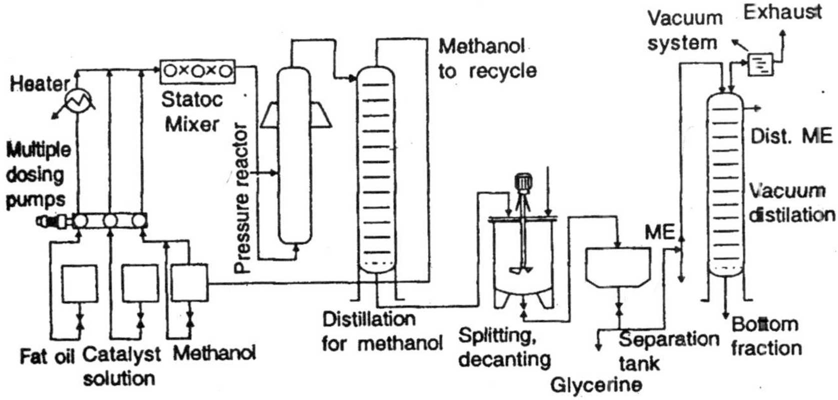

Fig. 9.5. Methyl ester production—continuous system.

Shell is also a large manufacturer of these alcohols—termed NEODOLS—through cobalt ligand 'oxo' chemistry, obtaining the base olefin stock—alpha olefins—from their proprietary SHOP process. This is an ethylene growth process using nickel catalysts. Shell's alcohols are slightly branched alcohols with odd and even-numbered alcohols. Detergents from these alcohols have properties and costs comparable with those of even numbered alcohols.

Ruhrchemie and Rhone Poulenc have developed a version of oxo chemistry with water-soluble rhodium complexes. This process is reported to yield alcohols of higher linearity than the Shell process.

Internal olefins manufactured through normal paraffin dehydrogenation with special catalysts are also reported to yield slightly branched alcohols through oxo-chemistry. Secondary alcohols are made in Japan through an n-paraffin oxidation process.

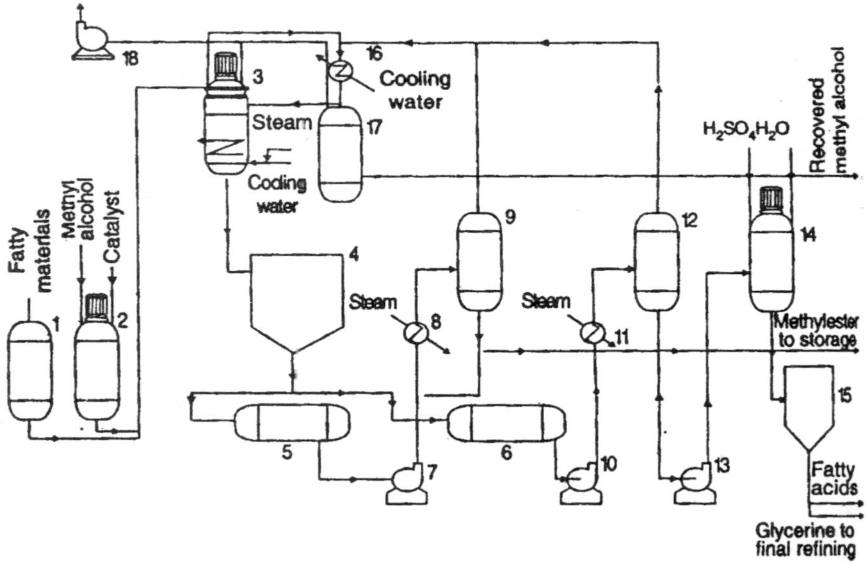

1. Fatty materials tank; 2. Methyl alcohol tank; 3. Interesterification reactor; 4. Settling vessel; 5. Methylester collecting tank; 6. Glycerine collecting tank; 7. Methylester transfer pump; 8.,9. Methanol evaporator; 10. Glycerine transfer pump; 11.,12. Methanol flash evaporator; 13. Glycerine transfer pump; 14. Soap spliting vessel; 15. Settling vessel; 16. Methanol condenser; 17. Condensed methanol collecting drum; 18. Vacuum pump.

Fig. 9.6. Ester interchange process—batch process.

Exxon Chemical also is a source for linear detergent-range alcohols, although they have been for long in the business for branched chain alcohols to the plasticisers industry and also Guerbet alcohols. It is reported that these alcohols are highly branched when compared to the modified Ziegler alcohols.

Alphaolefins (LAO)

Alpha olefins, often abbreviated as LAO, are linear mono-olefins with the double bond located at the terminal of a linear long-chain hydrocarbon. They differ from the 'internal mono-olefins' wherein the double bond is randomly located inside the hydrocarbon molecule. For detergent applications the carbon range of the raw materials used is C_8 to C_{18}. Apart from detergents, the alphaolefins figure in the production of oxo-alcohols for the plasticisers industry, in the manufacture of HDPE and LLDPE as co-monomers, in polybutene production, and as raw materials for polyalphaolefins (PAO) used as synthetic lubricants.

Alphaolefins production

The four main routes for the production of alphaolefins are :

(a) Through wax-cracking.

(b) Paraffin dehydrogenation.

(c) Ethylene oligomerisation.

(d) Shell's SHOP process.

Shell is the sole operator in Western Europe using the wax-cracking process, that too partially, to produce alphaolefins. Chevron, which operated this process in USA, abandoned it in the mid-eighties. The cracking of wax occurs thermally and a wide band of alphaolefins are produced, substantial volumes of which have little application. The process requires a special type of wax with highly linear hydrocarbon waxes which are reported to originate only from Libyan and Indonesian crude oils. Shell has also operated a paraffin chlorination-dehydrochlorination plant in USA to produce odd and even number C_{11} to C_{14} linear internal olefins of which a segment has been alphaolefins. They have been used for the manufacture of LAB and oxo-alcohols, but not for alpha-olefin based products.

By far, the most important of the processes to make alphaolefins are those based on Ziegler chemistry. In the classical process, an aluminium triethylene growth promoter (TEA)—catalyst—is used to build up long chains of low molecular weight ethylene polymers on the aluminium, the ethylene being inserted between the aluminium atom and the carbon. These are then displaced by more ethylene to yield a mix of alpha-olefins and TEA, the latter being recycled. The displacement involves dehydrometallisation followed by ethylene hydroalumination. Modifications of this process are the Gulf Process and the Ethyl Process. In the Gulf Process, the catalytic process is a one-step reaction producing a geometric distribution of alphaolefins. In the Ethyl Process, the one-step Gulf Process is changed to a two-step process carried out at lower and higher temperatures. By this method, using appropriate reaction conditions a stoichiometric distribution of alphaolefins of desired chain lengths can be produced.

Shell's SHOP process employed in plants in U.K. produces internal olefins for captive manufacture of oxo alcohols or LAB in Shell's plants. The alpha-olefins produced are for merchant sales. The SHOP Process is a variation of the Gulf Process with replacement of the aluminium catalyst by a proprietary nickel catalyst in a solvent like benzene or 1,4-butane-diol.

In India, Gujarat Godrej Innovative Chemicals whose plant is engineered by Lurgi, adopts a new route for alphaolefins. In this process, linear alcohols made from imported palm stearin are catalytically dehydrated and the alphaolefins produced are used as raw materials for alpha olefin sulphonates.

Ethylene Oxide (EO)/Propylene Oxide (PO)

Ethylene oxide is an important building block of the petrochemical industry and is used to manufacture ethylene glycol (for polyester fibre and bottles, antifreeze compounds), polyethylene glycols (brake fluids, cosmetic intermediates epoxides), glycol ethers (solvents) and surfactants. The EO based nonionic surfactants as well as other types of importance are alcohol ethoxylates (AE), alcohol ether sulphates (AES), alkylphenol ethoxylates (APE), ethoxylated fatty esters and acids and ethoxylated amines.

The glycols have been considered over the years as major outlets for ethylene oxide. However, currently nonglycol applications of EO are in the increase.

Manufacture

EO manufacturing processes are : (a) chlorohydrin process, and (b) direct oxidation of ethylene. The chlorohydrin process, in which ethylene is reacted with hypochlorous (chlorine and water) to give ethylene chlorohydrin which is treated with slaked lime or caustic soda to form EO, has been the traditional route to EO, but now this has been largely replaced by the direct oxidation process.

The direct oxidation of ethylene may be carried out over a silver catalyst in the vapour phase at about 245°C and 21 atmospheres of pressure. Either oxygen or air enriched in oxygen may be used for direct oxidation. The reaction may be represented as follows :

$$\underset{\text{Ethylene}}{CH_2 = CH_2} + \underset{\text{Oxygen}}{\tfrac{1}{2}O_2} \longrightarrow \underset{\text{Ethylene oxide}}{CH_2{-}CH_2 \; (\backslash O /)}$$

Propylene Oxide (PO) is produced either by the chlorohydrin or hydroperoxide process. ARCO Chemical USA is the largest producer of PO world over. Various modifications of these processes are used for the production of PO.

Fatty Amines

Nitrogen-based surfactants dominate the cationic types. Fatty amines comprising of a basic group of alkylamines—primary, secondary and tertiary, are important raw materials for these surfactants.

Primary, secondary and tertiary alkylamines—taking their names from the number of hydrogen atoms of the ammonia molecule substituted by one, two or three alkyl groups—are obtained by the reduction of nitriles which in turn are produced from fatty acids and ammonia in the presence of zinc oxide or manganese acetate catalysts. Alkyl group chain lengths may vary from C_8/C_{10} to higher. Whereas the primary amines are only obtained from nitriles, the secondary amines are obtained both from nitriles and from primary amines through further alkylation. The tertiary amines, the most important of this group in terms of volume and diversity of down-stream products, are produced through several routes such as :

(a) Reductive alkylation of a primary amine with formaldehyde and hydrogen.

(b) From alkyl chlorides and dimethylamine.

(c) From primary alkyl bromide and dimethylamine.

Tertiary amines are supplementary obtained from alpha-olefins.

Apart from the above types of oxygen-free amines, the fatty amines also comprise of oxygen-containing amines like ethoxylated amines. The production of nitrile and alcohol based amines in the Industrial Triad is of the order of 350-375,000 metric tons per annum.

The three groups of amines by themselves do not have any marked surfactant properties. About 20-25% of the amines and their salts are used directly and the balance converted to derivatives. Primary amines are predominantly used for the production of tertiary amines. Other uses of these amines are in metal extraction, as froth flotation collectors, as anti-caking agents for fert lisers, as filming amines in steam evaporators etc. Ethoxylated primary amines are used as cationic collectors in the flotation of zinc ore, as emulsification agents for pesticidal emulsions and in the petroleum industry. Secondary amines are the basic raw materials for the important range of dialkyl dimethyl quaternary ammonium salts used very largely as fabric softeners in home laundries and as textile conditioners in the textile industry. The major direct use of tertiary amines is in solvent extraction of metals. They are the basic raw materials for either classes of important nitrogen compounds, namely :

(a) Alkanolamides

(b) Quaternary ammonium compounds

(c) Polyamides

(d) Betaines

(e) Imidazolinium compounds

(f) Amphoteric surfactants

(g) Amine oxides

(h) Ethoxylated amines

All of these products are surface-active and are cationic in nature. The selection criteria for fatty amines and derivatives involve.

(a) Solubility in water, non-aqueous media and two-phase systems.

(b) Hydrophile—lipophile balance (HUB).

(c) Surface tension.

(d) Other surfactant properties like Forming, Krafts point, cloud point.

(e) Antimicrobial properties.

(f) Various physical and chemical properties.

Amines with bridging amids groups termed 'Amidoamines' are also building block amines. They are derived from fatty acids, i.e., the fatty acid is the source of the alkyl radical rather than the nitrile. The important economic advantage of the amids bridging is that these amines can be prepared at far lower levels of investment than are the basic amines which require the use of high pressures and expensive equipment. Also the amids group improves the multi-functionality of these amines. Many of these materials and their derivatives perform as effectively as the basic amines. In direct use they find application as flotation agents, asphalt emulsifiers and corrosion inhibitors and compete with the basic amines and their derivatives.

KEY FEATURES OF SURFACTANTS

Major Surfactants

Amongst the various types of surfactants major ones can be identified either by their large-scale use in industry or by their special chemical structures and characteristics. The products highlighted in this section are :

(a) Sulphonates—lignin sulphonates, petroleum sulphonates, alkylbenzene sulphonates, alkylnaphthalene sulphonates.

(b) Sulphates—alcohol sulphates, alcohol and alkylphenol ethersulphates.

(c) Polyhydric alcohol esters—sorbitan esters, glycerol esters, polyglycerol esters, glycols and glycol esters.

(d) Ethoxylates—Ethylene oxide/propylene oxide block copolymers, alcohol ethoxylates, alkylphenol ethoxylates, polyhydric alcoliol ethoxylates, lanolin ethoxylates, amine ethoxylates, polysiloxane ethoxylates.

(e) Alkanolamides.

(f) Fatty amine oxides.

(g) Acetylenic alcohol derivatives.

(h) Silicones.

(i) Fluorosurfactants.

(j) Alkyl polyglycosides.

(k) Sulphosuccinates and sulphosuccinamates.

(l) Phosphate esters.

(m) Amine based surfactants—imidazolines, quaternary ammonium compounds, betaines.

(n) Sarcosinates and taurates.

Lignin sulphonates

Although lignin sulphonates have low surface activity, they are used in many areas where a conventional surfactant can be used. They are obtained as by-products in the pulping of wood in the paper industry.

Lignin is one of the three major constituents of wood—the celluloses, pentagens and lignin. It represents 15-30% of the wood depending on the species. There is no clear understanding of the structure of lignin, but in general, propane units are bound through ether linkages to phenols with the molecular weight of the order of tens of thousands.

When wood chips are treated with sulphite liquor the cellulose and hemicellulose are not affected, whereas the lignin is partially sulphonated on the aromatic ring, with some degradation to pentoses and hexoses (sugars). The sulphonates and the sugars are all water-soluble and thus are easily separated from cellulose pulp. The sugars in the sulphite liquor are destroyed by fermentation and the residue, together with surplus sodium or calcium sulphite (depending on the pulping method used) is spray dried to the commercial product. Unlike other products of recovery processes, the lignosulphonates do not consume sulphonation chemicals. Various refinements on the raw, dried product yield products of different molecular weights, cation and chemical composition.

Petroleum sulphonates

The anionic petroleum sulphonates are obtained either as by-products of oil processing or by synthetic methods. Both materials are used in commerce competitively.

When high-grade petroleum oils (white oils) are prepared, reactive components and sulphonatable coloured bodies in the base oil have to be removed from the non-reactive portion, which is the desired material. One of the best ways of doing this is to sulphonate the oils with oleum or sulphur tri-oxide or both. The reactive components react with the acid to form sulphonates. The non-reactive components are naphthenic-paraffinic hydrocarbons. The sludge obtained in the sulphonation of base oils, termed 'green acids' contains the water-soluble sulphonates, excess acid and occluded oil. The products are largely disulphonated. After separation, the upper layer contains all unreacted oil and oil-soluble sulphonates termed 'mahogany' acids.

The oil is now given an alkaline wash and extracted with a low-boiling alcohol. The paraffinic-naphthenic fraction is not soluble in the alcohol whereas the sodium salts of mahogany acids are. When the alcohol is stripped from the lower layer, a high molecular weight sodium petroleum sulphonate results with some 30% unreacted oil. The sulphonates by and large are monosulphonated products.

Synthetic petroleum sulphonates are byproducts obtained in the Friedel Craft reaction to get detergent alkylates from benzene such as :

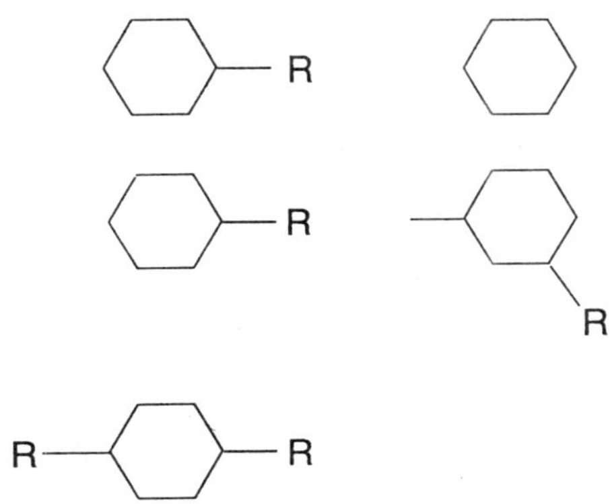

whose mixture is sulphonated with oleum. Both the natural and synthetic sulphonates are marketed as such or as overbased materials. The products marketed in largest volume are the alkaline earth salts produced by the double decomposition of the sodium sulphonate with an aqueous solution of barium, calcium or magnesium chlorides.

The petroleum sulphonates find application as emulsifiers for textile oils, dry cleaning solvents, degreases, soluble oils, metal working fluids, mold release agents and froth collectors in ore flotation. They are also used as dispersants (pigment dispersion in paints or sludge dispersion in fuel oil) and as rust inhibitors.

Alkylbenzene sulphonates

The largest used surfactant across the world are alkylbenzene sulphonates. There are two broad types of these products, namely:

(a) Linear alkylbenzene sulphonates (LABS), and

(b) Branched chain alkylbenzene sulphonates.

The branched chain product has poor biodegradability and as such does not figure in the household sector. The linear product is predominantly used in the household detergents and scourers, but the usage extends to I&I cleaners and industrial sectors. The length of the alkyl chain has profound influence on the detergency and solubility of the product.

The Most common method of sulphonating alkylbenzenes has been through oleum The disadvantage of the process is the need for the disposal of the spent acid. Air-SO_3, used predominantly for the sulphonation of long-chain alcohols is increasingly being applied to alkylbenzenes. The detergency properties of LABS (dirt removal power) are superior to those of the alcohol ethoxylates and moreover it is a cheaper product. However, it's high foaming tendency and higher efficiency only at higher temperatures are disadvantages for its use in the household sector.

There are a number of LABS manufacturers. A substantial portion of the product is for captive use. Firms active in sulphonation also undertake toll manufacture. The main usage areas are commercial dishwashing, emulsion polymerisation, petroleum production, textile industries and in pesticidal sprays.

Alkylnaphthalene sulphonates

Naphthalene sulphonic acid and salts are hydrotropes, i.e., materials which assist in solubilisation of associate actives without other impact on the system. In this respect they are similar to cumene, xylene and toluene sulphonic acids. They do not have any meaningful surfactant properties. With the introduction of alkyl side chains such as propyl, butyl and dipropyl surfactancy develops.

The sulphonates are prepared by condensing naphthalene sulphonic acid with formaldehyde. In this case the disulphonates are formed. If the nomosulphonates are desired naphthalene, oleum and formaldehyde are reacted together.

Alkyl naphthalene sulphonates and the alkyl naphthalene sulphonates— formaldehyde condensates are used in applications where lignosulphonates can also be used. Most importantly they are used as dispersing agents and stabilisers wherein particularly the condensates are superior performers. The areas of application are :

(a) As water reducers in the preparation of concrete (the formaldehyde and melamine formaldehyde condensates are the 'superplasticisers').

(b) As solubilisers in the production of SBR lattices.

(c) As pigment wetting and dispersion agents in the mixing of paints (sodium diisopropyl naphthalene sulphonic acid and condensates are used).

(d) As low-foam surfactants and dye dispersion aids in the textile industry.

(e) As pitch dispersants in paper industry.

(f) As syntans—leather tanning agents.

(g) As suspension and dispersion agents in the formulation of pesticide suspension concentrates and in the formulation of wettable powders.

(h) As dispersing agents in cure pastes in the plastics and elastomer industries.

(i) As compact dispersing agents in oil muds.

(j) As free flow additives in fertiliser mixtures and other dry materials.

(k) In carpet steam cleaners.

(l) In tank soak metal cleaners, and.

(m) In high foaming alkaline and acid cleaners.

Alcohol sulphates

Alkyl sulphates or alcohol sulphates are the first of the world's synthetic detergents, pioneered in Germany during the Second World War. They are currently produced by the sulphation of linear primary alcohols with air-SO_3 or chlorosulphonic acids, followed by neutralisation with a variety of cations. Most of the alcohol sulphates are made from natural alcohols because of their large use in personal care products. The alcohol's used range from C_8 to C_{16}. In the United States, they are derived from animal tallow base alcohols and as such are the least expensive anionics. The most-used product is lauryl alcohol sulphate. Secondary alcohol sulphates are also used as surfactants in industrial applications.

In general the alcohol sulphates are more hydrophilic than the sulphonates. Sodium lauryl alcohol sulphate has strong wetting, detergent and emulsifying properties. They are good foamers but are sensitive to hard water, necessitating effective builder support in consumer products. The major outlets for alcohol sulphates are in laundry powders, personal shampoos, in emulsion polymerisation of rubber lattices for textile and paper coatings, in wool scouring, kier boiling of cotton, as dye levelling agent for anionic dyes, as wetters for fruit processing, as pigment dispersion aids in paints and inks, in foaming of gypsum board, in soaking and degreasing of leather and in binding compositions for non-wovens.

Alcohol and alkylphenol ether sulphates (AES/APES)

The hydrophilicity of ethoxylate structures can be markedly enhanced by the sulphation/sulphonation of the—OH group. In the process the ethoxylates lose their nonionic nature and become anionic materials.

When the aromatic nucleus of a compound is sulphonated we have a 'sulphonated' product. If the reacting group in a hydroxyl group is an aliphatic compound, then the process is termed 'sulphation'.

In the sulphonation of an alkylphenol, while the primary reaction is sought at the active hydrogen site, some sulphonation of the aromatic nucleus also occurs. The ether sulphates are diversely known as ethoxysulphates or sulphated polyethers. AES and APES are used interchangeably in most technical applications.

The manufacture of the ether sulphates is based on sulphonation routes akin to those used for the manufacture of LABS. The heat of reaction is however higher and special types of reactors have to be employed. Common sulphonating agents used are oleum, chlorosulphonic acid and air-sulphur trioxide.

The alcohol ethoxylates, while soluble in water, produce turbidity at higher temperatures with likelihood of layer separation. AES overcome this problem. They are also high foaming products compared to the low foaming ethoxylates and are therefore of advantage where foaming action is required. In comparison with other anionic products they are excellently soluble, have good hard water tolerance and are more compatible with enzymes. They are extensively used in personal care products due to their mildness to the skin. In household detergents they are synergistic with LABS.

Virtually any sulphonator can make AES and APES. The basic markets for AES are in light-duty liquids, bath additives and personal shampoos. A sizeable quality is also used in household liquid surface cleaners. APES on the other hand is almost entirely consumed in the industrial sector. In most industrial operations the markets for AES and APES overlap. Major ones are in emulsion polymerisation of polyvinyl acetate and acrylic polymers, as foaming agents in the production of foam concrete and plasterboard and as foam booster in commercial dishwashing applications. The ether sulphates are also well known as dispersants for coating fillers in the paper industry, as foamers in drilling mud compositions, in the surfactant mixes for enhanced oil recovery and as wetting agents for primary backing compounds in the resins and elastomers industries.

Sorbitan esters

The surfactant field comprises of several nonionics belonging to the ester class. A wide variety of esters derived from alkanoic acids by reaction with polyhydric alcohols—sorbitan, glycerol and polyethylene/ polypropylene glycols have commercial significance.

The sorbitan esters with a wide range of hydrophilic and lyophilic properties are commercially produced. Sorbitol is a hexahydric alcohol derived from high purity dextrose. Sorbitan which is a mixture of anhydrosorbitols mainly consists of

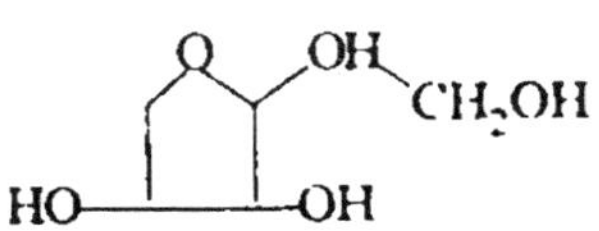

(1,4 Sorbitan)

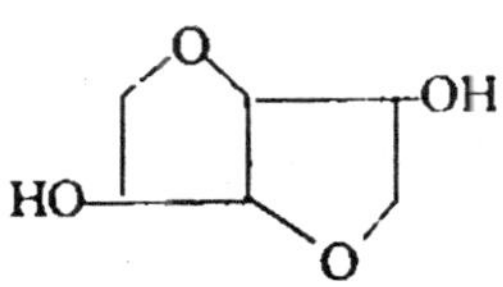

(Isosorbide)

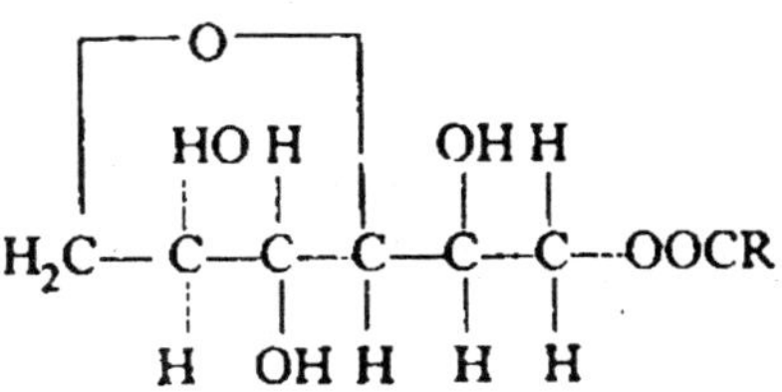

The sorbitan esters are not water-soluble but soluble in a wide range of mineral and vegetable oils, as sorbitan is not a strongly hydrophilic group. The lipophilic character of these esters aids tapping of water in oil to form water-in-oil (w/o) emulsions. Sorbitan mono, di and tri esters are derived by the reaction of sorbitan with fatty acids. The physical form and HLB are tailor-made by varying the type of fatty acid used and the degree of esterification. The products are approved for human ingestion and are used widely in foods, beverages and Pharmaceuticals. Their Hpophilic, emulsifying, solubilising, softening and lubricating properties are made use of in synthetic fibre manufacture, textile processing and cosmetics.

Glycerol esters

Glycerol esters form another group of polyhydric alcohol based nonionic surfactants derived by the esterification of glycerol with saturated and unsaturated fatty acids. Mono- and di-glycerides are made both through the esterification of glycerol with the appropriate fatty acid and through 'glycerolysis', the latter gaining prominence. In its modem batch version, glycerolysis involves reacting a suitable animal or vegetable fat with excess glycerol catalysed by NaOH or KOH at around 250°C. The reaction proceeds as follows :

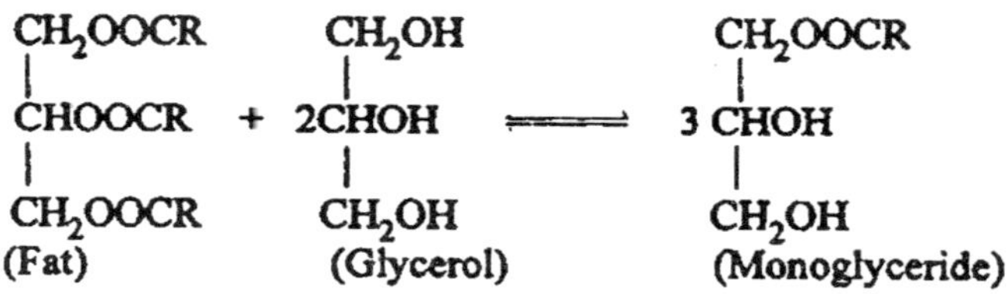

Excess glycerol is used to drive the reaction to the right and to slow down the reverse reaction. The position of the acyl radical—*alpha, beta, gamma*—depends mainly on the temperature of glycerolysis, but the *beta* product reverts to the *alpha* one on cooling. In place of fats, methyl esters are also used for glycerolysis. Fats used are soyabean oil, cottonseed oil, edible tallow and food grade triglycerides. Typically the commercial product analyses 40-48% monoester, 30-40% diester and 5-10% triester with low percentages of free fatty acid and glycerol. Product concentrations can be changed through molecular distillation of the mixed ester product or a mixture can be enriched with a pure or enriched monoester.

Both the solid and liquid type glycerol esters are hydrophobic materials which can be used as w/o emulsifiers, co-emulsifiers, lubricants, rust preventive additives, mould release agents and as solvents for dyes and pigments. They are used as components in lubricants and softeners for the leather industry, as anti-icing additives in fuels and as rust preventive additives in compounded oils. Other application areas of glycerol esters are in textiles, metals and plastics.

Glycerol monostearate is used as an emulsifier and pacifier in cosmetics. The glycerol esters are effective in building up viscosity in cosmetic systems. The non-dispersible grades are used as bases for creams and lotions. By adding other non-ionics such as sorbitan esters or ethoxylated polyol esters, anionics such as soaps or cationics such as quaternary ammonium compounds, the glycerol esters can be readily dispersed. The self-emulsifying grades are used as primary emulsifiers and in anti-perspirant formulations.

Table 9.4 Some typical commercial glycerol esters and their functions.

Ester type	Form	Mono %	Free glycerine	Acid value	Iodine value	HLB
Monocaprylate	Liquid	75	15	3	1	8.3
Monooleate	-do-	40	4	4	95	3.4
Monostearate	Flake	40	6	6	1	3.8
Distearate	-do-	-	-	5	-	2.4
Monostearate SE	Bead	30	4	4	3	8.4
Monolaurate	Solid	-	-	4	-	4.9
Dilaurate	-do-	-	-	5	-	4.0
Monococoate	-do-	50	5	4	10	3.8

Functions	**Application areas**
Lubricant	Textile staple fibres
Lubricant/Antistatic agent	In formulations for high speed processing of polyamide, polyester filaments.
Fabric softener	In textile industry
Emulsifiers/lubricants	Drilling and cutting oils, grinding and polishing pastes for metals.
Internal lubricant/thermal stabiliser/wetting agent for additives	PVC processing
Antistatic agents	Polyethylene, polypropylene, foamed polystyrene.

An important use of monoglycerides and diglycerides is in foods. They are widely used in breads, cakes, other bakery products, candies, ice creams, yeast, butter, whipped toppings and icings. Table 9.4 gives some typical commercial glycerol esters and suppliers of monoglycerides.

Other than the stearates, glycerol monocaprylate made from short chain coconut fatty acids is rattier unique. Due to its structure, it is an efficient solubiliser dissolving water upto 20% by weight. It has been used very effectively in the pharmaceutical industry as a solubiliser for vitamins, flavours and medicaments.

Polyglycerol esters

Compounds derived from the condensation products of hydrophobic groups containing an active hydrogen and glycidol constitute an important family of nonionics. They have the general formula :

$$RX(C_3H_5O)_nOH$$

where R is a typical surfactant hydrophobic group and X is O, N or another functionality capable of linking the glycidol to the hydrophobe. The maximum value of 'n' in the case of polyglycerol is ten as further reaction with the hydrophobic group becomes difficult. The existence of three possible isomers of diglycerol and increase in isomeric possibilities with each subsequent addition of glycidyl units leads to complexity of the products. Ranging from hydrophilic monoesters lipophilic diesters, the polyglycerol esters can be represented as :

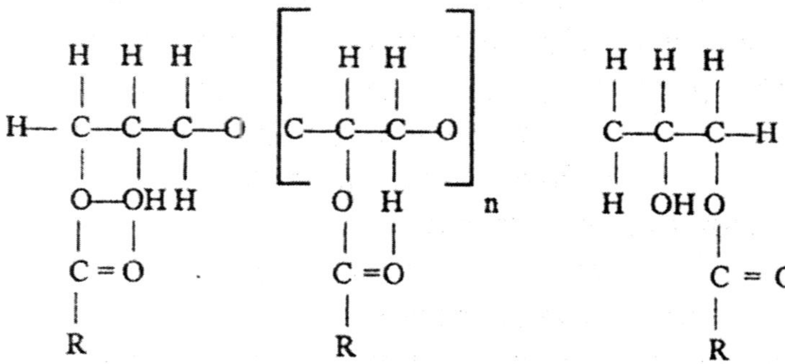

They are prepared by the esterification of polyglycerols with specific fatty acids. Polyglycerol can also be prepared by the alkaline dehydration of glycerol and then esterified with a fatty acid.

The polyglycerol esters are effective nonionic emulsifiers for both o/w and w/o emulsions. They are used in emollient creams and lotions, in pharmaceutical vehicles and due to their nontoxicity in food emulsions such as margarine and moisturising additives for bread and other baked goods. Typical polyglycerol esters are given in Table 9.5.

Glycols and glycol esters

Polyethylene glycols are condensation polymers of ethylene oxide represented by the formula :

$$HO(CH_2CH_2O)_nH$$

where n represents the average number of ethylene oxide units Ranging from molecular weight 200 to 3000, represented as PEG 200 PEG 400 etc. they exhibit good water solubility. Water is miscible in al proportions with PEG 200 through PEG 600. The polyethylene glycols are chemical intermediates for other nonionics. Being themselves nonionics they find applications as solubilisers, in coatings, adhesives lubricants, metal working, paper manufacture, petroleum production ceramic making, printing, electronics, solvents, cleaning formulations humectants and viscosity modifiers.

Surfactants of the glycol ester group are monoesters of either ethylene or propylene glycol. The extreme hydrophobicity of the diesters rende them unfit for use as surfactants. Since the simple glycol esters possess one unesterified hydroxyl group, they can be ethoxylated to increase their hydrophillic characteristics. Commercial polyethylene glycol esters contain varying proportions of monoesters, diesters and polyglycol. The physical properties of these esters vary with the type of fatty acid and the degree of ethoxylation.

The ethoxylates contain neaily 60% by weight of ethylene oxide to enable the solubilisation of the fatty acid at room temperature. Thei principle use is as emulsifiers in the textile industry for processing oils, antistatic agents and softeners. Other applications are as fibre lubricants as detergents in scouring operations and as emulsifiers for pesticides and cosmetic preparations.

Amongst the propylene glycol esters the most important is propylene glycol monostearate (PGME) which is almost wholly utilised fo manufacturing derivatised products which act as emulsifiers in the food industry. Table 9.6 gives some commercial polyethylene glycols and Table 9.7 some commercial fatty acid polyethylene glycol/polypropylene glycol esters.

Ethylene Oxide/Propylene Oxide Clock Copolymers

Amongst the ethoxylates ethylene oxide - propylene oxide (EO/PO block copolymers stand out as a unique class. In this class of materials

Table 9.5. Typical polyglycerol esters.

Ester	Form at 25°C	Hydroxyl value	Saponification value	Iodine value	HLB (+ 1.0)
Decaglycerol tetraoleate (Drewmulse 10-4-O)	Licuid	200-250	125-145	60	6.0
Decaglycerol octaolete (Drewmulse 10-8-O)	Licuid	25-50	150-180	80	4.0
Decaglycerol decaoleate (Drewmulse 10-10-O)	Liquid	20-60	160-190	90	3.0
Decaglycerol decastearate (Drewmulse 10-10-S)	Sclid	30-60	150-190	3	3.0
Hexaglycerol distearate (Drewmulse 6-2-S)	Solid	270-310	100-130	5	8.0
Triglycerol monostearate (Drewmulse 3-1-S)	Solid	315-345	120-140	3	7.0
Triglycerol monooleate (Drewmulse 3-1-Q)	Liquid	230-290	120-160	90	7.0

'Drewmulse' is the trade name of PVO International Inc. and corresponding Stepan Company products are designated 'Drewpo!'.

the careful control of monomer feed and reaction conditions allows the preparation of a series of surfactants in which the HLB, solubility, wetting and foaming properties can be closely and reproducibly controlled. The classification of these products is primarily based on the nature of the initiator employed in the formation of the initial polymer block, with subclasses determined by the compositions of the various blocks. The hydrophobicity is derived from one of the two polymeric blocks and typical initiators are monohydric alcohols such as butanol, dihydric materials such as glycol, glycerol, higher polyols or ethylene diamine.

Table 9.6. Some commercial polyethylene glycols.

Carbowax	Molecular weight	Specific gravity	Viscosity (Cst at 100°C)	Surface tension (dynes/cm)
PEG 200	190-210	1.1239	4.3	44.5
PEG 300	285-315	1.1250	5.8	44.5
PEG 400	380-420	1.1254	7.3	44.5
PEG 600	570-630	1.1257	10.8	44.5

(Con...)

Carbowax	Molecular weight	Specific gravity	Viscosity (Cst at 100°C)	Surface tension (dynes/cm)
PEG 900	855-900	1.0927 (60°C)	15.3	—
PEG 1000	950-1050	1.0926 (60°C)	17.2	—
PEG 1450	1300-1600	1.0919 (60°C)	26.5	—
PEG 3350	3000-3700	1.0926 (60°C)	90.8	—
PEG 4600	4400-4800	1.0926 (60°C)	184.0	—
PEG 8000	7000-9000	1.0845 (70°C)	822.0	—

Table 9.7 Some commercial fatty acid polyethylene glycol/ polypropylene glycol esters.

Glycol ester	Applications
PEG esters of lauric, oleic and stearic acids	Cosmetics, food, Pharmaceuticals, plastics, agriculture and others
PEG 600 distearate	Fabric softener
PEG 600 dioleate	-do-
Glycol stearate	Pearl shine agent for shampoos, shower and bath preparations, emulsions
Glycol distearate	-do-
Glycol stearate	-do-
Glycol distearate	-do-
Propylene glycol stearate	-do-
PEG 300 oleate	Emulsifier, lubricant, textile softener
PEG. 400 dilaurate	Emulsifier, lubricant, softeners, release agent for paper spin finishes.
PEG 300 monopelargonate	Coemulsifier
PEG 200 monolaurate	Defoamer in water based systems
PEG 600 monostearate	Emulsifier and viscosity modifier
PEG 400 monooleate	Emulsifier
PEG 6000 monooleate	Emulsifier, stabiliser, lubricant
PEG 400 sesquioleate	Emulsifier for kerosene in agricultural sprasy

Depending on the nature of the polymer blocks in the molecule this class of nonionics is made up of three subclasses, namely, 'all-block', 'heteric-block', and 'all-heteric' nonionics. Structurally the simplest form of the surfactants of this group is :

$$H—(EO)_m\,(PO)_n\,(EO)_m—H$$

In all-block surfactants each block is homogeneous—meaning that a single alkylene oxide is used in the monomer feed during each step in preparation. In heteric-block surfactants one portion of the molecule is composed of a single alkylene oxide, while the other is a mixture of two or more such materials, one of which may be the same as that of the homogeneous block portion of the molecule. In the preparation of such materials, the hetero portion of the molecule will be totally random. In the all-heteric block the monomer feed for the alkylene oxide in each step is composed of a mixture of two or more materials. These materials have a potential manufacturing advantage in that it is possible to vary the monomer feed composition during the reaction to continuously change the composition of the polymer as it grows on the initiator. The EO-PO block copolymers can belong to either of the classes :

$$I—A_m—B_n \text{ or } [B_nA_m]_x \; I' \; [A_m \; B_n]_y$$

where I and I' are the initiators. A is an alkylene oxide in which at least one hydrogen has been replaced by an alkyl or aryl group and B is an aqueous solubilising group such as oxyethylene, 'm' and 'n' are the degrees of polymerisation, usually greater than six. A wide variety of surfactant properties can be achieved by controlling 'm' and 'n'.

A method of manufacturing the EO-PO block copolymers is to form the polymerised PO—substrate and copolymerise the hydrophilic substrate onto it. The inverse type in which PO is condensed onto a polyethylene glycol substrate has also interesting properties. Other versatile group of products are made using ethylene diamine and synthetic C13 to C15 alcohols as starting materials.

EO-PO block copolymers encompass almost the entire spectrum of applications by the surfactants. Essentially they are defoamers, wetters, rinse aids, detergents, emulsifiers, emulsion stabilisers, dispersants, emulsifiers, antistats, antidusts and thickeners. Industrially they are prominent in three groups, namely:

(a) defoamers—in bottle washing, sugar production, fermentation of antibiotics, paper manufacture, in metal/phosphate cleaning, drilling muds, dishwashing, commercial laundry and inks.

(b) detergents—in hard surface cleaners, alkaline metal degreasing, wool scouring, cotton desizing, hand dishwashing, food and drink industry.

(c) Wetters—in agricultural chemicals, paper, leather and paints industries and commercial dishwashing.

The efforts to effect energy savings during the last decade frequently led to employing very high agitation rates to compensate for lower temperatures in many industrial operations. This led to greater use of low foaming surfactants. Apart from EO/PO block copolymers, ethoxylated and propoxylated linear alcohols (AEOPO) and alkylphenols (APEOPO) have been inducted for this purpose. Global production of EO/PO copolymers is around 140000 metric tons per annum.

Alcohol Ethoxylates (AE)

Alcohol ethoxylates (AE), also known as alcohol ethers, ethoxylated alcohols, polyglycol ethers, alkoxy alcohols, alcohol—EO adducts are ethers and are made through the catalytic reaction of one mole of a long chain alcohol with one or more moles of ethylehe oxide (EO). The reaction is exothermic and solid or liquid products result depending on both the molecular weight of the products and their distribution. The substrated alcohols used are popular detergent alcohols (C12-C18), obtained either from natural sources or petrochemical feedstock. Alcohol ethoxyiates with a low level of EO are usually sulphated to the anionic ether sulphates. For the ethoxylation, predominantly alcohols with mixed lengths comprising both linear and slightly-branched types are used.

Secondary reaction products, mainly polyethylene glycols (PEG) of molecular weight exceeding 200, are also formed in the ethoxylation of alcohols. The PEG content of a commercial product is of the order of 2-3%, Alcohol ethoxyiates are true surfactants with clear hydrophobic and hydrophilic moieties. They do not dissociate on dissolution in water and thus are nonionic surfactants. Alcohol ethoxyiates with 1-4 moles EO are oil-soluble, and water solubility begins to increase after 5-6 moles EO. The solubility decreases with increase in temperature and as such the cloud point of an alcohol ethoxylate is an important parameter in its utility for a particular application, The cloud point also is a good indicator of the foaming tendency of the alcohol ethoxylate. Commercial products have between 10-50 moles EO.

Replacement of EO by propylene oxide (PO) results in propoxylates. Just as the alcohol ethoxylates with low level of EO can be sulphated, they undergo phosphation to yield surfactants that perform as emulsifiers, detergents and dispersants. In general, the larger the EO chain, the higher is the HLB or hydrophilic character, pour point, viscosity, density, cloud point and flash point of the product. In the case of solid products the pour points can be reduced by adding a small amount of water to facilitate handling of the alcohol ethoxylate. Secondary alcohol ethoxylates, a subclass of alcohol ethoxylates and containing 3-40 moles EO per mole of alconol, remain fluid over a wider temperature range than primary alcohol ethoxylates and thus eliminate the expensive heating during storage and handling. Furthermore, they possess higher solubility in both water and hydrocarbon solvents than the primary alcohol ethoxylates.

The three most important industrial applications of alcohol ethoxylates are in industrial institutional cleaners, paper and textiles. In the cleaner sector they are used extensively in hard surface cleaners and in commercial laundry compositions. Other usage areas are as low-foam wetters for commercial dishwashing powders and rinse aids, as components of sanitiser formulations, in hand cleaning gels and in wax as well as silicone polishes. They are also excellent emulsifiers for degreasing of metals with solvents, In the paper industry, they are used for deinking of waste paper, as wax emulsifiers in chipboard manufacture, fluff pulp bulking agents and pitch dispersants. In textile industry they are used in the scouring of synthetic fibres and in ship finish formulations. Other applications are in agricultural sprays, as wetting agents for leather, as surfactants in emulsion polymerisation and for modification of PVC plastisol viscosities.

Alkyl Phenol Ethoxylates (APE)

Resembling alcohol ethoxylates in physical and performance properties. APE are chemically stable and highly versatile surfactants used in a large number of industrial products such as acid and alkaline metal cleaning formulations, detergents, wetting agents and efficient emulsifiers or co-emulsifiers. They are also used as dispersants, solubilisers, coupling agents and rewetting agents. Industrially their most important applications are in industrial institutional cleaners, emulsion polymerisation of paint emulsions, as wetting, scouring agents and detergents in many areas of textile processing, and as wetting agents and emulsifiers in the formulation of pesticidal concentrates. They are also used in recycling of paper (resin removal, deinking and wetting), concrete (plasticiser and foaming agent), gypsum board (foaming agent), leather tanning (wetting agent), formulation of hand cleaning gels, in coal dust suppression, filter cake dewatering, surface treatment in zinc and aluminium production, drilling mud chemicals and as raw materials for the anionic alkylphenol ethoxysulphates or ether sulphates.

The alkylphenol ethoxylates are represented by

$$RC_6H_4\,(OCH_2CH_2)NOH$$

where R is the alkyl group attached to the aryl group and n is the average number of EO moles, generally 5-40, in these products. Most important of the alkyl phenols is nonylphenol followed by octylphenol, dodecyl and other alkylphenols including those with more than one side chain. Nonylphenol with 4 moles of EO is insoluble in water, but soluble in hydrocarbons. With 6-7 moles EO the product becomes soluble in cold water and yet remains oil soluble. With 8—12 moles EO good water solubility results. Higher ethoxylates with 20 and more moles EO per mole of alkylphenol are used in specialty applications such as emulsion polymerisation.

The cloud point is a significant parameter in identifying various alkylphenol ethoxylates and their formulations. The larger the number of moles of EO in the molecule, the more soluble it is and the higher the cloud point. At 15 moles EO, the product will not cloud even in boiling water. The foaming tendency increases upto 18 moles EO and thereafter it begins to decline. The solubility of the alkylphenol ethoxylates is influenced by the level of calcium and magnesium ions. An important aspect of these products is their tolerance to water hardness. The surfactant properties are governed by the length of the alkyl chains. With an alkyl chain of 7-10 carbon atoms, good wetting and detergent action are favoured and with more than 12 carbon atoms these properties are lowered and the emulsifying properties predominate.

Polyhydric alcohol ethoxylates

Ethoxylated sorbitan esters (Polysorbates) and ethoxylated glycerides are two important categories in this class.

Ethoxylation of sorbitan esters leads to a series of more hydrophilic surfactants. All hydroxyl groups of sorbitan can react with ethylene oxide. A typical POE (20) sorbitan ester is represented by the structure :

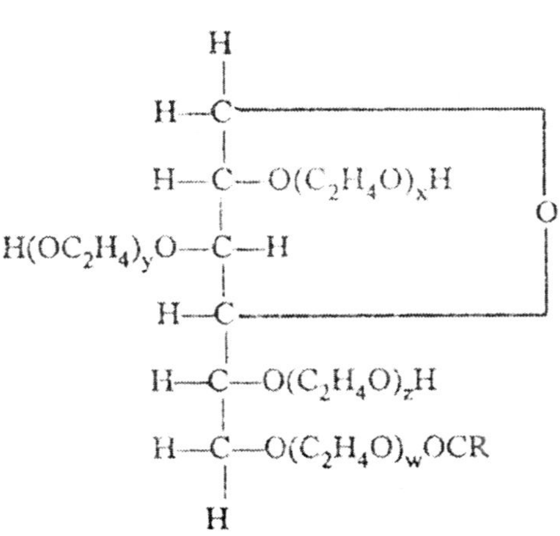

wherein w + x + y + zs equal to 20. The polysorbates either alone or with their counterparts, the sorbitan fatty acid esters, have a number of applications. Their properties are exploited in their uses as emulsifiers for w/o hydraulic fluid emulsions, in quenching emulsions for heat treated metal parts, in emulsion polymerisation, as dispersants for pigment colourants, in shampoos and other anti-irritant products in the cosmetics industry.

The ethoxylated glycerides comprise three chemically diverse groups of substances, all of which are derived from various acyl glycerides. One group is obtained by ethoxylation of monoglyceride. Thus POE 20 glyceryl oleate is obtained by ethoxylation of glyceryl oleate wherein both the OH groups present react with EO until the total level of polyoxyethylene (POE) equals 20. A second group is derived from OH group containing glycerides, which includes glyceryl ricinoleate, castor oil and trihydroxy stearin. The EO addition can occur on any available hydroxyl grouping. In addition some reactions can occur resembling those given below for the third type. When a natural glyceride is allowed to react with EO, a third type of ethoxylated glyceride results. Water solubility and HLB of products in the above referred three groups depend on the starting glycerides and the level of ethoxylation.

The ethoxylated glycerides, solids or liquids, are useful emulsifying agents, suspending and solubilising agents, skin conditioners and emollients. Typical members of this class are POE 4 castor oil. POE 120 glyceryl stearate and POE 6 triolein. The low HLB value products act as defoamers and w/o emulsifiers. The high HLB value products serve as o/w emulsifiers. Other applications are in metal working fluids, floor polishes, cutting oils, mold release agents, universal colourant vehicles in aqueous and non-aqueous systems for paints and inks, oilfield drilling fluids, hydraulic fluids and metal cleaners.

Lanolin Ethoxylates

Ethoxylated lanolin derivatives are intended to provide the benefits of lanolin in finished cosmetic products without imparting the unctuous characteristics of lanolin. They are formed by ethoxylation of the hydroxyl groups present in lanolin or its hydrogenation product—giving rise to complex mixtures of ethoxylated sterols, lanolin alcohols, lanolin fatty acids and unaltered lanolin. This complexity arises due to the presence of water in the lanolin and the transesterification reactions taking place during the ethoxylation. Most members of this group are waxy solids, water soluble due to the high levels of ethoxylation. Specific examples are POE 20 lanolin and PPG 12 POE 65 lanolin oil.

Ethoxylated Polysiloxanes

The introduction of the first organosilican block copolymers made it possible to lower the surface tension of many organic liquids that are not influenced by hydrocarbon surfactants. Organosilicon block copolymers emerged as commercial products at a time when new polymer chemistry and its applications were taking form and the technology of polyurethane had just begun to unfold itself. Nonionic silicone surfactants are the dominant stabilisers of polyurethane foam. Foam ingredient solubility is imparted to the silicone by such hydrogen bonding groups as the ether oxygens and hydroxyls of polyoxyethylene and polyoxypropylene glycols.

Silicone—oxyalkylene block copolymers typified by Union Carbide 'Silwet' surfactants are of two distinct structural types. The major class is a polydimethylsiloxane to which polyethers have been grafted through a hydrosilylation reaction. This process results in an alkyl pendant type (AP type) copolymer in which the polyoxyalkylene groups are attached along the siloxane backbone through a series of hydrolytically stable Si-C bonds. These products have the general formula :

$$Me_3Si0\ (Me_2SiO)_x\ (Me\ SiO)y\ SiMe_3$$

$$|$$

$$PE$$

wherein Me is CH_3 group and PE is $—CH_2CH_2O(EO)_m(PO)_nZ$. EO and PO are ethylene and propylene oxides and Z is either hydrogen or a lower alkyl group. The second class is a branched polydimethylsiloxane to which polyethers have been attached through condensation chemistry. This creates an alkoxy-end-blocked (AEB) type copolymer in which the polyoxyalkylene groups are attached to the ends of the silicone backbone through Si-O-C bonds. This linkage offers limited resistance to hydrolysis under neutral or slightly alkaline conditions, but breaks down quickly in acidic environments. These products have the general formula

$$(MeSi)_{y-z}\ [(O\ Si\ Me_2)^{x/y}\ O—PE]_y$$

wherein Me is CH_3, PE is $—(EO)_m\ (PO)_n$ R, R being a lower alkyl group.

A broad range of this class of surfactants has been developed by varying x, y, m and n values in the above formula. These products offer unique properties and performance that are not achievable with conventional organic surfactants. The ethoxylated polysiloxanes are especially used in the cosmetic industry as emulsifiers for silicones. The low surface tension, high wetting, superior dispersing, emulsifying, lubrication, sheen, gloss enhancing, static suppressing, moderate prefoaming, broad range of aqueous cloud points and solubility, good thermal stability and good compatibility with other surfactants and system components, are the various parameters taken advantage of in the applications of these products. Their low toxicity, environmental acceptability and their cost effectiveness due to their performance at low concentrations are added advantages. Other than cosmetics, end uses are in adhesiyes and sealants, agriculture, automotive specialties, coatings, fibres, hydrocarbon antifoams, mineral processing, paper, petroleum extraction and processing, pigments and dyes, plastics and

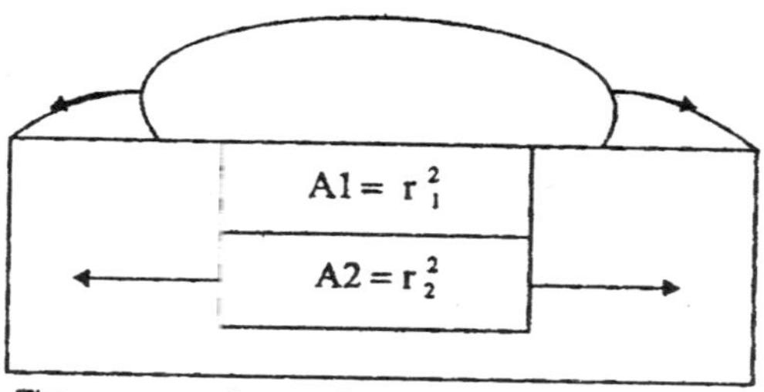

The process of spreading wetting

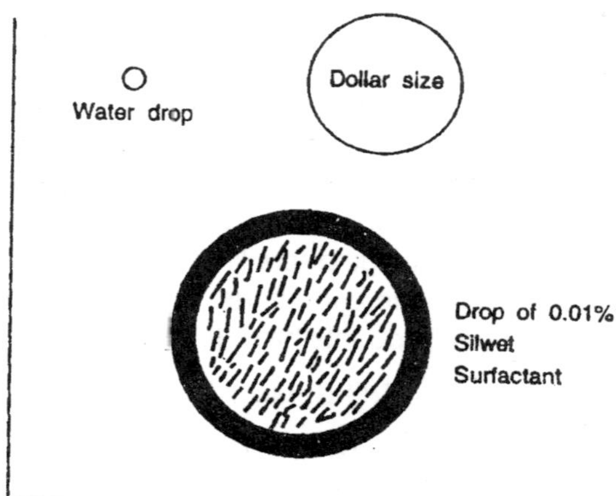

Fig. 9.7. Wetting and spreading of silwet surfactants.

rubber, pharmaceuticals, printing inks and textiles. A significant application is in their role as emulsifying agent in the formation of flexible urethane foams smoothening the reaction between polyol, isocyanate and water. In rigid urethane foams also they contribute to structural soundness.

Commercially available Union Carbide 'Silwet' brand products are indicated in Fig. 9.7.

Alkanolamides

The alkanolamides are another class of major nonionic surfactants comprising of:

(a) Monoalkanolamides

(b) 2:1 knitchevsky diethanolamides

(c) 1:1 superamides, and

(d) The mixed ratio amides.

Monoalkanolamides are made by condensing one mole of a monoalkanolamide with one mole of fatty acid or ester at 180°C according to the equation :

$$RCOOH + NH_2CH_2CH_2OH \longrightarrow R\,CO\,NHCH_2CH_2OH + H_2O$$

With monoisopropanolamine the corresponding mon-oisopropanolamide is obtained. This reaction also produces a mono-ethanolamide ester byproduct, thereby restricting the product purity to around 95%. A 99% purity product can be obtained by reacting two moles of fatty acid with one mole of monoethanolamine to give a fatty acid acrylaminoethyl ester and transesterifying this intermediate with a further mole of the amine. The superior hydrolytic stability and viscosity build up properties of monoisopropanolamide makes it the product of choice in shampoos in the United States. In Western Europe the moderate foaming characteristics of monoethanolamides and their solid form boost their use in powder laundry detergents.

Diethanolamides of commercial interest are the 2:1 knitchevsky amides and the 1:1 superamides. The 2:1 products are made by reacting two moles of diethanolamine with one mole of fatty acid at 140-170°C The use of fatty acid esters and sodium methylate catalyst also gives the 2:1 diethanolamides of mixed composition. The product purity is thus only 60-65%. These alkanolamides are liquids and are used in water-based systems. The 1:1 superamides with purity around 90% are obtained at 100-110°C and pressures atmospheric or lower by reacting equimolar quantities of methyl ester and diethanolamine using alkaline sodium methylate catalyst. In this process, methanol is continuously removed using explosion-proof equipment. Typical compositions of the 2:1 and 1:1 amides are as follows :

Composition	Percent by weight	
	2:1 knitchevskyn amide	1:1 superamide
Diethanolamide	65	90
Free diethanolamine	22	5
Amine salt	10	Trace
Amide ester	1	4
Water	2	Trace
Methanol	-	0.2
Methyl ester	-	0.8

The superamides are gels or soft, low melting solids with slight solubility in water. The viscosity building properties of these amides are directly related to their water solubilities and in this respect the lauric isopropanolamide is superior to the lauric diethanolamide.

The alkanolamides figure in a number of applications. In detergent and cosmetic formulations they basically perform as foam quality improvers, foam stabilisers, viscosity builders and detergency synergists. They are used in light duty washing liquids, heavy-duty laundry detergents, and home and institutional cleaners, including carpet cleaners. In the formulation of shampoos, bubble baths, synthetic toilet bars and institutional scrub soaps they are used directly. Ethoxylated alkanolamides and sulphosuccinates derived from their reaction with maleic anhydride are also used in cosmetics. Their asset in shampoos is due to their effectiveness in the presence of high levels of grease. The alkanolamides are compatible with other nonionic and anionic surfactants. Thus a 5% addition of alkanolamide in a formulation containing 20% anionics and 75% builders enhances the detergency of the product. The superamides are excellent foam boosters and valuable constituents in handwash detergents and shampoos. The addition of fatty alkanolamides to surfactant formulations reduces the 'Zein number' of the formulation, rendering it thereby skin non-irritant. Other applications are as bases for deodorant sticks, as textile greasing agents, and as rust inhibitors in drilling and cutting oils. Lauric acid based alkanolamides dominate the market.

Fatty Amine Oxides (FAO)

The substitution of the traditional alkanolamides as foam boosters in dishwashing liquids was the specific instance, which brought recognition to the nonionic fatty amine oxides. These are produced by reaction of tertiary amines and hydrogen peroxide or peroxyacids. Their general structure is given by :

$$R\,R'\,R''\,N^{+}\,O^{-}$$

wherein R, R' and R" may be alkyl, aryl or any or several other structures with at least one being a fatty acid residue. Two typical reactions showing their formations are :

$$C_{12}H_{25}(CH_3)_2N + H_2O_2 \longrightarrow C_{12}H_{25}(CH_3)_2N \longrightarrow O + H_2O$$

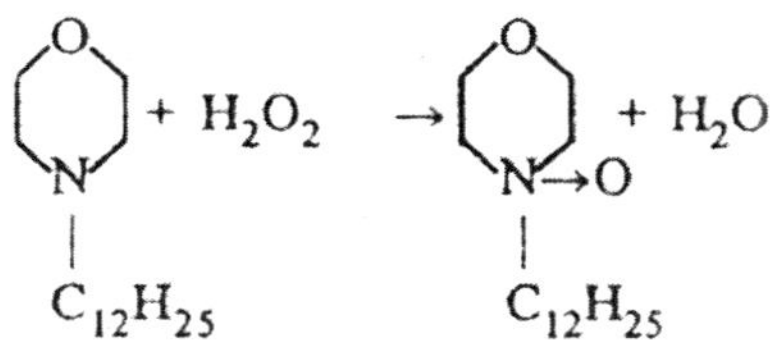

These materials while possessing a formal charge separation on the nitrogen and oxygen atoms behave as electrolytes. In aqueous solution FAO exhibit nonionic or cationic properties depending on the pH. At lower pH the weakly cationic form precipitates metathetically with anionic surfactants such as sodium dodecyl benzene sulphonate. Under neutral or alkaline conditions they exist in solution as non-ionised hydrates.

The most common amine used for the production of FAO is the alkyldimethylamine where the alkyl group contains 12 to 16 carbon atoms. In turn, the alkyldimethylamines are derived from either linear alpha-olefins or detergent alcohols. The synthesis of FAO involves the conversion of the alpha-olefin to the primary alkyl bromide which when reacted with dimethylamine gives the corresponding alkyldimethylamine.

FAO are good foam stabilisers, thickeners and emollients, emulsifiers and conditioning agents exhibiting mildness towards the skin. In dishwashing liquids they show superior foam stabilisation properties, when used along with alcohol ether sulphates in presence of grease, compared with the more commonly used fatty alkanolamides. Other applications are as rinse additives in laundering, shampoo formulations, waterless hand cleaners and hair conditioners.

Acetylenic Alcohol Derivatives

Surfactants based on acetylenic diols are a series of products under the trade name 'Surfynols' marketed by Air Products Co. The core member of this group, Surfynol 104, is a nonionic molecule containing a hydrophili portion in the middle of two symmetric hydrophobes. Chemically, it can be represented as:

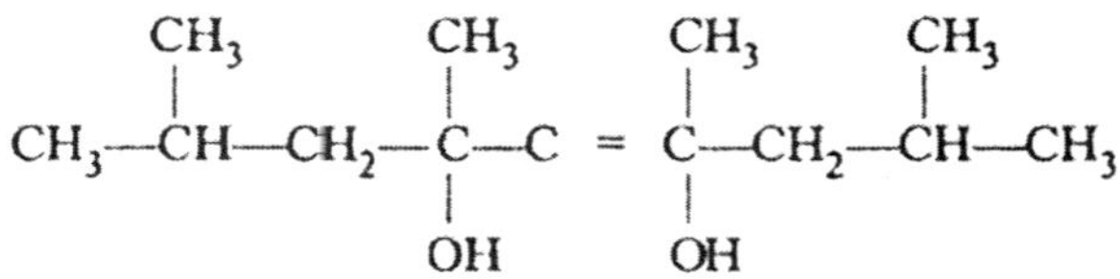

(2,4,7,9-tetramethyl-5-decyn-4,7-diol)

This unique chemical structure allows Surfynol 104 to provide multifunctional properties such as surface tension and foam control. Other members of the Surfynol group are other acetylenic alcohols and diols and ethoxylated products. Surfynol 104 effectively reduces the surface tension of water to 33.1 dynes/cm under dynamic conditions at a concentration of 0.1%. In this respect it is superior to the performance of Triton X. Surfynol 104 does not have a cloud point and as such functions as a defoamer over a very broad temperature range. Table 9.8 gives the application areas in which the wetting, defoaming and dispersant properties of some Surfynols are exploited.

Table 9.8. Application areas of 'Surfynol' surfactants.

Applications	Surfynol types					
	61	82S	104A	440	465	485
Coatings						
(a) (Acrylic, alkyl, epoxy SBR, polyurethane)	WD	—	WD	W	W	W
(b) Powder	—	WG	—	—	—	—
(c) Radiation curable	—	—	W	W	W	W
(d) Paper (SBR, PVA)	—	—	WD	WD	—	—
Graphic arts						
(a) Flexographic & gravureinks	WD	—	WD	W	W	W
(b) Overprint varnish	W	—	WD	W	—	—
Dyes/pigments						
(a) Pigment dispersion	WD	—	WD	—	—	—
(b) Dye milling	—	—	WD	—	—	—
(c) Crystallisation & filtration	—	—	WDC	—	—	—
Adhesives (acrylic, PVA, phenolics, styrene butaeidne	—	—	WD	W	W	W
Foundry	—	—	WD	—	—	—

(Con...)

Applications	Surfynol types					
	61	82S	104A	440	465	485
Emulsion polymerisation	—	—	WD	W	E	E
PVC production/plastisols	—	—	WD	—	—	—
Agricultural chemicals	W	W	WD	W	W	W
Oilfield chemicals	W	—	WD	WD	—	—
Hard surface cleaners	W	W	WD	W	W	W
Metalworking fluids	—	—	WD	W	W	—
Textiles	W	—	WD	W	W	—
Cement/Concrete	—	—	WD	WD	—	—

W- low or nonfoaming wetting agents; D-defoaming, anti-foaming and/or deair entrainment agents; G-pigment grinding aid or dispersant; C-crystallisation enhancer; E-emulsifier; 61-3, 5 dimethyl-l-hexyn3-ol; 82-S - 3,6-dimethyl-4-octyne-3,6-dio ; 104A-2, 4, 7, 9 tetramethyl-5-decyne-4,7 diol; 440-104 + 3.5 moles EO; 465-104 + 1C moles EO; 485-104 + 30 moles E0.

Silicones

Like all true surfactants the silicone surfactants possess two moieties termed 'lipophilic' and 'lipophobic', rather than 'hydrophilic' and 'hydrophobic' as is the case with hydrocarbon surfactants. The variety of solubilising groups with which the silicones can be reacted permit tailoring a silicone surfactant for specific systems. The generalised structure of a silicone surfactant is wherein X is any of the hydrophilic groups of anionic,

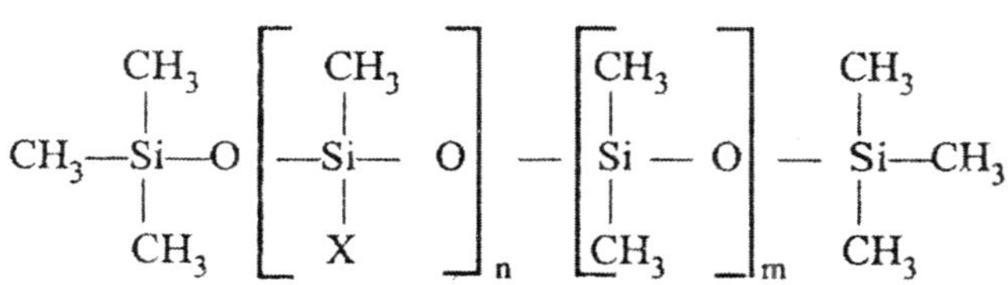

cationic or nonionic character or organophilic groups such as esters, amides and polyethers. Unlike most common organic surfactants, silicone surfactants are multifunctional. The many possible combinations of siloxane molecular weight, functionality and polyether composition control the HLB and molecular geometry, the primary influences of surfactant behaviour. The silicone backbone can be considered, as a 'Super-hydrocarbon' because of the density of methyl groups present, and is very stable and very flexible. Most silicone surfactants thus are liquids and remain so even at high molecular weights. Major applications of silicone surfactants are as wetters, emulsifiers for silicone fluids and concrete mould release agents.

Other silicone based surfactants are fluorosurfactants and ethoxylated polysiloxanes, referred to in other sections.

Fluorosurfactants

A fluorosurfactant consists of a hydrophobic and oleophobic perfluorinated tail and a hydrophilic or organophilic head group, structurally represented as

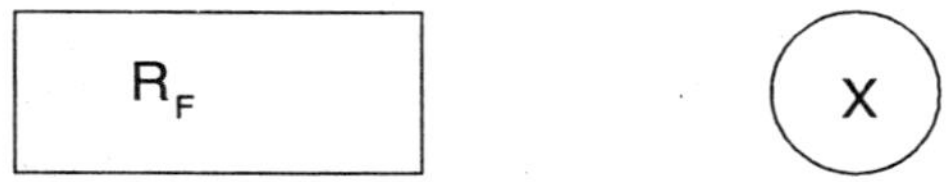

The fluorochemical tail, R_F consists of the stable perfluorocarbon group. This group can be modified in length and structure to meet end use heeds, and provides exceptional resistance to thermal and chemical attack. This fluorochemical portion is basically responsible for its capacity to dramatically reduce surface tension as well as being the major difference between fluorosurfactants, conventional hydrocarbon surfactants and silicone surfactants. The head group X is commonly a water- soluble group but can also be designed to be oil-soluble for use in non-aqueous systems. The nature of X can be varied to give anionic, cationic, nonionic or amphoteric surfactants such as:

$$R_FSO_3\text{-}K^+;\ R_FNH_3^+Cl\text{-};\ R_F(CH_2CH_2O)_nH;$$

$$R_FN^+H(CH_3)\ CH_2\ COO\text{-}$$

The fluorosurfactants can be made commercially by the following processes

(a) *Simons electrochemical fluorination process (ECF)*

$$HF + C_8H_{17}SO_2F_{18} \xrightarrow{ECF} C_8FI_8SO_2F + H_2$$

followed by conversion of $C_8F_{17}SO_2F$ to various types of surfactants

(b) *Telomerisation process*

$$C_2F_5I + n\ (CF_2—CF_2) \longrightarrow C_2F_5\ (CF_2CF_2)_n\ I$$

followed by conversion of the telomer iodides to surfactants

(c) *Anionic oligomerisation of fluorine monomers*

$$n\ (CF_2 = CF_2) \longrightarrow (C_2F_4)n$$

followed by reaction of the oligomers with alcohols, phenols, oleum or polyethylene glycols leading to various surfactants.

The advantages of fluorosurfactants are lower surface tension in aqueous systems, better effectiveness at very low concentrations, excellent stability in hostile environments and good surface activity in organic media. Areas of application include floor polish emulsions, photographic processes, production of fluoropolymers, electroplating bath additives, electronic coatings, as additives for oil/gas well stimulation, in battery electrolytes, in fire-fighting foams and as additives in paints, coatings, inks and adhesives.

Alkyl Polyglycosides

The abundance of carbohydrates and the fact that they are both natural and renewable has evoked fresh interest in the last few years in carbohydrate derived surfactants. Nonionic alkyl glucosides, commonly known as alkyl polyglycosides (APG), have attracted attention as highly efficient and mild surfactants. They are obtained by the reaction of glucose with fatty alcohol, starch providing the source for glucose. APG has a generic structure :

$$C_nH_{2n+1}O\,(C_6H_{10}O_5)_x\,H$$

where x ranges from 1 to 4.

APG is reportedly more soluble than a typical alcohol ethoxylate or alkylphenol ethoxylate designed for household laundry applications. Detergent formulations based on APG are also more stable than the above-referred ethoxylates over a wider range of temperatures.

Consequently its liquid detergent formulations require less solubilising agent and can be formulated with higher levels of soluble builders. Liquid dishwashing formulations incorporating it reportedly require no foam booster. Its mildness to the skin promotes its use in hand dishwashing personal care applications. APG can also be used effectively in combination with anionic surfactants. Henkel is the major producer of this type of nonionic surfactant.

Sulphosuccinates, Sulphosuccinamates

The sulphosuccinates are made by forming a maleic ester and then sulphonating it. The starting raw materials for these anionics are maleic anhydride and a fatty alcohol, alcohol ethoxylate or an alkanolamide as the second reactant. If amines are used in the reaction replacing the alcohols, then sulphosuccinamate surfactants are produced. The products obtained in these reactions can be half esters or diesters. For the half ester an aqueous solution of sodium sulphite is used as the sulphonating agent and for the diester, sodium bisulphite. Typical half ester and diester sulphosuccinates are illustrated below :

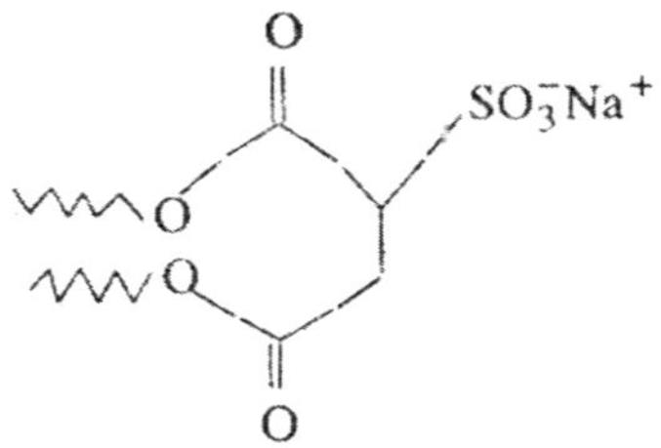

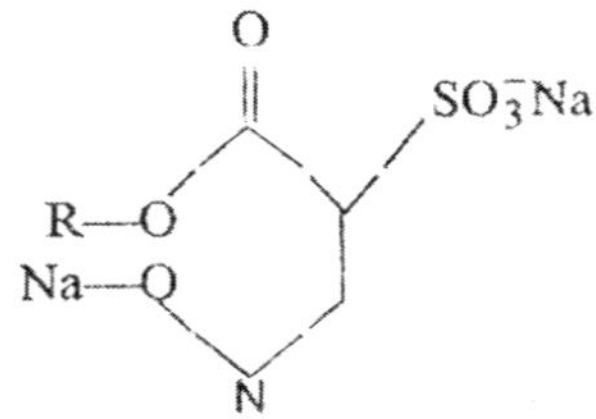

Diester sulphosuccinate

Half ester sulphosuccinate

The sulphosuccinamates are typically manufactured by the reaction:

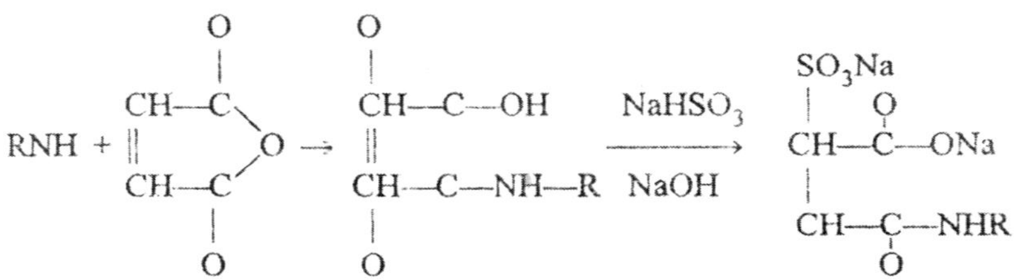

Primary Maleic anhydride
amine

involving a primary amine and maleic anhydride, and then adding sodium bisulphite across the double bond.

The sulphosuccinates are good to excellent foamers and wetting agents. The half esters have application in household detergents, but the sodium dialkylesters are industrially used in the following areas :

(a) Emulsion polymerisation of PVA emulsions and PVC dispersion resins.

(b) Foam stabilisers in rug shampoos.

(c) As components of solvent degreasers for metals.

(d) As solubilisers in industrial dry cleaning formulations.

(e) Dewatering of mineral slurries.

(f) Mineral flotation.

(g) Oil-spill chemicals.

(h) Pigment dispersion and wetting agents in paints.

(i) Foaming agents for secondary foam backings,

(j) Coatings of textiles, leather and leather-cloth.

(k) Modification of plastisol viscosity.

Phosphate Esters

Analogous to the sulphate esters, the phosphate esters are reaction products of phosphoric acid with alcohols or ethoxylates resulting in an anionic product. As it is difficult to phosphate an alcohol with orthophosphoric acid, pyrophosphoric acid is used. Likewise, oleum replaces sulphuric acid. It is possible this way to generate mono, di and polyphosphoric esters. Aromatic phosphate esters are also feasible and these can be further ethoxylated. The phosphated and ethoxylated esters form an important group of industrial surfactants.

The phosphate esters find application primarily in their exploitation as:

(a) Detergents

(b) Dispersants

(c) Emulsifiers

As detergents they are used in industrial and institutional cleaners. As dispersants they are used in paper coatings, paints and inks, textile dyeing and pesticide/herbicide suspension concentrates. As emulsifiers they are used in emulsion polymerisation of lattices, cutting oils, drilling aids, crop protection chemical concentrates. They also are used in dry cleaning, as corrosion inhibitors, and as antistats in textile cleaning formulations.

Amine Based Surfactants

Amines are the building blocks for the entire train of cationic surfactants as illustrated below :

The amines find direct application as surface-active agents in ore flotation, filming amines for corrosion inhibition and as anti-caking agents for granular and blended fertilisers.

Amine ethoxylates

These are prepared by ethoxylation and the products contain 2-50 EO units. Their uses are as :

(a) Cationic collectors in ore flotation and frothing agents.

(b) Part of filming amine formulations.

(c) Additives for lubricating oils and gasoline.

(d) Emulsifiers for agricultural sprays.

(e) Emulsifiers for textile spinning oils.

(f) Emulsion breakers.

(g) Dye-levelers and textile finishing agents.

(h) Corrosion inhibitors.

(i) Antistats.

Quaternary Ammonium Compounds (QAC)

The quaternary ammonium compounds are commercially the most important of the group of cationic and amphoteric surfactants accounting for 45-50% of the total market for this class. There are over 200 QAC in commercial use. The QAC are made by 'quaternising' primary, secondary and tertiary amines with four different types of quaternising agents:

(1) Methyl chloride or bromide.

(2) Dimethyl or diethyl sulphate.

(3) Benzyl chloride.

(4) Ethylene oxide or diethanolamine.

Products obtained by the use of different quaternising agents have different properties and serve widely different markets. The alkyl, benzyl or ethoxy groups attach themselves to the nitrogen atom of the amine.

The counterion is the halide or the methosulphate group. Alkyl chain lengths are determined by fatty acids used in preparing the amine and profoundly affect the properties of the product. If a symmetrical tertiary amine is the starting material and methyl chloride is used as the quaternising agent, a symmetrical QAC : is obtained. Distearyldimethyl ammonium chloride (DSDMAC) is the most important QAC and is used as fabric softener. It is also used in the preparation of organic-modified clays used in petroleum drilling, as thixotropic agents in paints and inks, and also for its bacteriostatic properties.

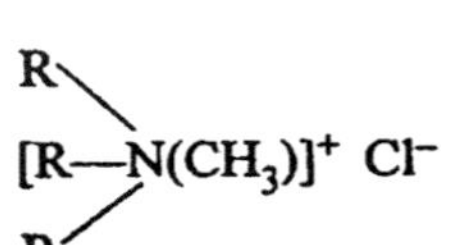

When monoalkyl type QAC are quaternised with benzyl chloride, compounds known as 'benzyl quats' are obtained. They have the structure :

$$[R\text{-}N(CH_3)_2.CH_2.C_6H_5]^+ Cl^-$$

These quaternaries form a special class of biocides, sanitisers etc., used in hospitals, restaurants, food processing centres and swimming pools.

The other groups of QAC, namely,

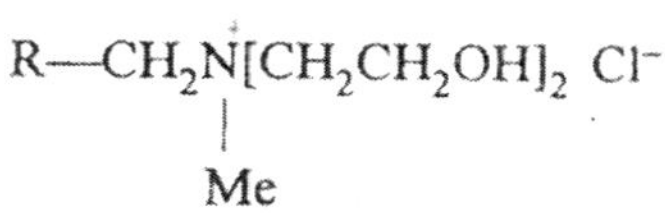

and

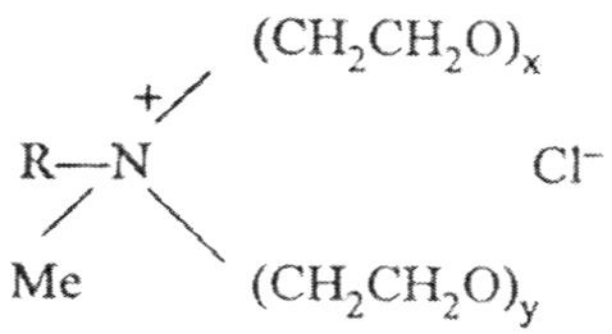

are obtained by quaternising with diethanolamine and ethylene oxide. They have a wide range of hydrophilicity. They are important in the formulation of asphalt/bitumens, in vehicle cleaning formulations and as emulsifiers in pesticide formulations.

Imidazolines and Polyamines

The cationic properties of amines are greatly improved by the incorporation of additional nitrogen atoms into their structures, resulting in polyamines of the type :

$$H_2N\,CH_2\,CH_2\,NH_2\,CH_2\,CH_2\,NH_2$$

diethylenetriamine

They are made by reducing the product obtained by the cyanoethylation of primary and other amines with acrylon trile. Their difunctional character makes them very effective corrosion inhibitors.

Polyamines react with fatty acids and dimer/trimer acids to form the imidazolines such as :

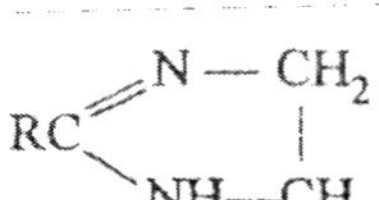

These, with various substituents, are used in fabric softeners, corrosion inhibitors in oil-field applications and other areas.

Betaines

As already pointed out, the amphoteric betaines are special members of the ring opened imidazcline derived surfactants. They differ from other amphoterics with regard to their solubility and electrical nature in alkaline solution. They are compatible with anionics at all pH values. The carboxyl containing betaines are insensitive to water hardness. They are used as levelling and wetting agents in textile processing, detergents, scrubbing compounds, antistatic agents, as fabric softeners, as lime soap dispersants and in personal care products. Coconut fatty acid amidopropylbetaine is pa-ticularly used in hair shampoos, foam baths, shower foams and liquid soaps where a high, creamy foam is required. It has a good skin tolerance.

The most common route to carboxyl-betaines is through the quaternisation of long-chain alkyldimethyl tertiary amines with chloroacetic acid :

$$R(CH_3)_2\,N + ClCH_2COOH \longrightarrow R(CH_3)_2N^{+}CH_2COO$$

There are several commercial producers of cocoamido-propylbetaine and other betaines. The betaines play an important role in the amphoterics market which in United States alone is currently around 12000 metric tons per annum.

Sarcosinates and Taurates

The sarcosinates and taurates are two fairly important groups of surfactant products with amino acid moieties in their structure. They were initially introduced by IG Farben.

The sarcosinates are condensation products of fatty acids with N-methyl glycine (sarcosine). They are manufactured from fatty acid chlorides and sodium sarcosine :

$$R—\overset{\overset{\displaystyle O}{||}}{C}—Cl + \overset{\overset{\displaystyle CH_3}{|}}{NH}—CH_2COONa \xrightarrow{-NaCl} R—\overset{\overset{\displaystyle O}{||}}{C}—\overset{\overset{\displaystyle CH_3}{|}}{N}—CH_2COONa$$

The alkyl groups in the sarcosinates are usually lauryl or oleyl, the former dominating. These products are anionic foam boosters and are used in hair conditioners and shampoos, rug shampoos, tooth paste, hand soaps and pharmaceuticals. They are also used in emulsion polymerisation and in window cleaning formulations. They are important as emulsifying agents for the removal of certain anti-corrosive agents on metal prior to their further processing.

The taurates, also referred to as taurides and N-acylmethyl taurates, are made in a manner similar to that of the sarcosinates with the reaction occurring between N-methyl taurine and fatty acid chlorides under a kaline conditions :

$$R{-}\overset{\overset{\displaystyle O}{||}}{C}{-}Cl + \overset{\overset{\displaystyle CH_3}{|}}{N}H{-}CH_2{-}CH_2{-}SO_3Na{-}R{-}\overset{\overset{\displaystyle O}{||}}{C}{-}\overset{\overset{\displaystyle CH_3}{|}}{N}{-}CH_2{-}CH_2{-}SO_3Na$$

Coconut oil fatty acids and oleic acid, again, are the preferred fatty feedstocks but in this case oleic acid is the preferred fatty acid. Both sodium and potassium salts prevail. The taurates combine the properties of soap (foaming power and emulsifying property) with those of the alkylaryl sulphonates (greater insensitivity of hard water). The taurates are particularly water-soluble. They are used as additives in all areas of cleaning materials and in cosmetics and Pharmaceuticals.

The global consumption of sarcosinates is of the order of 55 00-6000 metric tons per annum with the United States accounting for 60% of this volume. The global consumption of taurates is in the range 3500-4000 metric tons per annum, Japan being the major user.

TECHNOLOGIES FOR MANUFACTURE OF SURFACTANTS

Important Physico-chemical Characteristics of Surfactants

When one considers the impact of surface science in general, and emulsions, dispersions, foaming agents, wetting agents etc., in particular, on our day-to-day existence; one begins to realise the overwhelming extent to which these areas of chemistry and chemical technology permeate our lives. Although surfactant science and technology is a wide field, some specific aspects of these materials related to their application are highlighted in this section. These are:

(a) The HLB system
(b) Surfactant solubility and the Kraft temperature
(c) Emulsion stabilisation
(d) Foam stabilisation
(e) Wetting and related phenomena
(f) Dispersion.

The HLB system

Quantitative correlation of the chemical structure of surfactant molecules with surface activity to facilitate their choice in a given formulation, although has not been possible in respect of all their areas of applications, has to a large degree proved fertile in establishing such a criteria in the field of emulsions. The HLB of an emulsifier is an expression of its Hydrophile-Liphophile Balance (HLB) i.e., balance of the size and strength of the hydrophobic polar groups and the lipophilic nonpolar groups of the emulsifier. The HLB system developed by Griffin employed certain empirical formula to calculate the HLB number in a range of 0-20 on an arbitrary scale. Hydrophilic surfactants which possess high water solubility and generally act as good solubilising agents, detergents and stabilisers for oil in water (o/w) emulsions lie at the high end of this scale. Surfactants with low water solubility which act as

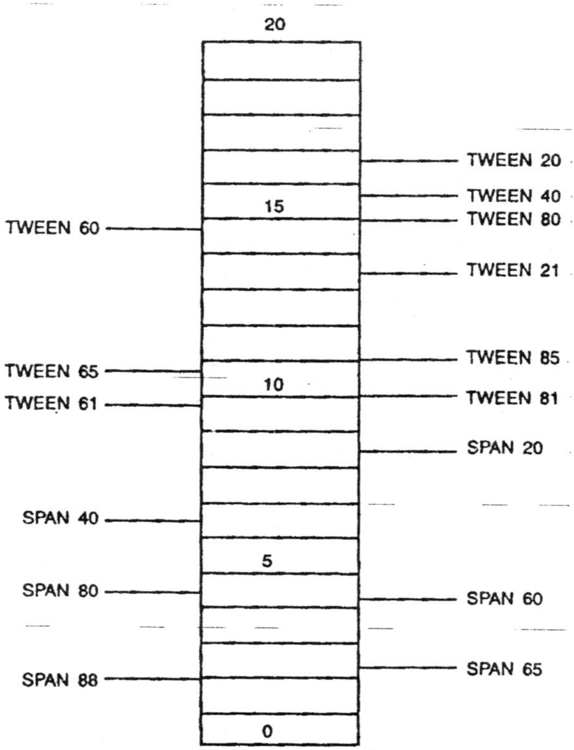

Fig. 9.8. HLB scale of typical atlas emulsifiers.

solubilisers of water in oils and good water in oil (w/o) emulsion stabilisers lie at the low end of the scale. The effectiveness of a given surfactant in stabilising a particular emulsion system would depend on the balance between the HLB values of the surfactant and the oil phase involved. For nonionic surfactants with polyoxyethylene (POE) solubilising groups, the HLB is calculated from the formula :

HLB = (mole per cent hydrophilic group)/S.

In this scheme an unsubstituted polyethylene glycol would have an HLB of 20.

Surfactants based on polyhydric alcohol fatty acid esters such as glycerol monostearate can be handled by the formula :

$$HLB = 20\ (1\text{-}S/A)$$

where S is the saponification number of the ester and A is the acid number of the acid. A typical surfactant of this type—Tween 20 (POE 20 sorbitan monolaurate) with S = 45.5 and A = 276—would have an HLB of 16.7. The HLB scale of typical ICI Tween and Span brand emulsifiers is given in Fig. 9.8. The HLB values for typical nonionic surfactant structures are given in Table 9.9. For materials which are not saponified an empirical formula of the type :

$$HLB = (E + P)/S$$

is employed. In the above formula, E is the weight per cent of oxyethylene chains, and P is the weight per cent of polyhydric alcohol.

Table 9.9. HLB value for typical nonionic surfactant structures.

Surfactant	HLB
PEG-4 dilaurate	7.4
PEG-4 dioleate	6.0
PEG-4 distearate	5.0
Sorbitan monolaurate	8.6
POE sorbitan tristearate	10.5
Glycerol monostearate	3.2
POE 4 - lauryl alcohol (BRIJ 30)	9.7
POE 2 - oleyl alcohol (BRIJ 92)	4.9
POE 100 - stearyl alcohol (BRIJ 700)	18.8

Con...

Surfactant	HLB
Sorbitan monooleate	4.6
POE 16 sorbitan tristearate	10.0
POE 8 stearate (MYRJ 45)	11.1
POE 40 stearate (MYRJ 52)	16.9
POE 12 tridecyl alcohol	14.5
POE 10 nonylphenol	13.3
POE 9 octylphenol	13.2
Sorbitan trioleate (SPAN 85)	1.8
Sorbitan monopalmitate (SPAN 40)	6.7
POE 5 stearic acid	9.2
POE 10 oleic acid	12.2
POE 20 sorbitan monolaurate (TWEEN 20)	16.7
POE 20 sorbitan monooleate (TWEEN 80)	15.0
Sorbitan tristearate	2.2
POE 20 sorbitan monooleate	15.0

The Griffin system while proving useful for surfactant formulations had its limitations. In surfactant systems of nonionic mixtures, emulsion stability tests, interfacial tension, gas liquid chromatography, cloud point determinations and phase inversion temperature (PIT) studies have shown that the HLB of the system does not bear a linear relationship as generally assumed by the equation :

$$HLB_{mix} = f_a\, HLB_a + (1\text{-}fa)\, HLB_b$$

where f_a is the weight fraction of surfactant A in the mixture. Several other approaches based on group contributions using group numbers given in Table 9.10 and the formula :

HLB = 7 + Σ (Hydrophilic group numbers) — Σ (Hydrophobic group numbers) and correlations involving Hildebrand solubility parameters and heat of hydration of the surfactant have been evolved.

Table 9.10. Group numbers for the calculation of HLB.

Group	HLB
Hydrophilic	
— SO_4Na	38.7
— COOK	21.1
— COONa	19.1
— N (tertiary amine)	9.4
ester (sorbitan ring)	6.8
ester (free)	2.4
— COOH	2.1
— OH (free)	1.9
— O	1.3
— OH (sorbitan)	0.5
Hydrophobic	
— CH	-0.475
— CH_2 —	-0.475
— CH_3—	-0.475
— CH—	-0.475
— CF_2—	-0.870
— CF_3 —	-0.870
Miscellaneous	
— (CH_2CH_2O) —	0.33
— $(CH_2CH_2CH_2O)$ —	0.15

Table 9.11. HLB ranges and numbers for several emulsion ingredients.

Application	HLB range
W/O emulsions	3-6
Wetting	7-9
O/W emulsions	9-18
Detergency	3-15
Solubilisation	15-18
Oil phase	*Normal HLB for O/W*
Lauric acid	16
Oleic acid	17
Cetyl alcohol •	14
Decyl alcohol	14
Benzene .	15

Con...

Application	HLB range
Castor oil	14
Kerosene	14
Lanolin	12
Beeswax	9
Carnaubawax	12
Paraffin wax	10
Chlorinated paraffin	8
Pine oil	16
Dimer acid	14
Mineral oil aromatic	12
Mineral oil paraffinic	10

However, in most general applications, HLB ranges and HLB numbers for several emulsion ingredients as given in Table 9.11 are commonly used.

The HLB numbers are most significant in the case of nonionic surfactants. In practice, as oils, waxes and solvents from various sources vary in properties and emulsifying characteristics, a formulator should make a series of trial emulsions with its ingredients using emulsifier combinations of known HLB value and establish the required HLB for this set of ingredients. Apart from knowing the right HLB it is also essential to identify the particular chemical type for maximum effectiveness. This is evident from the fact that an oleate type emulsifier is more suited for unsaturated oils and a stearate type emulsifier for saturated oils. Instead of using a single emulsifier, blends of emulsifiers give most stable emulsions. HLB values of some blended ICI surfactants are given in Table 9.12 and it can be noted that different blends can give the desired HLB. The emulsifier concentration and chemical type are important in attaining the emulsion stability. The importance of HLB can be judged from Table 9.12 which indicates the use of single or blended surfactants in specific industrial applications. While the formulae mentioned earlier for HLB calculation are satisfactory for many nonionic surfactants, those containing propylene oxide, butylene oxide, nitrogen and sulphur show anomalous behaviour. The HLB values of these, as well as ionics which do not follow the 'weight percentage' HLB basis, have to be determined experimentally which is often difficult and time consuming. A rough estimate of HLB in these cases can be made from the water solubility of the emulsifier or its dispersability characteristics on the following basis :

No dispersibility in water	HLB 1-4
Poor dispersion	HLB 3-6
Milky dispersion after vigorous agitation	HLB 6-8
Stable milky dispersion	HLB 8-10
Translucent to clear dispersion	HLB 10-13
Clear solution	HLB 13 and above

Surfactant solubility and the kraft temperature

The nature of surfactant molecules, having both hydrophilic and hydrophobic groups, is responsible for their tendency to concentrate at interfaces and thereby reduce the energy of the system in which they interact. The primary mechanism for energy reduction in most cases will be adsorption at various interfaces. However, when all available interfaces are saturated, the overall energy reduction may continue through other mechanisms. The physical manifestation of one such mechanism is the crystallisation or precipitation of the solute from solution. An alternative is the formation of molecular aggregates or 'micelles' that remain in "solution" as thermodynamically stable, dispersed species with properties distinct from those of the monomeric solution.

Table 9.12. HLB values of some blended surfactants.

Blends	HLB of blend composition						
	100/0	80/20	60/40	50/50	40/60	20/80	0/100
1. Span 20/Tween 20	8.6	10.2	11.8	12.6	13.4	15.1	16.7
2. Span 40/Tween 40	6.7	8.5	10.2	11.1	12.0	13.8	15.6
3. Span 60/Tween 60	4.7	6.7	8.8	9.8	10.8	12.9	14.8
4. Span 80/Tween 80	4.3	6.4	8.5	9.6	10.7	12.8	16.0
5. Brij 30/Brij 35	9.7	11.2	12.5	13.2	13.8	15.3	16.9
6. Brij 52/Brij 58	5.3	7.3	9.4	10.5	11.6	13.7	16.7
7. Brij 72/Brij 78	4.9	6.9	9.0	10.1	11.2	13.3	15.3
8. Brij 92/Brij 98	4.9	6.9	9.0	10.1	11.2	13.3	15.3

1—Laurate. 2—Palmitate, 3—Stearate. 4—Oleate. 5—POE lauryl alcohol, 6—FOE cetyl alcohol, 7—POE stearyl alcohol, 8—POE oleyl alcohol Span—Sorbitan fatty acid esters; Tween—POE sorbitan fatty acid esters; Brij—Polyoxyethylene alcohols.

For many ionic materials it is found that the overall solubility of the material in water increases as the temperature increases. That effect is the result of the physical characteristics of the solid phase, i.e., the crystal lattice energy and heat of hydration of the material being dissolved. In the case of ionic surfactants, it is often observed that the solubility of the material will undergo a sharp, discontinuous increase at some characteristic temperature, Tk, commonly referred as the Kraft temperature. Below Tk, solubility of the surfactant is determined by the crystal lattice energy and heat of hydration of the system. The concentration of the monomeric species in solution will be limited to some equilibrium value determined by those properties. Above Tk, solubility of the surfactant monomer increases to the point at which micelle formation begins and the aggregated species becomes the thermodynamically favoured form. The formation of micelles favours an increase in solubility. The concentration of surfactant monomer may increase or decrease slightly at higher concentrations (at a fixed temperature), but micelles will be the predominant form of surfactant present above a critical surfactant concentration. The total solubility of the surfactant, then, will depend not only on the solubility of the monomeric material, but also on the "solubility" of the micelles. A schematic representation of the temperature/solubility relationship for ionic surfactants is shown in Fig. 9.9.

The Kraft temperature of a number of common surfactant types show that Tk can vary as a function of both the nature of the hydrophobic group and the character of the ionic interactions between the surfactant and its counterion. Nonionic surfactants, however, do not exhibit a Kraft temperature, because of their different mechanism of solubilisation. They

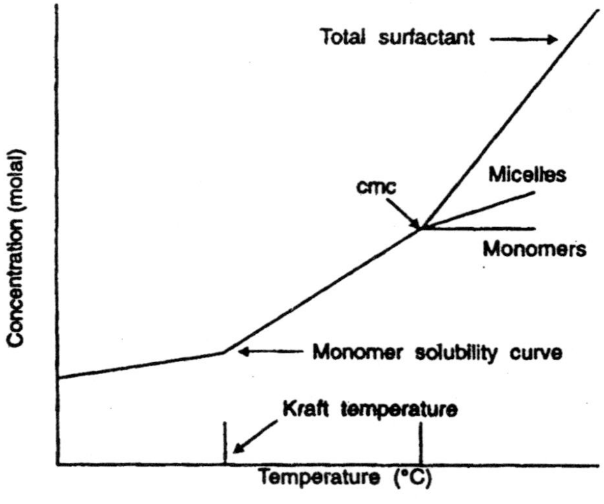

Fig. 9.9. Temperature/solubility relationship for typical ionic surfactants. Data are listed for nonionic surfactants.

do, however, have a characteristic temperature/solubility relationship with water in which they become less soluble as the temperature increases. In some cases phase separation and formation of a cloudy suspension results. This temperature is the 'cloud point'.

Emulsion stabilisation

Emulsions are used in a large number of applications namely, food, cosmetics, medicinals, agriculture, paints and numerous industrial processes. In most of these cases, the emulsion form is used because it represents a convenient means of achieving delivery of some active material to this site, at some convenient concentration and frequently at some convenient area of coverage or controlled rate of release.

An emulsion can be defined as a heterogeneous system consisting of at least one immiscible liquid dispersed in another in the form of droplets whose diameters in general exceed 0.1 mm. Such systems possess minimal stability, which may be accentuated by additives such as surfactants. An emulsion may be either oil-in-water (o/w) or water-in-oil (w/o), where the first phase mentioned is the dispersed phase and the second, the continuous phase.

The preparation of an emulsion requires the formation of a very large amount of interfacial area between two immiscible phases. The work (W) required to generate 1 cm^3 of a new interface is given by :

$$W = \gamma_i \Delta A$$

where γ_i; is the interfacial tension between the two liquid phases and AA is the change in interfacial area between the two immiscible phases. If the interfacial tension between oil and water is assumed to be 52 mv/m (as for a hydrocarbon liquid), the reversible work required to carry out the dispersion process will be of the order of 2×10^8 ergs. Since that amount of work remains in the system as potential energy, the system will obviously be thermodynamically unstable and will rapidly result in transformations like coalescence, creaming, breaking and flocculation to attain a minimum interfacial area. If some material can be added to the system to reduce the value of γ_i the magnitude of W will be substantially reduced. A true stable system should have γ_i (and hence W) equal to zero. However, thermodynamically this is not possible to achieve, and most useful emulsions achieve their stability by kinetic pathways which can play a dominant role over a short term.

In nature, as well as man-made technology, macromolecular emulsifiers and stabilisers play a major role in the preparation and stabilisation of materials. The major class or emulsifiers and stabilisers is that of monomeric surfactants that adsorb at interfaces and produce electrical, mechanical and steric barriers to drop coalescence, in addition to their role in lowering the interfacial free energy between the dispersed and continuous phases. Because of the role of the interfacial layer in emulsion stabilisation, it is often found that a mixture of surfactants with widely differing solubility parameters will produce emulsions with enhanced stability. In terms of HLB (0-20), at the high end of the scale lie hydrophilic surfactants which possess high water solubility and generally act as good solubilising agents, detergents and stabilisers for o/w emulsions. At the low end of the HLB scale are surfactants with low water solubility which act as solubilisers. The effectiveness of a good surfactant in stabilising a particular emulsion system will depend on the balance between the HLB values of the surfactant and the oil phase involved.

Recently, multiple emulsions of the type w/o or o/w have become of practical interest in controlled drug delivery, emergency drug overdose treatment, waste water treatment and separation technology. Such systems are more unstable than conventional emulsion systems and the choice of surfactants to stabilise these systems is complex.

The sensitivity of emulsions to temperature led to the suggestion that 'Phase Inversion Temperature' (PIT) be used as a possible method for emulsion preparation. It is generally found that the same circumstances that affect the solution characteristics of nonionic surfactants (their micelle size, critical micelle concentration, cloud point etc.) will also affect the PIT of emulsions prepared with the same materials. For typical ethylene oxide based nonionics, increasing the length of the polyoxyethylene chain will result in a higher PIT, as will a broadening of the polyoxyethylene chain length distribution. The use of PIT, therefore, represents a very useful tool for the comparative evaluation of emulsion stability. The effects of variables on the relationship between PIT, surfactant structures and emulsion stability have not been clearly defined in a quantitative way. However, it has been found that there is an almost linear correlation between the HLB of a surfactant under a given set of conditions and its PIT under the same circumstances. The process of selecting the best surfactant or surfactants for the preparation of an emulsion has been greatly simplified by the development of the more-or-less empirical approaches exemplified by the HLB and PIT methods. However, each method has its limitations and cannot eliminate the need for some amount of trial-and-error experimentation.

Foam stabilisation

Foams and emulsions have a great deal in common with regard to the basic physical principles controlling their stability. Their major differences lie in the natures of the dispersed phases, liquid or gas, and in the fact that foams will generally involve a much higher volume fraction of the dispersed phase than that encountered in emulsions.

Foams have wide technical importance in the fields of fire fighting, polymeric foamed insulation, foamed rubbers, foamed concrete, mineral separation and electroplating operations. They also have certain aesthetic utility in many detergent and personal care products. Unwanted foams may be a nuisance in sewage treatment, coating applications and crude oil processing.

A foam is produced by the introduction of air or other gas into a liquid phase, during which time the bubbles become encapsulated in a film of the liquid. The thin liquid film separating two or more gas bubbles is referred to as a lamellar film indicating that the film structure has two essentially identical interfaces in close proximity. The ability of a surfactant to perform as a foaming agent is dependent primarily on its effectiveness at reducing the surface tension of the solution, its diffusion characteristics, its properties with regard to disjoining pressures in thin films and the elastic properties it imparts to interfaces. The amount of foam that can be produced in a solution under given conditions will be related to the product of the surface tension and the new surface area generated during the foaming process.

Surfactants play a key role in foam formation, suppression as well as stabilisation. While all foams containing fluid phases are thermodynamically unstable, their degree of stability, commonly referred to as 'Resistance', can vary from seconds to weeks. More or less permanent foams can be produced in presence of extremely small amounts of surfactants. Maintenance of the foam is as important as its original formation. The static aspects of foam stability are related to the action of surfactant molecules and additives at the various interfaces in the system, while the dynamic characteristics are controlled primarily by the dilatational viscosity of the interfacial layers and the bulk rheological properties of the system. The choice of surfactant or surfactant formulations, therefore, must take these factors into account in the context of the system being prepared.

Wetting and related phenomena

The adsorption of surfactants onto a solid surface from solution is an important process in many situations such as detergency, waterproofing and dispersion stabilisation. In these and many other related applications of surfactants, the ability of the surface active molecule to situate itself at the solid-liquid interface and produce the desired effect is controlled by the chemical natures of the components of the system—the solid, the surfactant and the solvent. A similar role can be played by surfactants on essentially infinite surfaces related to wetting, spreading, adhesion and lubrication. Classically, there are three classes of wetting phenomena—adhesional wetting, spreading wetting and immersional wetting. The distinctions amongst these, although may seem subtle, are significant from a thermodynamic and phenomenological point of view.

It has been found that surfactants with symmetrically located internal head group substitution and ortho-substituted alkylbenzene sulphonates are better wetting agents than their straight-chain and para-substituted analogs. The enhanced wetting activity of the nonlinear materials is generally associated with their more compact structure, allowing for further diffusion to the solid-liquid interface and greater relative adsorption efficiency. The presence of additional polar groups in the molecule like ester and amide linkages or POE chains usually result in loss of wetting power. Nonionic surfactants such as polyoxyethylenated alcohols and fatty acids show lesser and lesser wetting power as the POE chain is increased. For a given hydrophobic chain length, the maximum in wetting power will occur for the POE chain length for which the cloud point lies just above the test temperature. As a rule POE nonionics with an effective hydrophobic chain length of 11 methylene units and POE chain length of 6 to 8 will exhibit optimal wetting power. In addition, POE alcohols and thioethers are generally found to be superior to equivalent POE fatty acids.

A number of external factors that can affect the wetting power of surfactants include temperature, electrolyte content, pH and the addition of polar organics and cosurfactants. An increase in solution temperature will generally reduce the wetting power of most ionic surfactants. Electrolytes that cause a reduction in surface tension of a surfactant in solution will produce improvements in wetting power. The addition of long-chain alcohols and nonionic cosurfactants increases the wetting properties of many nonionic surfactants. Solution pH becomes important to wetting characteristics when weakly acidic or basic groups are present in the surfactant molecule.

Wetting plays an important role in many technologically important processes, and an understanding of the part played by surfactants can go a long way towards solving the problem of choosing the proper surfactant for the job. Some of these areas are detergency and soil removal, enhanced oil recovery (EOR) and suspension of solids in liquids.

Dispersion

Dispersion is everywhere. Be it foods, pharmaceuticals, cosmetics, paints or printing inks and many such industries, no new products would have ten developed without dispersion, i.e., a process of reducing particles into a uniformly distributed submicron size and distributing them also uniformly in a suitable liquid medium. The paint industry represents a vital area where dispersion processes play a crucial role. Irrespective of quality and quantity of surface treatment received by pigment/extender powders, and no matter how favourable the resin molecular architecture is for dispersion, the wetting agents or surfactants are indispensable to achieve complete dispersion.

The range of surfactants available are so large that it is almost impossible for a paint technologist to choose the right surfactant or surfactant mix and its dosage for achieving dispersion for the given formulation at optimum cost with optimum energy and efficiency. While the role of surfactant in dispersion process is well conceived, its requirements are rigid. The interesting classes of surfactants giving high performance in dispersion process are:

(a) Chemical surfactants based on fluorine and silicon

(b) EO/PO polycondensates

(c) Surpynols (Acetylenic diol based surfactants)

(d) Polymeric hyperdispersants

(e) Innovative class of hyperbranched and dendrite structured surfactants

The evolution of various classes of surfactants became necessary as the dispersion of pigments in hi-tech resins posed problems. Epoxides, polyurethanes, polyesters and powder coatings do not offer ease of dispersion. Polymeric dispersants have been developed for sophisticated low molecular weight, low viscosity, high solid coatings. Unlike alkyds, for achieving dispersions in such difficult resins, dispersants must have anchoring groups with high functionality like carboxylic acids, sulfonic acids, amino acids, amine, pyridyl, acetyl etc. which will have strong bonding to the pigment surface and also soluble polymeric chains more or less identical to the main binder of the paint system. Dispersion has been a challenge to the paint industry from the beginning and this challenge persists with the emergence of new technologies.

Technologies

Technologies of major important to surfactant manufacture are :

(a) Sulphonation and sulphation

(b) Ethoxylation and propoxylation

(c) Esterification

(d) Condensation

10

Manufacture of Synthetic Detergents

The bulk of detergent materials are eventually converted into powders and cakes by one process or another. The problem in the production of powders is that all active detergent materials, with only a few exceptions, are not in themselves solids. It is, therefore, necessary to combine them with the builders and filling materials in such a way that the finished powder does not tend to cake or lump and remains dry to the touch. For each detergent raw material there is a limit of active material that can be incorporated into a powder, and the method of production of the powder also limits its active matter.

The principal methods of producing powders are :

(a) adsorption of a liquid detergent onto inorganic salts;

(b) simultaneous absorption and neutralization of a sulphonic acid by soda ash;

(c) dry-mixing of previously dried concentrated detergents with the other powder ingredients;

(d) spray-drying;

(e) drum-drying

Simple Absorption

If the detergent is available in the form of a water solution, containing not more than 40 per cent active matter (i.e. it is of relatively low viscosity), then 8 per cent active matter calculated on the final powder can easily be incorporated, and with special manipulation, up to 12 per cent can be achieved. If the detergent is in a more concentrated form, for example, a non-ionic detergent, which is usually available in 100 per cent concentration, 5 per cent active matter is usually the practical limit.

The plant required for this method is any one of the conventional bladed powder mixers available, such as ribbon mixers, plough mixers, screw mixers, crutchers etc.

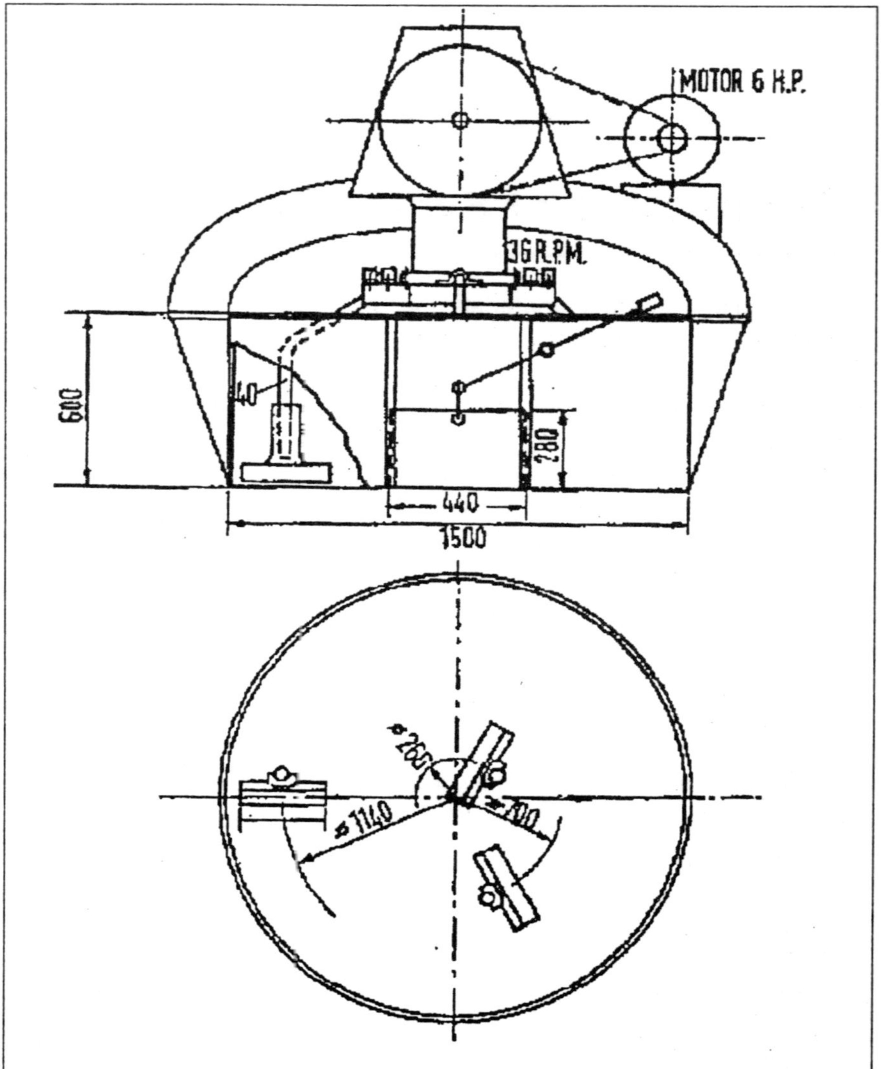

Fig. 10.1 : Bladed power mixer

In these methods, anhydrous inorganic salts, which can be hydrated, are used, and on the addition of the detergent solution the salts are partially hydrated and the active matter is dispersed with this water of crystallization. It is essential that the detergent solution be of very low viscosity and that it contain more water than active matter.

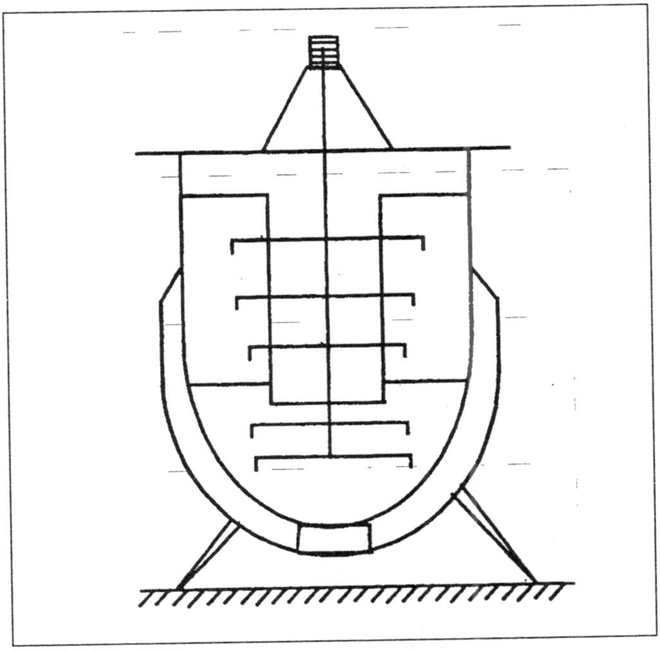

Fig. 10.2 : Soap crutcher.

However, if low concentrations of active matter are to be incorporated, this condition need not necessarily be fulfilled. In this case, the detergent is merely absorbed on to the surface of the inorganic material. To obtain the higher concentrations of active matter, it is necessary for the formula to contain a large proportion of soda ash, as it can theoretically absorb as water of crystallization 170 per cent of its weight of water. The same effect can be achieved by the use of borax. either in the anhydrous or pentahydrate forms. Borax is, more expensive than soda ash but has two added advantages in that it is a better builder and can also to a certain extent eliminate stickiness.

As mentioned above, if a 40 per cent active-matter solution is used, 8 per cent active matter can easily be incorporated. If, the vessel is steam jacketed, or if the mixing blades are hollow and can be steam-heated, powders containing up to 11 per cent active matter can be produced.

The method of producing powders is to charge a mixer with the dry ingredients, start the mixing, and to pump (or pour) the solution through a jet into the powder slowly while mixing. The rate of addition of the liquid

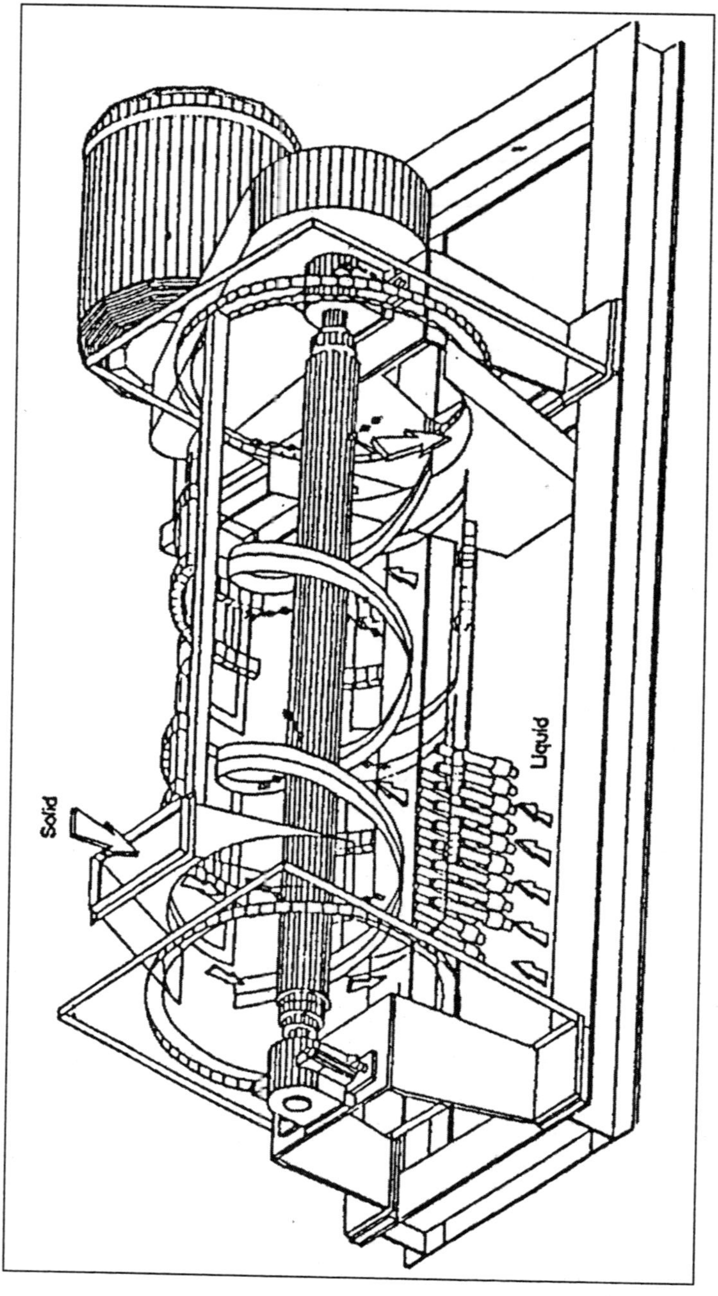

Fig. 10.3 : Blender normally used for manufacturing high density detergent powder.

must be adjusted so that the liquid is absorbed as it reaches the surface of the powder; if not, hard crystalline lumps will be formed.

After all the liquid has been added, mixing is continued for at least 15 minutes and the powder is discharged on to a concrete floor to age for 12-24 hours. If the total amount of liquid is small (not more than 5 per cent) this ageing can be dispensed with, but in general the ageing serves the purpose of allowing the crystals to form and cool.

By these methods a free-flowing powder, free from lumps is be obtained. If any of the\original dry ingredients contained an appreciable amount of lumps, it will be necessary to pass the power through a hammer mill or cage mill after ageing. This grinding can be obviated by charging the powders into the mixer through a 60-mesh sieve. In this case, the lumps are screened out and can by themselves be milled to recover for use in future batches.

Combined Absorption of Neutralisation

The method of neutralization and absorption is more versatile than that of simple absorption. The process depends on the utilization of an unneutralized linear alkyl benzene sulphonic acid, and neutralizing it with soda ash which has previously been dry mixed with all the other dry ingredients of the formula. It is immaterial whether this sulphonic acid is of the 90 per cent or 100 per cent types. It should be pointed out that if material other than 100 per cent sulphonic acid is being used, precautions against iron pick-up must be taken in storage and transport.

By this method there is obviously no lower limit to the amount of active material that can be incorporated into the powder. The upper limit of active matter is generally 20 per cent, but it is possible to achieve as much as 24 per cent.

The plant required are plough mixers, ribbon mixers and screw mixers, but in this case no heating arrangements are required. Although, theoretically, the powder produced by this process should not need to be ground, in practice a better appearance is obtained if the finished powder is passed through a hammer or cage mill. If perborate is to be added, the powder after manufacture can be mixed with perborate and enzymes if required.

The method of manufacture is as simple as that for the absorption process. The dry materials are charged into the mixing vessel and the mixer started. The sulphonic acid is now poured in slowly while the mixer is running. If 90 per cent sulphonic acid is being used, the acid immediately reacts with the soda ash present to form the sodium salt, and the sulphonic acid should be run in at such a rate that no large unabsorbed excess of the acid is allowed to form. If 100 per cent sulphonic acid, which is more inert, is being used, it will not react so easily with the soda ash, and it can be added fairly fast and the mixer will merely disperse the acid. When the sulphonic acid has been well dispersed, i.e. when there is a uniform brownish-blue discolouration of the powder, 2 per cent of water, based on the final weight of powder, is added. This water renders the sulphonic acid reactive and almost immediately the powder will assume a light-yellow colour without any dark lumps of sulphonic acid. The sodium silicate can now be added, followed by the optical brightener, if the formulation calls for it.

In this reaction of alkyl benzene sulphonic acid with soda ash, no carbon dioxide is liberated, as in every case the formulation is arranged so that at least double the amount of soda ash is present over the stoichiometric amount and the reaction proceeds only as far as :

$$C_6H_4C_{12}H_{25}SO_3H + Na_2CO_3 = C_6H_4C_{12}H_{25}SO_3Na + NaHCO_3$$

Therefore, only one sodium atom of the two in the soda ash is utilized to form the sodium salt of the sulphonic acid and the soda ash is converted to sodium bicarbonate. If this were not the case, the evolution of carbon dioxide would cause the mixture to overflow the vessel. For this reason, when the 100 per cent type of sulphonic acid is used, it is necessary to disperse the acid well, so that no local concentrations are formed before the water is added.

Once the reaction is completed, which in practice should not take more than 30 minutes for a 300-500 kg. batch, the powder is discharged onto a concrete floor and allowed to age overnight. After the ageing period, the powder is fed into a hammer or cage mill to break up any lumps and is then ready for packing.

Powders made by this process will have a cream to light-yellow colour, the exact shade depending on the colour of the sulphonic acid used. If a whiter powder is required, this can be achieved by bleaching it with sodium hypochlorite. When 100 per cent sulphonic acid is used, a 10 per cent solution of sodium hypochlorite is employed instead of the water, and when 90 per cent sulphonic is being used, the sodium hypochlorite is added thus :

The mixer is charged with all the powdered ingredients, except the optical brightening agent, and the mixing started. As soon as the powders are uniformly dispersed, the sulphonic acid (either 90 per cent or 100 per cent) is added. When the sulphonic acid has been well mixed in, the sodium hypochlorite solution, calculated at the rate of 2 per cent on the final weight of powder, is added. This will help to disperse the sulphonic acid, trigger the reaction with the soda ash and simultaneously bleach the powder. The silicate of soda is added after the bleaching is completed.

When sodium hypochlorite is used for bleaching of powders, the optical brightening agents should not be added to the mixing vessel immediately after the neutralization, as the hypochlorite will attack the dyestuff. If perborate is to be added to the powder, the optical brightener can be incorporated simultaneously with the perborate. If the perborate is not to be added, after the reaction of the sodium hypochlorite has ended, the powder can be quantitatively checked for active chlorine. If this test is negative, the optical brightener can then safely be added. If this test is positive, 50 g. of an 'anti-chlor' (sodium thiosulphate, sodium sulphite or sodium bi-sulphite)/300 kg. batch of powder are added, the mixing continued for 3-5 min. and then the optical brightener can be added with safety. The qualitative test for chlorine could even be dispensed with and the anti-chlor added as a routine, but one must stress that the anti-chlor can only be added after the powder has been bleached to the required shade, as otherwise it will interrupt the bleaching reaction.

Sodium perborate, if called for in the formulation, cannot be added prior to the ageing or grinding (unless one of the modern powder mixers is used) whether sodium hypochlorite is used or not. If sodium hypochlorite is not used, the perborate will start decomposing when the powder is damp, prior to ageing, if it is introduced initially into the mixing vessel, or it will start decomposing in the hammer mill as a result of the heat of friction in the grinding process. If sodium hypochlorite is used, the hypochlorite and perborate (peroxide) ions are mutually incompatible (so much so that perborate can be used as a rather expensive form of anti-chlor if nothing else is available. Sodium perborate can only be added after the ageing and grinding processes by reintroducing the powder into the mixer and adding the requisite amount of perborate. It is preferable to make use of a separate simple powder mixer for this operation.

The active ingredient by this process need not necessarily be only alkyl benzene sulphonic acid, but this can be mixed with any other active material desired to give special properties. These other materials can be non-ionics of the ethylene oxide condensate type, alkylolamides (the preferred types being lauric acid monoethanolamide or monoisopropanolamide) and even fatty acids to form a soap *in situ.* If the material to be mixed with the sulphonic acid is a solid at room temperature, it should be warmed by about 10°C above its melting point, then added to the sulphonic acid immediately before the addition to the powders. By this method the reaction of the sulphonic acid with the soda ash causes the fatty acid, if used, to be saponified completely and eliminates the need for the pre-saponification of fats or fatty acids prior to their incorporation into powders of this sort. To obtain this 'auto-saponification' the fatty acid should be of the distilled grade with a minimum of 1½ per cent neutral oil (triglyceride) or unsaponifiable matter present. If neutral oil is present it will not be saponified under these conditions and will tend to make the powder stick if present in too large quantities.

It is often required to dye powders to a colour other than white. This can be done by dissolving a water-soluble dye in the water naturally being added to the powder or to disperse with the powders finely divided lakes or pigments, e.g. Monstral blue, In general, if a light coloured sulphonic acid is used, it will not be necessary to bleach the powder prior to dyeing so that no complication about the use of sodium hypochlorite need arise. However, if the combination of the neutral colour of the sulphonic acid and the colour of the dye or pigment produces a 'muddy' appearance, it is necessary to bleach the powder before adding the colouring matter, to give a bright colour. Inorganic pigments are, in general, not affected by sodium hypochlorite, but lakes can be, so again it is necessary to treat the lake in the same way as the optical brightener when sodium hypochlorite is used.

Perfume is generally added to household powders. If sodium hypochlorite is not used, the desired amount of perfume can be sprayed into the powder towards the end of the mixing process. Sodium hypochlorite can destroy perfume material; so, if the powder is being bleached, it is advisable to add the perfume in the same manner as the optical brightener.

On occasion it is required to manufacture powders containing more than the practical limit of 20 per cent active matter. This is achieved by the use of highly absorptive special silica. This silica will tend to absorb onto its surface all the stickiness that a high active matter will cause. The powder is manufactured in the normal way as described above without the addition of the silica and when completed prior to its being discharged for ageing 1-2 per cent silica is added. The actual amount is dependent on the actual formulation and can be as low as ½ per cent and should rarely exceed 2 per cent.

Some formulations and procedures using both 100 per cent and 90 per cent alkyl benzene sulphonic acids are given below. It should be pointed out that 100 per cent sulphonic acid never contains 100 per cent of the acid. The term 100 per cent means 100 parts of the sulphonic acid when neutralized to the sodium salt will yield between 99 and 101 parts of active matter. Similarly, for 90 per cent sulphonic acid, 100 parts of the acid will yield 90 parts of active matter after neutralization to the sodium salt. These two figures, however, are very variable. One hundred per cent sulphonic acidimade by the sulphonation of alkyl benzene with SO_3 gas does not usually deviate seriously from the practical limits, but for acid or oleum sulphonated material, unless special precautions are taken with the separation of the spent acid, the available active matter very rarely exceeds 88 per cent.

This process can be used to manufacture a cheap, heavy duty household powder:

Charge and mix together	100% sulphonic acid	90% sulphonic acid
Light soda ash	58	58
C.M.C. (66% active)	2	2
Sodium tripolyphosphate	15	15
then add with mixing		
LAS	18	20
followed by		
Water and	2	—
Sodium silicate (40% solution)	5	5

The powder is now discharged on to the floor to age and on the following day is passed through a hammer mill. In practice, several batches can be prepared on the first day and all of these can be combined prior to milling. After milling, the powder is weighed into the some (for another) mixer and sodium perborate and the optical brightening agent are added in the following proportions :

Milled powder	89.9
Sodium perborate	10.0
Optical brightening agent	0.1

This is mixed only for a few minutes and is then ready for packing.

If linear alkyl benzene sulphonic acid is used, the addition of toluene sulphonate and/or colloidal silica will obviate stickiness.

For a whiter powder than that produced by this method the water is replaced by sodium hypochlorite solution containing 10 per cent available chlorine. The formula then becomes :

White Households Heavy-day Washing Powder

	100% sulphonic acid	90% sulphonic acid
Light soda ash	58	57
C.M.C. .	2	2
Sodium tripolyphosphate	15	15
LAS	18	20
Sodium hypochlorite solution	2	2
Sodium silicate (40% solution)	5	—
Sodium silicate (54% solution)	—	5

Dry Mixing of Powders

Concentrated spray-dried or drum-dried detergent powders, containing at least 40 per cent active matter, often more than 60 per cent, are available. They are merely blended with the other required ingredients, in a powder mixer, dry blender or similar equipment.

If it is desired to preserve as far as possible the characteristics of a spray dried powder, this can be achieved by using spray dried sodium tripolyphosphate in addition to the spray dried detergent concentrate. In this way more than half of the ingredients are already of the spray dried type. When mixing the ingredients care must be taken to avoid (as far as possible) physical breakage of the beads; a cube mixer is eminently suitable for this purpose.

As this is a dry mixing process, it is not advisable to incorporate silicate solutions into the powder. Finely divided, partially hydrated colloidal silicates are available or sodium metasilicate can be used if the high alkalinity will not adversely affect the final properties of the powder. Alternatively, some concentrated detergent powders are available with sodium silicate already included in the beads.

Spray Drying of Powders

The vast majority of household detergent powders are manufactured by the spray-drying process, because spray-dried powders have many advantages over the other types. However, spray drying is expensive and cannot be considered for SSI.

The bulk of household powders are perfumed. Perfume can be added in two ways, either as a powder (concentrated powdered perfumes are available for this purpose) in which case the powder is treated like perborate or enzymes.

The choice of the perfume for detergent powders is important and the following points should be borne in mind:

(a) The type of perfume. Perfumes have both an immediate and residual odour and both need to be considered.

(b) Whether the contents of the powder will adversely affect the perfume on storage.

(c) The volatility of the perfume under the particular conditions of packaging and storage.

(d) Whether the perfume will leave a residual smell on the washing. This is not always a requirement but account must be taken of this possibility.

Liquid Detergents

Liquid detergents can be made from a variety of starting materials, but in every case the plant is the same. A vessel equipped with a slow speed stirrer is all that is required and the stirrer should be positioned so that it is well under the surface of the liquid, so as not to cause foaming. It is, however, necessary that the vessel be of a non-corrodible material. Stainless steel is satisfactory, but expensive; concrete or asbestoscement vessels are eminently suitable, and so are wooden vessels where wood is a cheap article of commerce.

The choice of active ingredient depends on the requirements of the finished liquid, but here particularly, the versatility of alkyl benzene sulphonic acid is of particular value. Other anionic raw materials are available as the already neutralized salt, with or without the presence, whether incidental or not, of various non-detergent materials.

Light-duty liquid detergents can be based on alkyl benzene sulphonic acid, alcohol sulphates, non-ionics as such, or sulphate non-ionics, or amphoteric detergents, or combinations of two or more of these materials.

Except when sulphonic acids are used, all the other components are available as concentrated (from 40 -100 per cent) neutralized material which needs only to be diluted down to the required activity. With sulphonic acid, however, the manufacturer has the choice of varying his neutralizing agent to give his liquid any property he wants, from a low viscosity to a thixotropic gel.

If non-ionics of the ethylene oxide condensation type are being used in liquid detergents, either alone or in combination, it should be borne in mind that this type of material has a peculiar cloud point, in that it forms a cloudy solution when the temperature is raised and not (as is usually the case) when the temperature is lowered. It is thus important that products should be tested extensively, taking into account the highest possible temperature that the liquid may encounter on storage.

Heavy duty liquids are coming more and more into use and require special formulation techniques. The problem here is to incorporate into the liquid active matter, sequestering agents, silicates, anti-redeposition and optical brightening agents. To achieve all this and to retain the finished material as a clear liquid with a low cloud point is not easy. If at a moderately high temperature the liquid 'clouds', it is an indication that separation into at least two phases is taking place and each phase will contain different proportions of each of the ingredients.

This problem is best overcome by producing the heavy-duty liquid as a lotion or gel, but this must be formulated so that it will not separate into two phases at the higher ambient temperature to which it may be subjected.

Toilet Preparations

As hair shampoos, shaving creams and bath preparations are all basically detergents, more and more detergent manufacturers are manufacturing either ready-made cosmetic preparation of this type or a concentrate for supply to the cosmetic manufacturer. The alcohol and ether sulphates have proved themselves over the years to be dermatologically safe for this type of preparation.

For hair shampoos the choice depends on the desired physical form of the product. For a cream the sodium salt of one of the fatty alcohol sulphates is recommended. For a liquid an ether sulphate is used or else an ethanolamine salt of a fatty alcohol sulphate. The latter has the disadvantage in that it cannot normally be obtained with as light a colour as the ether sulphate and it also foams less, but this can be enhanced by the use of a foam booster. The pearlescent type of shampoo can use as a base either an ether sulphate or sodium salt of the alcohol sulphate.

In addition to the well-tried sulphated alcohols and ethers, more and more use is being made of the amphoteric detergents (Miranol) as either a portion or all of the active ingredient in shampoos etc. If they are used as the sole ingredient an additional advantage is that cationic detergents can be incorporated as bactericides.

Perfumes used in shampoos should all be dermatologically tested and in addition preservatives used to be added as fungi and yeasts grow in detergent solutions. All formulations should be made up to include perfume, dyes and preservatives and subjected to extensive storage tests as no hard and fast rule can be laid down for the interaction of the micro constituents. Furthermore, it is best to add a small portion of a chelating agent (¼ per cent or so) as traces of iron may have an adverse effect on dyes in storage.

Some basic formulae for shampoos are given below :

1. Cream Shampoo

Sodium fatty alcohol (C_{12-14}) sulphate (50% paste)	25
Coconut monoethanolamide	2
Thickening agent	1
Sodium chloride	2
Chelating agent	0.25
Perfume, dye, preservative	q.s.
Water	to 100

The thickening agent is predissolved or dispersed in a portion of the water in accordance with the manufacturer's instructions. The sodium chloride is added to increase the viscosity if desired.

2. Liquid Shampoo

Sodium ether sulphate (C_{12-14}, 2 E.O.) (100% basis)	12.5
Thickening agent	q.s.
Sodium chloride	2
Perfume, dye, preservative	q.s.
Chelating agent	0.25
Water	to 100

The thickening agent is added as required because hard and fast rules cannot be given as very often the concentrated ether sulphate contains ethyl alcohol or propylene glycol both of which drastically lower the viscosity.

3. Liquid Shampoo

Triethanolamine fatty alcohol sulphate (40% concentrate)	35
Coconut diethanolamide	3
Chelating agent	0.25
Perfume, dye, preservative	q.s.
Water	to 100

In place of the triethanolamine salt, the monoethanolamine neutralized fatty alcohol sulphate can be used. This will give a higher viscosity.

A pearlescent effect can be obtained by adding to the paste ethylene glycol stearate, diethylene glycol stearate, polyethylene glycol stearate, magnesium stearate or myristic diethanolamide.

4. Pearlescent Shampoo

Sodium fatty alcohol sulphate (50% concentrate)	25
Coconut monoethalamide	2
Ethylene glycol stearate	1
Chelating agent	0.25
Perfume, dye, preservatives	q.s.
Water	to 100

The alcohol sulphate, the glycol stearate, the monoe-thanolamide and the water are charged into the vessel and warmed with gentle stirring until a clear solution free disperse particles is obtained. This is then cooled to 50°C and the other ingredients added and passed to packing. When cold the pearlescence will have developed.

5. Bubble Bath Preparation

Sodium ether sulphate (100% basis)	20
Triethanolamine fatty alcohol sulphate (100% basis)	8
Chelating agent	0.25
Perfume, dye, preservative	q.s.
Water	to 100

PASTE DETERGENTS

In certain parts of the world detergents are used in a finished or semifinished form as pastes of varying concentrations. Certain detergent raw materials are sold as pastes: for example, the sodium salt of lauryl alcohol sulphate in a concentrated form without any addition of inorganic fillers.

The detergent manufacturer who wishes to manufacture a paste can do so very easily from alkyl benzene sulphonic acid, again either from the 100 per cent or 90 per cent varieties, depending on which is available to him. Production of a snow-white paste from 90 per cent sulphonic acid can only be achieved if the acid is neutralized immediately after sulphonation, and not stored. The 100 per cent sulphonic acid can produce a snow-white paste even though stored for many months.

The manufacture of the paste can be done in a soap crutcher, or in a specially built neutralizer, equipped with a cooling jacket as shown in fig. 10.4. The neutralizing vessel should preferably be built of stainless steel, but if precautions are taken so that the pH of the paste does not fall below 7 during the process of manufacture, a mild-steel vessel can be used.

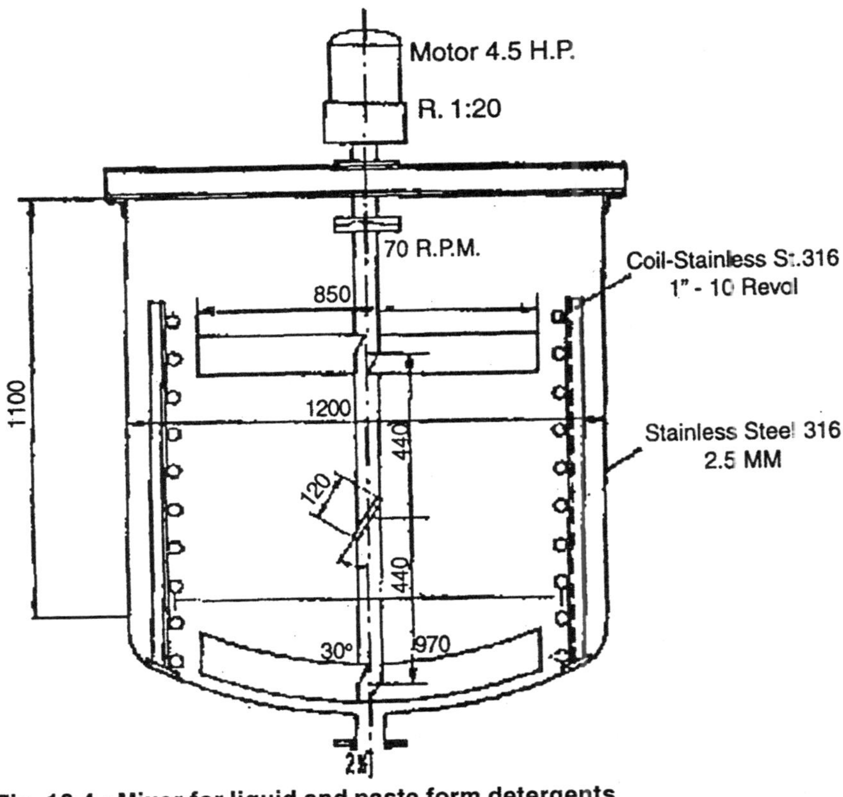

Fig. 10.4 : Mixer for liquid and paste form detergents

Because sodium alkyl benzene sulphonates are not completely miscible with water, various materials must be used to prevent separation into two phases. This can be done by the use of hydrotropes, small proportions of C.M.C. or alkylolamides. However, hydrotropes will tend to produce thinner pastes and this will mean adding inorganic salts to make them stiffer again, depending, of course, on the requirements of the market.

These inorganic salts can be sodium chloride, sodium sulphate, tetra sodium pyrophosphate or sodium silicate solution, or a combination of these. To achieve a stiff paste, it is very rarely necessary to add more than 3 per cent in total. Sodium chloride is the cheapest and gives the greatest stiffening effect, but is corrosive to iron or steel. Sodium sulphate and tetrasodium pyrophosphate suffer from the disadvantage that in cold weather they might crystallize out from the paste into needle-like crystals, while both the tetra sodium pyrophosphate and the sodium silicate raise the pH of the paste, but add to the detergency. The high pH can be regulated by using some of the sulphonic acid to neutralize a portion of the alkalinity of these two materials. Neutralization is done in this instance by caustic soda only, the amount required depending on its acid value. The acid value will vary not only with the average molecular weight of the alkyl benzene but also with the method of manufacture (i.e. oleum, sulphuric acid or SO_3) and finally according to the individual manufacturer.

For this reason although the acid value is usually expressed as the amount of milligrams of caustic potash required to neutralize 1 gm. of acid is better to consider the acid value as the number of grams of caustic soda required to neutralize 100 gm. of acid. This can readily be calculated from the internationally accepted acid value by the formula:

Acid value in gm. NaOH/100 gm. acid =

$$\frac{\text{Acid value in mgm. KOH/gm. acid}}{14}$$

The method of manufacture depends on whether a stainless steel or mild steel vessel is being used.

If C.M.C. is to be included in the formulation, it is necessary to dissolve it separately. If a separate mixing vessel with a slow speed stirrer is available, water to the amount of ten times the weight of the C.M.C. is charged into the container and the C.M.C. poured in slowly with stirring. The stirring is continued until all the lumps of C.M.C. are dispersed, concurrently with the process of the manufacture of the paste.

If a mixing vessel is not available, the solution can be made in the same way in a 45 gal. drum and the C.M.C. added while stirring with a hand crutcher. This dispersion is best prepared the day before it is required and left to swell and dissolve by itself overnight.

The C.M.C. dispersion, if in contact with iron or steel, will tend to corrode the vessel and also will become discoloured by the rust formed. It is therefore essential to produce this dispersion in a non-corrodible vessel — stainless steel, asbestos cement or steel clad with plastic or rubber. The stirrer itself should also be noncorrodible.

If a mild steel neutralizing vessel is being used for the manufacture of the paste, all the remaining water called for in the formula (all the water if no C.M.C. is to be added) and the requisite amount of caustic soda solution, with organic salts if they are to be used, are run into the vessel. Mixing and cooling is started and the sulphonic acid added at such a rate that the temperature does not rise above 65°C (If 100 per cent acid is used the heat of reaction is low and the temperature will not rise very high, provided that an efficient cooling coil or jacket is available. If 90 per cent acid is used, the heat of reaction is considerably higher and the rate of addition of the sulphonic acid must be adjusted).

When about 80 per cent of the sulphonic acid has been taken up and the paste is still distinctly alkaline, the requisite amount of sodium hypochlorite solution is added and mixed in. The balance of the sulphonic acid is now added, taking care that the pH of the paste does not fall below 7. Mixing is continued until the paste is uniform and the C.M.C. solution (if called for) is added, or, if an alkylolamide is to be used, this can now be put in. If a hydro trope is employed, this can be added with the sulphonic acid.

When a stainless steel neutralizing vessel is being used, the procedure is similar, except that the sodium hypochlorite can be put in at the beginning with the water and caustic soda and no special precautions need be taken about not passing to the acid pH. If an acid pH is reached, the desired pH of 7.5 - 8 can be achieved by the addition of a litre or two of caustic soda solution.

A slight variation of this paste procedure occurs when a highly concentrated liquid is required. This is done by neutralizing the sulphonic acid with an ethanolamine.

In this instance, the requisite water (which depends on the final concentration desired) and the ethanolamine are charged into the vessel.

The sulphonic acid is added slowly with intermittent stirring so as not to generate foam. The reaction is instantaneous. The only precautions that need be observed are to avoid the production of foam and to keep the temperature from rising above 60°C.

Cake detergents are usually manufactured in three forms for the following different application:

(a) toilet cakes;

(b) household scrubbing;

(c) 'one-shot' addition to washing machines

(a) Detergent toilet cakes

The manufacture of a detergent toilet bar comparable with soap is fraught with many difficulties, and is the subject of many patent applications throughout the world. Not many of these patents have been successfully exploited commercially for technological or economic reasons, or both. A few toilet detergent bars have been put on the market, but not all of them have captured the sales that the manufacturers had hoped for.

One hundred per cent of detergent active matter is considerably more expensive than 100 per cent soap. This does not matter when detergents in liquid or powder form are being marketed, as 20-25 per cent active matter in a well-made powder can compete very favourably with a 40 - 60 per cent fatty acid soap powder. To be sold in the same price range as soap a detergent bar cannot have much more than 40 per cent active matter. If only 40 per cent active matter can be used the mass needs to be filled to 100 per cent with relatively inexpensive materials and this causes the problem. The use of soluble inorganic salts is precluded because the cake will be heavy compared to soap and will tend to effloresce. Talc, although not efflorescent, will again make the cake extremely heavy and hard to the feel.

A detergent used as a soap will tend to defat the skin overmuch and 'superfating' or retarding agents need to be incorporated into the bar.

One of the big disadvantages to overcome is the behaviour of a detergent tablet when wet compared to a soap tablet. When soap is wetted, water is absorbed over the whole surface of the soap and the viscosity of the water soap mixture drops dramatically and then increases with further dilution to form the viscous 'middle soap'. Thus when a wet tablet of soap is placed in a soap dish this viscous middle phase prevents water from penetrating into the tablet and the soap remains dry inside, the outside surface gradually drying out by evaporation. This middle phase does not occur with detergents and therefore the water in a wet detergent tablet under the same conditions will penetrate right to the centre of the mass, making it soft and slimy.

For all that, synthetic toilet tablets have one very big advantage in that because of the chemistry of synthetic detergents they do not make a scum or leave a ring in the bath tub. A toilet detergent tablet should therefore not be readily soluble or should not disintegrate, and should have the feel of soap when wet; it should lather freely and when stored should not crack or effloresce. Finally, it should be possible to work the mass in normal soap-milling and stamping machinery.

The bulk of these problems have been overcome by the use of a soap detergents mixture, but although this improves the detergency of the cake it does not do away with the disadvantages of soap.

There are a few detergent cakes on the market and these are based on sulphonated monoglycerides, fatty alcohol sulphates and sulphated fatty acids. To these active raw materials are added plasticizers such as fatty alcohols, the phosphate and phthalate esters, and polymrized ethylene glycols and binders such as starch and take.

Manufacture is the subject of many patents and trade secrets, but the process consists of using raw material in as nearly an anhydrous form as is possible to maintain, melting it with plasticizers, adding the binders, and then milling, plodding and stamping in the normal soap making machinery

Household Detergent Cakes

Historically, in this field again the first attempts were based on a detergent which had been available as a water solution. Binding the water was done with materials such as bentonite and sodium stearate, i.e. soap produced *in situ.* Because the starting material contained at least as much water as active matter, the final bar or cake contained the same ratio of water to active detergent matter. This limited the amount active matter added, the more water appeared in the final product. Nowadays a bar of this type can be manufactured at any concentration desired by the use of alkyl benzene sulphonic acids.

The sulphonic acid is mixed with the dry ingredients in a dough-mixer (a plough-mixer such as that suggested for the manufacture of powders is also suitable provided that the arms and motor are strong enough to withstand the resistance of the material) and the neutralizing agent is either soda ash or a concentrated caustic soda solution. If caustic soda is used, a percentage of water is automatically added to the material, but the final product can be controlled to have a neutral pH. Although a neutral pH is not essentially, as it would be for bars meant for toilet use, nevertheless the bar will still come into contact with the hands, and must not be too alkaline. The pH can be lowered by having a large amount of bicarbonate in the formula or by the addition of sodium acid pyrophosphate after the neutralization has been completed.

After neutralization, and the addition of any special ingredients, the mass is allowed to age. This ageing process varies with the formulation and further manipulation. If a bar of high active-matter content (60 per cent or so) is being made, the mass should be aged for at least 12 hours. If a low active matter material (40 per cent) is being manufactured, the mass can be transferred to the next stage immediately. In fact, it is not advisable to allow it to age, as it will set hard and become unworkable. (If by any chance a low active-matter bar has set hard before it can be worked, it is possible to regenerate the plasticity by warming it to 50 - 60°C in a soap drying room).

Low active concentration bars or tablets are not recommended because they are both inefficient and uneconomical in use. However, in certain of the emergent countries it is considered that the unit cost of a bar might be too high if it contains the normal amount of active matter. This is a false consideration because the filling materials as well as the extra manipulations involved all cost money. For all that, bars of 25 per cent active matter or less are being produced.

To make bars of this type filling materials need to be used. Plain water cannot be used alone as this will make the bar too soft. If inorganic salts alone are used the bars become heavy, hard and unattractive in appearance and are also subject to efflorescence on storage. These problems can be partially overcome in various ways.

Paraffin wax at the rate of 2 per cent can be added. The wax needs to be melted separately and poured on the mass while mixing, before the temperature has fallen to 60°C. The addition of the paraffin wax gives a better feel to the tablet and to a certain extent hinders the defatting action of the detergent on the human skin. This skin-protecting action can be enhanced by using a blend of paraffin wax and polyethylene wax. In this instance the polyethylene wax (which has a melting point of the order of 100°C) needs to be dissolved in the molten paraffin wax. Surprisingly enough, this addition of waxes in no way detracts from the detergency of the bar or tablet.

Another method is to use 5 per cent starch and to include in the basic formula a total of 15 per cent water. After the reaction is completed, the starch is added and the mass heated to a minimum of 80°C to solubilize the starch.

Finally, a combination of both the above methods can be used and also on occasion talc is added to improve the feel of the tablets.

After the requisite ageing period, the mass is passed through a soap mill. In certain factories this milling is dispensed with and the aged mass is fed directly into a plodder. However, the appearance and texture of the finished product is definitely inferior if it is not passed through a mill.

If the mass is to be milled, the ageing period can be shorted, as it is desirable to feed the mass into the mill while it is still very plastic. If no milling is to be done, the mass should be less plastic. In some factories the mass is allowed to set hard and then chipped in a soap-chipper and then passed into a mill or direct into the plodder.

After milling, the chips are fed into a plodder and extruded into the required shape, cut on soap-cutting tables and then stamped.

There is also a different approach to the manufacture of synthetic laundry bars (and also to a lesser extent toilet cakes). The method is to compact the ingredients (in a dry form) in a special tablet forming press to give a synthetic tablet directly from powder.

'One-shot' Tablets for Washing Machines

Tablets of this sort are usually manufactured high in active matter and fillers and with the minimum of inert builder. The size is adjusted so that one tablet is sufficient for a washing machine taking an average amount of clothing for wash. The tablets should be fabricated so that they both disintegrate and dissolve quickly in water so that valuable washing time is not lost while they are dissolving. They can be made by pressing in a tableting machine similar to that used for the manufacture of pharmaceutical tablets, or by plodding a plastic mass. To increase their speed of solubility they are made with binders that readily dissolve on contact with water. Polyethylene glycols or polyvinyl alcohols can be used as binders, or a small amount of any crystalline acid or acid salt, such as citric acid or sodium bisulphate, can be incorporated into the tablets dry with an equivalent amount of sodium bicarbonate. On contact with water the acid and bicarbonate generate CO_2 which disintegrates the tablet into small particles which will then dissolve more readily.

If a water soluble binder is employed, the material is made as for laundry bars, using soda ash for neutralizing, and the binder is added in a water solution.

If the acid-soda system of disintegration is to be used, the materials are dry mixed, using as a base a concentrated spray-dried powder of LAS. If of a concentration of over 60 per cent active matter, this powder has sufficient neutral tackiness to bind the tablets if pressed in a tablet press.

Spray-dried heavy duty household hand-washing powder

Sodium alkyl benzene sulphonate (or equivalent)	25
Sodium tripolyphosphate	15
Tetra sodium pyrophosphate	10
C.M.C. (66% basis)	2.5
Sodium metasilicate (anhydrous)	15
Optical brightening agent	0.2
Sodium sulphate	32.7

and to this powder after spray-drying add sodium perborate at the rate of

Spray-dried powder	90
Sodium perborate	10

Heavy duty fully automatic washing machine powder

Non-ionic detergent (low foaming)	10
Sodium tripolyphosphate	20
Tetrasodium pyrophosphate	10
C.M.C. (66% basis)	1.5
Sodium metasilicate (anhydrous basis)	10
Optical brightening agent	0.2
Sodium sulphate (can be partially replaced by soda ash)	43.7

Low-foaming machine powder for soft water areas

Mix together with warming to 45°C

A.	LAS (100 per cent)	11.6
	Distilled tallow fatty acid	6.4

In the powder-mixer, mix together

	Sodium tripolyphosphate	10
	Tetra sodium pyrophosphate	5
B.	Soda ash light	55
	C.M.C. (66 % basis)	2

When uniform, add A with mixing. When the LAS tallow fatty acid mixture has been dispersed, add immediately in order

Sodium hypochlorite	2
Sodium silicate 40 per cent	8

This is mixed for a few minutes until the reaction is seen to have been completed, and then discharged for ageing. Next day the powder is ground and recharged to the mixer in the following proportions :

Milled powder from above	90
Sodium perborate	10
Optical brightening agent	0.15

and mixed until uniform and then sent to packing.

To manufacture the same formula using ready made soap powder the formulation is :

Low-foaming machine powder for soft water areas using ready-made soap powder

Mix together :

Sodium tripolyphosphate	10
Tetra sodium pyrophosphate	5
Soda ash light	53.7
C.M.C. (66% basis)	2

and add in order

LAS (100%)	11.4
Sodium hypochlorite	2
Sodium silicate	8

and when the reaction is completed add:

High titre soap powder 82 % fatty acids	7.7

Thereafter process as in above.

The same powder can of course be made by spray-drying.

Spray dried household low-foaming laundry powders

	A	B
Sodium dodecylbenzene sulphonate (100% basis)	15	7
Tallow soap, soda based (100% basis)	10	5
Low foaming non-ionic detergent	—	7
Sodium tripolyphosphate	15	15
Tetrasodium pyrophosphate (optional, can be completely replaced by sodium tripolyphosphate)	10	10
Sodium silicate (anhydrous basis, ratio 1:2.5)		
C.M.C. (66% basis)	2.5	2.5
Optical brightening agent	0.2	0.2
Soda ash	0-20	0-20
Sodium sulphate	to make	100

Sodium perborate is added at the rate of 10 per cent (or more if desired) after drying.

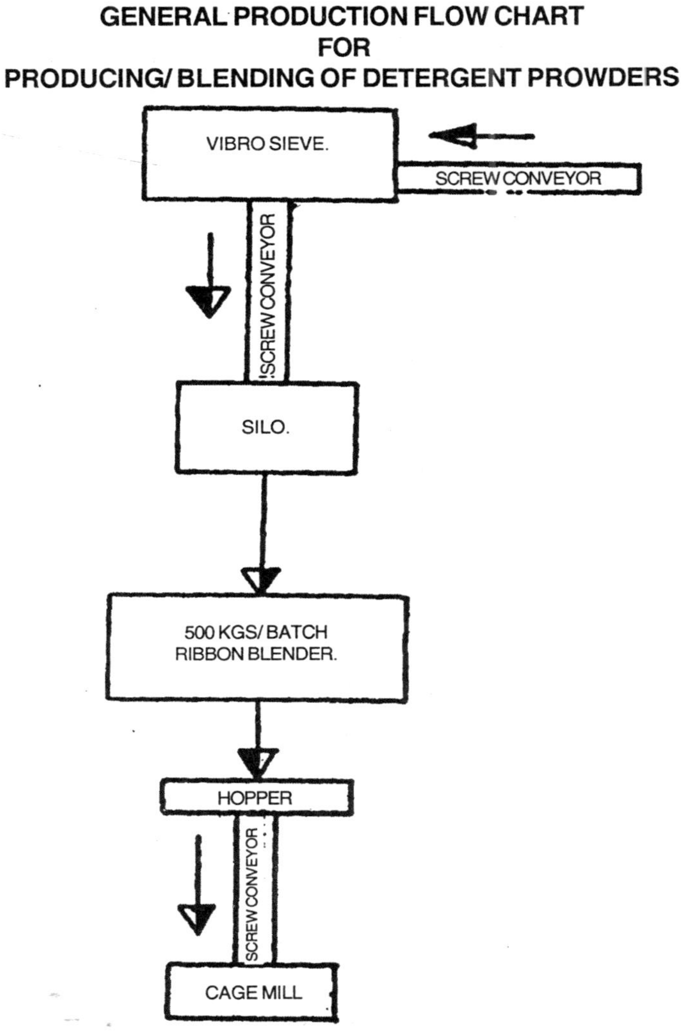

Fig. 10.1. General production flow chart for producing/blending of detergent powders.

LAYOUT BOX DIAGRAM FOR POWDER PLANT

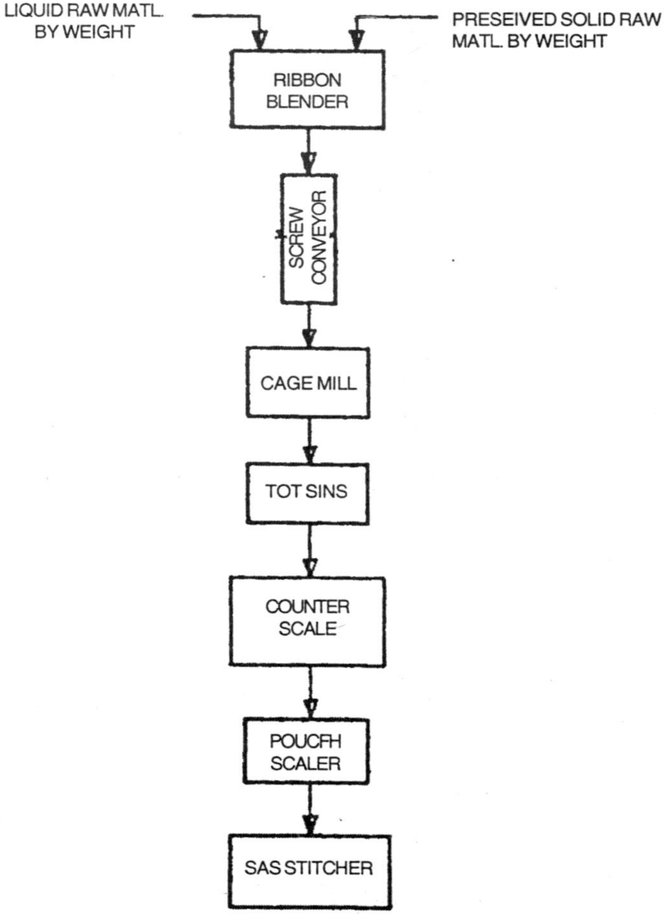

Fig. 10.2. Layout box diagram for powder plant

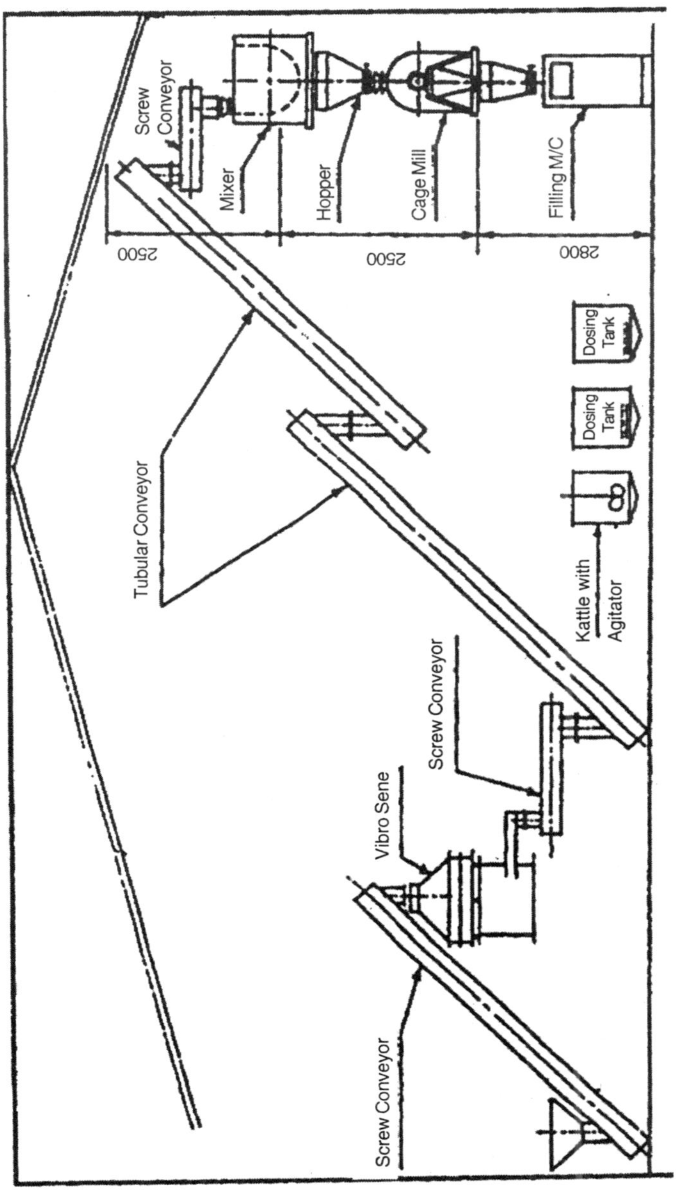

Fig. 10.3. Elevation plan of compact detergent powder

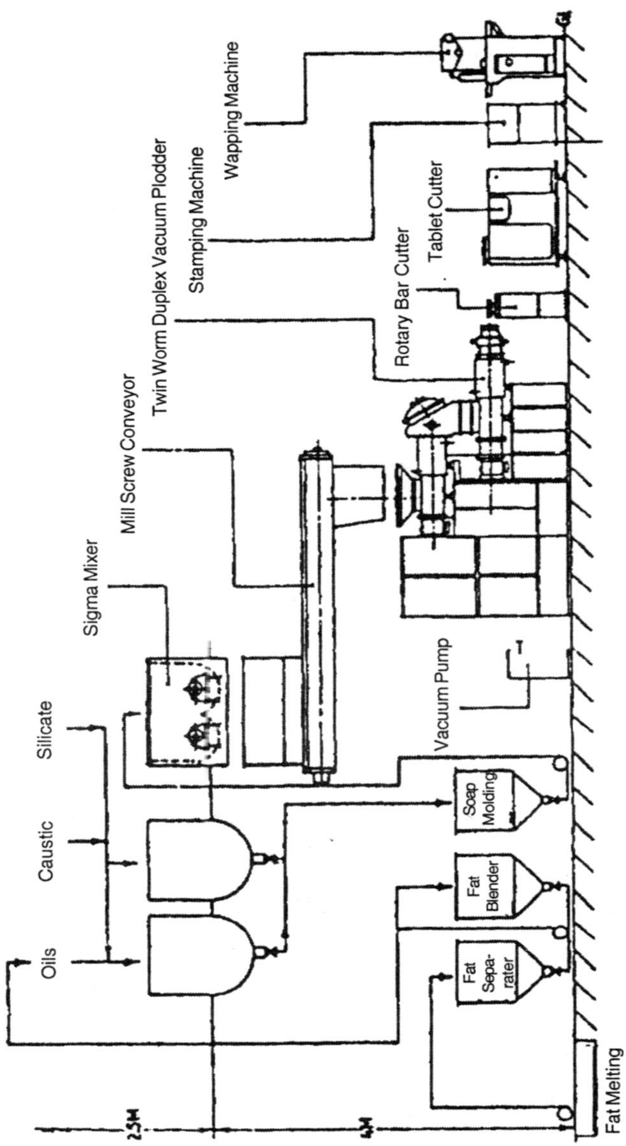

Fig. 10.4. Laundry soap (crutcher route) plant

11

Detergent Soap and Additives

ALKYL ARYL SULPHONATE

(Dodecyl Benzene Sulphonic acid)

CAS NO.

27176-87-0

MOLECULAR FORMULA

$C_{18}H_{30}O_3S$

PROPERTIES

A synthetic anionic detergent containing a minimum of 40% sodium alkyl aryl sulphonate approximately, 2% moisture, 1% unsulphonated oil and the balance sodium sulphate.

Physical Form	—	Amber, Reddish - amber, Reddish brown, brown coloured viscous liquid with characteristic SO_3 odour.
Density	—	8.7 to 8.84 lb/gal.
Specific gravity	—	1 to 1.06
Viscosity	—	100 Cps to 20,000 Cps.
Flash Point	—	> 200 °F
Acid No	—	180 to 182
pH of 1% solution	—	1.6
Stability	—	Good in hard and soft water, strong alkalis and strong acids. Stable to acids and alkalis.
Solubility	—	Soluble in oil and water.

MANUFACTURING PROCESS

From Dodecyl Benzene and Sulphuric Acid

Dodecyl benzene sulphonic acid (acid - slurry) is manufactured by the sulphonation of linear chain alkyl benzene with a mixture of sulphuric acid and oleum at controlled temperature.

Raw Material

Basis	—	1 Ton dodecyl benzene sulphonic acid (85% sulphonic acid).
Dodecyl benzene	—	725 Kg.
Sulphuric acid (98%)	—	1000 Kg.
Oleum (22%)	—	130 Kg.

Charge dodecyl benzene to the reactor, add mixture of oleum and sulphuric acid slowly to the reactor. Maintain the reaction at 55 - 66 °C for four hours and stir for further two hours at 60-65 °C for digestion. Transfer the product to a lead lined separator. In the separator, dilute the mass with ice cold water to bring down the spent-acid concentration to 75% at 55 to 60 °C. Allow the product to settle in separator by gravity. Settling time varies from 8 to 16 hours. Remove the bottom layer of spent acid and collect top layer of dodecyl benzene. The active content is 85 to 90%. Yield will be 1.45 times of dodecyl benzene.

REACTION

$$C_6H_5C_{12}H_{25} + H_2SO_4 \longrightarrow C_{12}H_{25}C_6H_4\,SO_3H + H_2O$$

FLOW DIAGRAM

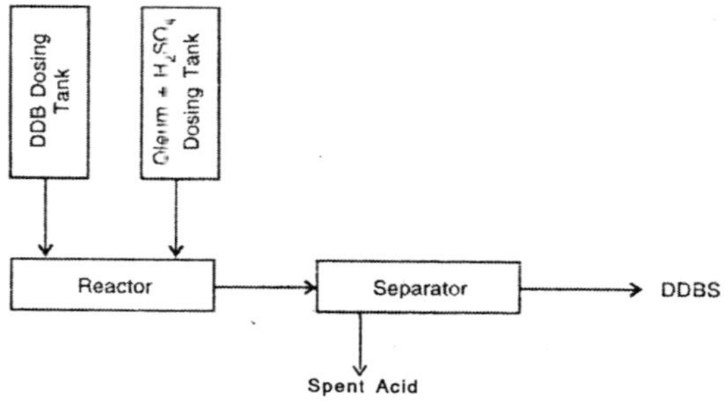

Note

In continous process, carry out the sulphonation in a scrapped surface heat exchanger reactor (votator). Inject oleum into an alkylate stream at several points along the rotating scraper - shaft. As the result of immediate interphase contact, the reaction will be 90% complete within 30 seconds at 27°C. Complete the reaction in digester and dilute the mass with water. Remove the spent acid.

Useful Data

Three important classes of synthetic detergents are

(a) anionics

(b) nonionics

(c) cationics

The anionics are by far the most important class of synthetic detergents and represent 80 per cent of production. Two thirds of these anionics are classified as alkyl aryl sulphonates. Another 10 per cent of the anionics are the fatty alcohol sulphates, example - sodium lauryl sulphate. The next most important class of surfaceactive agents 20 per cent of production are the nonionics, which do not ionize in water. Advantages are compatibility with either anionic or cationic types, marked stability, and the nonfoaming characteristics of some members. Typical nonionics are polyoxyethylene derivatives of fatty acids, amides, or amines. The cationic surface active agents are less in use example: quarternary ammonium salts. Synthetic detergents are usually marketed as a mixture with builders, such as sodium tripolyphosphate, and diluents such as sodium sulphate. Household detergents may also contain various additives such as sodium carboxymethyl cellulose to prevent soil redeposition, and an optical whitner.

USES

It is used as household detergent & industrial detergent.

GRADES

Alkyl aryl sulphonates are usually marketed as blends with a diluent or additives. Percentage active ingredient varies from 15 to 98 per cent. Common grades are 30,40,65, 85 and 96 per cent in the form of flakes, beads, powder, granules, paste and liquid.

TOXICITY

Moderately toxic by ingestion. When heated to decomposition it emits toxic fumes of sulphur trioxide. Corrosive, skin and eye irritant.

DETERGENT

A detergent is a formulation comprising essential constituents (surface active agents) and subsidiary constituents (builders, boosters, fillers and auxiliaries).

Typical Properties of Linear Alkyl Benzene, produced by the Pacol Process

Bromine no.	0.02
Saybolt colour	+30
Alkyl benzene content	97.4%
Doctor test	Negative
Unsulphonatable matter	1.0%
Water 0.1%	
Special gravity 15°C	0.8612
Refractive index	1.4837 at 20 °C
Flash Point	138 °C
Average molecular weight	240
Distillation range °C	
IBP	281
50 vol %	290
EP	309
2-Phenyl isomer	20%
Biodegradability	95%

MANUFACTURING PROCESS

Detergents are very complex mixtures of many substances, all chosen to impart a particular action in cleaning.

By Sulphonating Linear Alkybenzene

The most widely used detergent is a heavy-duty granule.

Raw material requirements

Synthetic Detergent Granules	—	1 ton basis
Linear Alkylbenzene	—	70 Kg.
Fatty alcohol (from tallow)	—	70 Kg.
Oleum	—	140 Kg.
Sodium Hydroxide solution	—	200 Kg.
Corrosion inhibitor Sodium silicate	—	120 Kg.
Builder		
Sodium tripolyphosphate	—	500 Kg.
Miscellaneous additive	—	30 Kg.
Water	—	500 Lit.

The sulphonation conversion is extremely fast.

Introduce LAB continuously into the sulphonator with the requisite amount of oleum, maintain the temperature at 130°F. Add fatty tallow alcohol and more oleum and maintain temperature at 120 to 130 ° F. Neutralise the sulphonated-sulphated product with NaOH solution under control temperature to maintain fluidity of the surfactant slurry.

The surfactant slurry can be mixed with following compounds.

Suds Regulators

A suds regulator either a stabilizer or suppressor is often used with a surfactant. Example of stabilizer surfactant systems are lauric ethanolamide-alkylbenzene sulphonate and lauryl alcohol-alkyl sulphate. Suds suppressors are generally hydrophobic materials, some examples of which are long - chain fatty acids, silicones, and hydrophobic nonionic surfactants.

Builders

Builders boost detergent power, and complex phosphates, such as sodium, tripolyphosphate, have been used most extensively. These are more than water softeners which sequester water-hardening calcium and magnesium ions. Polyphosphates (e.g., sodium tripolyphosphate and tetrasodium pyrophosphate) have a synergistic action with the surfactant and hence reduce the overall cost, together with an enhanced effectiveness.

Surfactants, such regulators, and detergency builders make up the basic surfactant detergent formulation, however, small amounts of additives are necessary (3% or less).

Additives

Corrosion inhibitors, such as sodium silicate, protect metal and washer parts, utensils, and dishes from the action of detergents and water. Carboxymethyl cellulose has been used as an antiredepositton agent. Tarnish inhibitors carry on the work of the corrosion inhibitor and extend protection to metals. Fabric brighteners are fluorscent dyes which make fabrics look brighter because of their ability to convert ultraviolet light to visible light.

After mixing surfactant slurry with above compounds, take into the crutoner, remove excess water and spray under high pressure to get heavy duty granule. Separate granules in cyclone, screen and perfume. Perfume has become an accepted ingredient, and compositions & fragrances vary widely.

Note

(1) The sulphonation conversion is extremely fast. The use of oleum in both cases reduces the sodium sulphate in the finished product. However, the oleum increases the importance of control to prevent oversulphonation.

(2) The most significant development in the detergent industry in recent years is the addition of enzymes to household washing powders. Enzymes are of many types and sub-types, but the three which are of interest to the detergent industry are :

Proteases which act on protein to form amino acids;
Amylases which convert starches into dextrins;
Lipases which attack fats and oils.

Enzymes are sensitive materials and the base powder had several a prior conditions. The moisture content of the powder had to be below 5 per cent, the pH of the powder was best between 8 and 9.5, and no oxidizing agents could be included.

REACTION

Linear alkylbenzene sulphonation

1. Main reaction

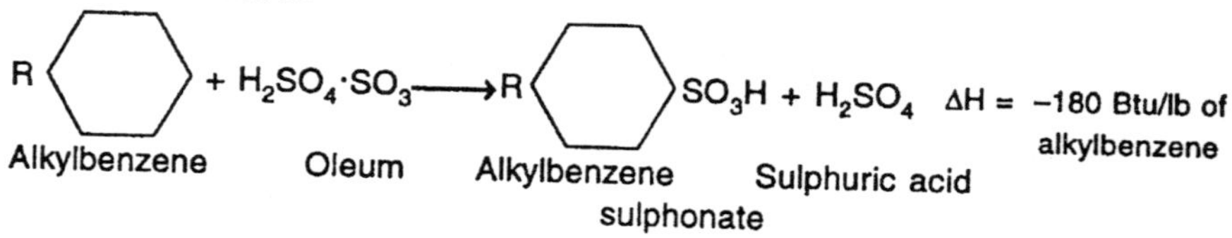

2. Secondary reaction

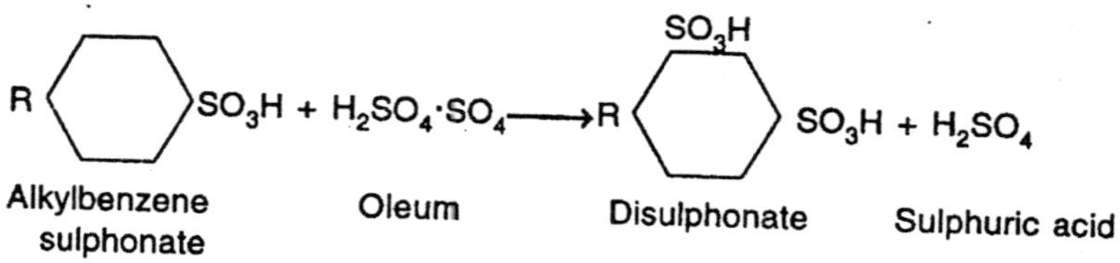

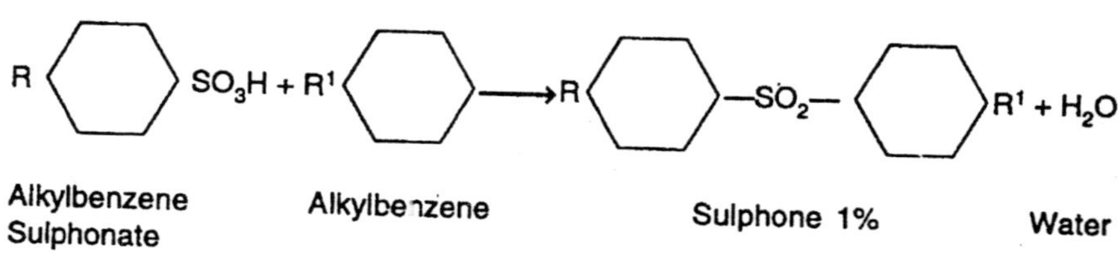

FLOW DIAGRAM

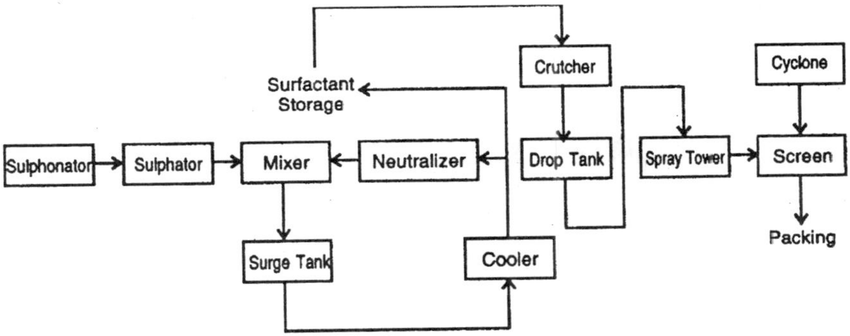

12

PLANT ECONOMICS OF LIQUID SOAP

Rated Plant Capacity	6000.00 Kgs./Annum
Land & Building (Area 500 Sq. Mt.)	Rs. 16,45,000.00
Plant & Machinery	Rs. 4,60,000.00
Working Capital for 1 Month	Rs. 2,30,490.00
Total Capital Investment	Rs. 24,80,490.00
Rate of Return	**46.51 %**

PLANT & MACHINERY

1. Reaction Kettle with open top. Jacketes with agitator arrangements Madeofmild steel,epoxycoted.caplton
2. Storage Tank
3. Filter Press with Accessories
4. Baby Boiler
5. Pump set
6. Automatic weighing filling and sealing machine

13

PLANT ECONOMICS OF NEROL LAUNDRY SOAP

Rated Plant Capacity	300.00 MT/Annum
Land & Building (Area 500 Sq.mts.)	Rs. 22,50,000.00
Plant & Machinery	Rs. 2,41,000.00
Working Capital for 3 Months	Rs. 20,94,390.00
Total Capital Investment	Rs. 46,67,390.00
Rate of Return	27.00%

PLANT S MACHINERY

1. Cauldron for Mixing, Cooking at various stages.
2. Moulds.
3. Coal Fired open hearths.
4. Automatic Soap Cake Cutting Machine
5. Soap Stamping Machine.
6. Miscellaneous viz. Weighing Slabe
7. Testing Equipment, Fire Fighting

14

PLANT ECONOMICS OF WASHING AND LAUNDRY SOAP

Rated Plant Capacity	1500000 BARS OF 200 GM./YR.
Land & Building (Area 1250 Sq.Mtrs)	Rs.36,50,000.00
Plant & Machinery	Rs. 3,18,500.00
Working Capital for 1 Month	Rs. 9,51,673.00
Total Capital Investment	Rs.50,21,123.00
Rate of Return	87.52 %

PLANT & MACHINERY

1. WASHING SOAP:
2. Iron pan for oil heating jacketed with steam coil
3. Iron pan for dissolving caustic soda
3. Iron pan for mixing various ingredients (equipped with weighing unit)
4. Kettle for preparing washing soap
5. Baby Boiler
6. Soap cutting machine
7. Soap Stamping machine
8. Soap dies and moulds (wooden)
9. LAUNDRY SOAP:
   Amalgamator (with mixing sys.-5 H.P motor (made of AISI 316 St.Steel.)
10. Milling machine equipped with 3 rolls
11. Twin Worm duplex Vacuum machine (Bitra-slab type) with 5 H.P. Motor
12. Vertical cooling tunnel (TRV-Duplo type)
13. Wrapping machine
14. Miscellaneous

15

PLANT ECONOMICS OF TOILET SOAP FROM SOAP NOODLES

Rated Plant Capacity	600000.00 Kg
Land & Building Area 600 sq.mt.	Rs. 18,00,000.00
Plant & Machinery	Rs. 31,78,500.00
Working Capital for 1 Month	Rs. 15,86,026.00
Total Capital Investment	Rs. 67,74,526.00
Rate of Return	50.03 %

PLANT S MACHINERY

1. Sigma Mixer
2. Hopper made
3. 150 mm Twin Worm Simplex Plodder
4. Roll Mill
5. Belt Conveyer Roll Mill to Plodder
6. 200 mm Twin worm Duplex Plodder
7. Automatic Soap Stamping Machine
8. Bar Cutter
9. Automatic Size Cutting Machine
10. Pedal Stamping Machine
11. Misc. Tools, Jigs, "fixture etc.

16

PLANT ECONOMICS OF BAR SOAP

Rated Plant Capacity	300000.00 KGS Annum
Land & Building (Area 2000 Sq.Mtrs)	Rs. 52,97,500.00
Plant & Machinery	Rs. 72,22,950.00
Working Capital for 1 Month	Rs.1,39,22,880.00
Total Capital Investment	Rs.2,82,43,330.00
Rate of Return	79.58%

PLANT & MACHINERY

1. MACHINERY TO PRODUCE TOILET SAOP (FROM SOAP NOODLES) (COMPLETE FINAL SOAP
2. Soap mixer (sigma type) with heavy duty "ZS" reduction gear box system electric motor
3. electric panel board, all standard accessories,etc.
4. Heavy duty noodler (simplex) plodder complete with reduction gear box systems
5. and electric motor,electric panel board, all standard accessories,etc
6. First soap three roller machine with reduction gear box system, water circulating device (etc.)

17

PLANT ECONOMICS OF WASHING SOAP

Rated Plant Capacity	300.00 MT Annum
Land & Building (Area 500 Sq.Mtrs)	Rs. 14,75,000.00
Plant & Machinery	Rs. 1,87,900.00
Working Capital for 1 Month	Rs. 5,54,500.00
Total Capital Investment	Rs. 23,22,400.00
Rate of Return	48.76 %

PLANT S MACHINERY

1. Iron Pans
2. Iron Moulds
3. Tanks (tanki)
4. Manual Mixer mixing
5. Manual Mixer
6. Cutting M/C.
7. Misc. jigs, tools, fixtures, etc.

18

PLANT ECONOMICS FOR DETERGENT CAKE & POWDER

Rated Plant Capacity	12000.00 MT/Annum
Land & Building (Area 6000 sq.mtrs)	Rs. 2,41,00,000.00
Plant & Machinery	Rs. 35,00,000.00
Working Capital for 2 Months	Rs. 3,44,57,688.00
Total Capital Investment	Rs. 6,54,67,688.00
Rate of Return	83.79 %

PLANT AND MACHINERY

1. Detergent Cake mixture (M.s.)
2. Automatic Plodder Machine (10"size)
3. Automatic Cutting Machine
4. Automatic Stamping Press
5. Conveyor Systems 1 Lot
6. Tripple roll mill size (6" x 18"),
7. Automatic Wrapping and Sealing Machine with all accessories
8. Pipes, fittings, Pumps, Valves, Structures and Others
9. Laboratory Equipments
10. Weighing Balance (Plat Form)
11. D.P. Mixture Ribbon blender
12. Automatic Weighing, Filling and Pouch Sealing Machine for 1 kg. 1/2 kg size pouches.

19

PLANT ECONOMICS OF DETERGENT POWDER

Land & Building (Area 1500 sq. rnts.)	Rs. 39,50,000.00
Plant & Machinery	Rs. 22,50,000.00
Working Capital for 1 Month	Rs. 51,25,900.00
Total Capital Investment	Rs. 1,19,25,900.00
Rate of Return	73 %

PLANT AND MACHINERY

1. Mixing machine with sigma blade motor
2. Weighing scale plat form type
3. Bucket elevator
4. Automatic sieving machine
5. Automatic weighing, filling, sealing pouch packing machine
6. Laboratory testing equipment
7. Miscellaneous equipment, fittings
8. Conveyer Belt

ALL FOLLOWING PROJECT REPORTS ARE READILY AVAILABLE

AUTOMOBILES, MECHANICAL, STEEL & IRON & METALLURGICAL

- Agricultral Equipments
- Aac & Acsr Aluminium Conductors (All Aluminium Conductors)
- Agricultral Equipments Including Threshers
- Air Brake Helical Coil
- Air Cooler
- Air Filters (For Scooter Car & Excavators Etc.)
- Aluminium & Aluminium Alloys From Aluminium Scrap To Make Utensils (Induction Furnace Melted)
- Aluminium Alloy Wheels
- Aluminium Alloys From Aluminium Scrap To Make Utensils (Induction Furnace)
- Aluminium Hot & Cold Rolling Mill
- Aluminium Conductors
- Aluminium Bottle Manufacturing (Cold Extrusion Of Aluminium)
- Aluminium/Copper Cable Lugs
- Aluminium Cans For Beer Pkgs.
- Aluminium Cans For Capacitors
- Aluminium Caps For Injection Vials
- Aluminium Extrusion
- Aluminium Furniture & Hardware
- Aluminium Sheet Rolling Mill
- Alloy Steel Casting (Foundry)
- Aluminium Utensils
- Aluminium Utensils & Schooi Boxes
- Aluminium Wire Drawing And Super Enamelling For Winding
- Anodised Aluminium Utensils
- Anodizing Of Aluminium
- Antimony Oxide From Lead Scrap
- Anti Scale Compound For Adding In Sugar Boilers
- Arc Welding Filter Glass
- Aluminium Foil Cutting & Roll Making
- Auto Flaps For Trucks & Buses
- Automobile Workshop (Garage & Service Centre)
- Auto Bulb
- Auto Electrical Parts (Armature)
- Auto Gears
- Auto Horns
- Auto Leaf Spring
- Auto Tubes
- Auto Piston Ring
- Auto Piston
- Auto Parts (Electricla And Electronic)
- Auto Rubber Parts And Turned Components Silent Block Bush And Ceiling Fan Shaft+
- Auto Wire Outer (Outer For Auto Wire)
- Bakery And Biscuits Equipments Fabrication
- Ball Point Pen Refills
- Ball Roller & Taper Bearing
- Band Saw Blades
- Barbed Wire
- Barrels (Oil)/(Metalliic Barrels)
- Bath Fittings, Turned Components (All Type) Sheet Metal (Job Work) And Hdpe/Pp Moulded Articles
- Battery For Car (Dry)
- Battery Operated Three Wheelers
- Benefication Of Chromite Ore Processing Charge Chrome
- Bicycle Spokes
- Bicycle Assembly
- Brake Lining Asbestoes/Resin Based & Asbestoes Free
- Brass Artware/Hollow Ware Casting (With Thehelp Of Phenolic Resin)
- Brass Casting
- Brass Pipes From Brass Sheet With Longitudinally Welding
- Brass Ware By Casting Method (Brass Articles Viz. Brass Pooja Lamps And Other Casted)
- Bright Bars
- Buffing And Polishing Industry (Job Work)
- Butt Hinge (Brass Sheet)
- Carbon Brush Holder & Slip Ring
- Co Welding Wire Electrodes (Copper/Copper Alloy Coated M.S.Wire)
- Carbon Film Resistors
- Car Dealership (Hyundai)
- Carburettors
- Cast Steel Body Valve
- Cast Steel Panes For Melting Furnace
- Ceramic Coated Steel Pipes
- Chemical Etching Of Stainless Steel
- Chemical Resistant Iron & Steel
- Concast Steel Bars
- Cold Form Section Mill
- Cold Rolled Forming Of Section And Other Sections
- Cold Rolling Of Ms Strip
- Cold Twisted De-Formed Ribbed Steel
- Cold Rolling Mill
- Compressor (Hermetic) For Air Conditioners
- Compressed Natural Gas (Cng Kit) For Autovehicle
- Continuously Cast Steel Wire Rods (5 Mm)
- Continuous Casting Copper Wire Rods
- Conveyor Beltings
- Conveyor Belt, Transmission Belt & V Belts
- Cooking Ranges
- Copper/Brass Sheets,Circle & Utensils
- Copper Foil
- Copper Ingots, Rods Making & Wire Drawing
- Copper Products From Copper Scrap
- Copper Smelting Plant
- Copper Wire Rods From Copper Scrap
- Corrugated Box Making Machinery And Other Their Parts
- Cylinder Liner For Automobiles
- Disposable Plastic Razors
- Door Locks/Pad Locks
- Drill Bits & Tool Bits
- Drum Closures
- Erw Steel Pipes And Tubes
- Erw Steel Conduit Pipe
- Earth Moving Eqpt.
- Engine Valves For Automobiles
- Fabrication Of Heat Exchanger
- Fabrication Of Storage Tanks And M.S. Drum
- Ferrous Alloy Ni-Hardy I.V Casting
- Ferrous Mn Alloy Casting By Alumina Thermic Process
- Ferro Alloys
- Ferro Silicon & Ferro Manganese From Dolomite (Sms Grade)
- Fire Extinguishers
- Fire Fighting Equipments And Appliances
- Flip-Tone Cans
- Forged Conecting Rod
- Forging Unit
- Fountain Pen Nibs
- Foundry Sand
- Free Wheels, Free Wheel Bushes And Free Wheel Plates For Autorickshaws
- Fuel Briquettes From Agro Waste
- Fuel Injection System
- Fused Magnesia
- Generator Canopy
- Galvanized M.S.Strips
- Galvanizing Plant
- Galvanized Iron Wire (G.I. Wire)
- G.I. Pipes
- Gas Welding Torches And Nozzles
- Gasket Sheet
- Gate Grills & Window Frames
- Generating Set (Diesel)
- Hard Anodised Aluminium
- High Pressure Cylinder

ALL FOLLOWING PROJECT REPORTS ARE READILY AVAILABLE

- Steel Furnitures And Electrical Appliances
- Steel Furniture And Fire Fighting Equipments
- Steel Furniture And Room Cooler
- Steel Wire Drawing And Galvanizing
- Steel Wire/Rod
- Steel Wool
- Ston Scrusher And Screening Plant
- Submerged Arc Welded Pipes
- Submersible Pump Manufacturing
- Super Enamelled Copper Wire
- Super Enamelled Copper Wire (From Copper Cathode Rod)
- Three Wheelers
- Tie-Rod Ends
- Tin Containers
- Toolroom And Sheet Metal Products
- Trolley (Shopping) For Carrying Of Stores At Super Market And Ware Houses
- Tractor Trailers
- Transmission Power Fitting
- Tubular Poles
- Tyre Retreading By Cold Process
- Super Enamelled Copper Wires
- Trolley (Shopping) For Carrying Of Stores At Super Market & Ware Houses
- Tmt Bars
- Tubular Poles For Electrical Transmission (By Fabrication Process)
- Tubular Poles Of M.S. & High Tensile Steel
- V- Belt
- Vacuum Cleaners
- Vacuum Flask (Stainless Steel)
- Valves For Refrigeration And Air-Condition
- Vehicle Welding & Painting
- Venetion Blind
- Washing Machines (Automatic & Computerised)
- Water Controller (Automatic)
- Watch Straps/Chains/ Bracelets/Belt Brass & Stainless Steel
- Water Coolers
- Welded Wire Mesh
- Welding Electrodes
- Wheel Barrow
- Wick Stoves
- Wind Mill Window Frame (Ferrous & Non-Ferrous)
- Wrist Watch

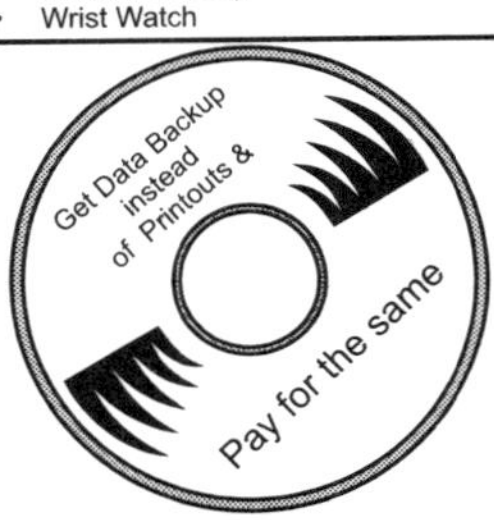

CHEMICALS (ORGANIC & INORGANIC) WITH PETROLEUM PRODUCTS

- Acetic Anhydride
- Acetic Acid (Glacial)
- Acetic Acid From Ethanol
- Acetone
- Acetylene Black
- Acetyl Chloride
- Acetylene Gas
- Acetylene Gas & Oxygen Gas (Integrated Unit)
- Acid Black Dye
- Acid Slurry
- Activated Alumina
- Activated Bleaching Earth (Activated Fullers Earth)
- Activated Carbon From Cashewnut Shell
- Activated Carbon From Rice Husk
- Activated Carbon From Rice Husk, Coconut Shell & Coconut Powder
- Activated Carbon From Wood
- Activated Carbon Powder & Granules From Coconut Shell
- Activated Carbon & Sodium Silicate From Paddy & Rice Husk
- Alcohol From Broken Rice
- Alum For Water Treatment
- Adhesive (Fevicol Type)
- Aerosol Insecticides Spray (Baygon, Hit, Mortein Type)
- Agarbatti Synthetic Perfumery Compounds
- Alcohol From Potato
- Alcohol From Rice Grains
- Alcohol From Rice Husk
- Alcohol From Molasses
- Alcohol, Beer, Starch, Liquid Glucose, Dextrose, Sorbitol, Vitamin-C,
- Alcoholic Beverages And Vinegar From Coconut Water
- Germ Oil, Cattle Feed Etc. From Maize
- Alkyd Resin
- Alkylated Phenol Likenonyl Phenol, Dodecyl Phenol
- Alum (Non Ferric)
- Alum (Ferric)
- Aluminium Chloride From Aluminium Ore
- Alum Cake
- Alum From Aluminium Hydrate
- Aluminium Ingot By Bauxite
- Aluminium Phosphide
- Aluminium Phosphate
- Aluminium Sulphate (Non Ferric Alum) 17% - 18% Alumina Content In Granules (2 Mm To 4 Mm) And Flakes
- Amines & Allied Products
- Amino Acid
- Ammonia Gas

- Ammonia Gas Bottling
- Ammonia Liquor
- Ammonium Nitrate
- Ammonium Chloride (Pure & Technical)
- Ammonium Sulphate
- Annato Seed Extraction And Processing
- Anti Corrosion Chemicals
- Anthranilic Acid From Phthalic Anhydride
- Anesthesia (All Types) Used In Hospitals
- Aniline
- Argon Gas
- Ariel Type Detergent Powder
- Anthraquinone
- Antimony Trioxide
- Atenolol
- Auramine "O"
- Azodicarbonamide
- Baking Soda From Ash
- Barium Carbonate
- Barium Compounds
- Barium Nitrate
- Barium Peroxide
- Barium-Thio-Sulphate Banzene
- Baryte Powder
- Bar Soap (All Varieties) Using Soap Noodles
- Beer Plant
- Belt Paste
- Beneficiation Of Chromite Ore Processing Charge Chrome
- Benzyl Acetate, Benzyl Benzoate, Benzyl Alcohol
- Beta Naphthol
- Bentonite Powder
- Benzoic Acid
- Benzidine
- Biofertiliser From Mother Culture
- Bio Oil For Power Generation From Coffee Husk
- Bio Gas Plant
- Bio Gas Filling In Cylinder
- Bio Tech Unit
- Bi-Chromate Of Sodium, Potassium & Ammonium
- Bi-Functional Black Mfgr.Reactive Dye (Dye From Cotton Yarn Dyeing)
- Bio-Fuel (Jatropha Cultivation And Extraction)
- Bituminous Roademulsion
- Black Phenyl
- Black Sulphur
- Bleaching Powder (Stable)
- Blue Detergent Powder
- Bone Crushing Plant
- Bone Meal (Calcined) Enrichment With Calcium & Phosphorus
- Boric Acid
- B.O.N. Acid
- Bromine Gas Plant
- Brandy
- Butanol
- Butyl Rubber For The Manufacture Of Tubes For Truck And Car Tyres
- 1,4, Butanediol
- Butyl Acetate
- Caffein From Tea Waste
- Calcined Lime (Dead Burnt Dolomite)

ALL FOLLOWING PROJECT REPORTS ARE READILY AVAILABLE

- Integerated Complex Of Easter & Allied Products (D.O.P, D.B.P, Ethyl Acetate Wire Enamel & Cable Jelly)
- Insta Whitening System (Ujala Type)
- Imfl (Whisky) & Country Liquor
- Imfl (Whiskey) From Potato
- Iron Oxide For Making Feritte
- Iron Sulphide
- Jatropha (Biodiesel) Cultivation And Extraction
- J. Acid
- Jute Batching Oil
- Kesh Kala Tel (Hair Dye Lotion) (Vasmol 33, Black Nite Type)
- L-Lysine Monohydrochloride
- Lactic Acid From White Sugar By Fermentation Process
- Ldpe Granules From Virgin (Ldpe Resin)
- Lead Extraction From Battery Scrap
- Lead Oxide
  (A) Lead Monoxide
  (B) Lead Tetra Oxide
  (C) Greylead Oxide
- Liquid Glucose & Its By Products
- Liquid Gold (In Paste Form)
- Lemon Oil From Lemon
- Liquid Oxygen Bottling Plant
- Liquid Shoe Polish
- Liquid Floor Polish
- Lithium Based Grease
- Linear Alkyl Benzene Sulphonate
- Lube Oil Viscosity Improved For P.P.G/P.E.G.
- Lube Oil And Greases
- Lube Oil From Cnsl To Reduce Friction
- Lubricants Ashless 100% Combustion
- Maize Oil
- Magnesium Carbonate And Magnesium Bicarmonate
- Magnesium Hydroxide Powder
- Magnesium Silicate
- Magnesium Sulphate
- Malachite Green
- Maleic Acid
- Maleic Anhydride
- Manganese Sulphate
- Manufacturing Of Carbon Mono-Oxide Water Gas
- Menthol Bold Crystals From Flakes
- Menthol Crystal & Mentha Oil
- Mercuric Oxide
- Metal Pre-Treatment Chemicals
- Methyl Chloride
- Methyl Cinnamate
- Methane Gas By Sodium Acetate & Soda Lime
- Methyl Acetyl Ricinolate
- Methyl Parathion 2% Dust Powder
- Methyl Stearate
- Metol
- Metol From Hydroqui-None & Methylamine
- Micanite
- Micro Crystalline Wax
- Micro Nutrient Mixture
- Mineral Water
- Mineral Water And Pet Bottilng Plant
- Mineral Water In Bottles, Glass And Pouches
- Mini Cement Plant (By Rotary Kiln Process)
- Mixed Fertilizer
- Mosquito Repellent Vaporiser (Liquid Mosquito Destroyer)
- Mosquito & Flies Repellent Agarbatti (Incense Sticks)
- Monochloro Acetic Acid
- Monocrotophos (Technical)
- Mosquito Coil
- Mosquito Coil & Mat
- Mosquito Mat
- Mosquito Net
- Mosquito Coil Agarbatti
- Mother Tincture & Bio Chemic Medicines
- Naphthalene & Phenyl (Integrated Unit)
- Natural Mineral Water By Reverse Osmosis Process
- Nickel Plating Brightner (Primary Or Carrier Brightner & Secondary Brightner)
- Nickel Sulphate
- Nicotine From Tobacco Waste
- Nicotine Sulphate From Tobacco Waste
- Nitro Benzene
- Nitro Cellulose Sanding Sealer/Lacquer
- Nitro Musk
- Nitrogen & Oxygen Gas Plant
- Non-Ionic Surfactant (Wetting Agent)
- No-Carb Paste
- Npk Mixed Fertilizer (Molasses Based)
- N.P.K Fertilizer
- Octanol
- Oleoresin From Chilly And Ginger (Extraction)
- Oleoresins From Marigold Petals (Extraction)
- Organic Fertiliser
- Ortho Nitro Phenol
- Ortho Phthalic Polyester
- Oxalic Acid From Molasses
- Oxalic Acid From Rice Husk
- Oxalic Acid From Tree Bark
- Oxalic Acid From Waste Vegetables
- Oxygen Gas Plant
- Oxygen And Nitrogen Gas Plant
- Oxygen Gas Plant (Air Seperation Method)
- Para-Amino Benzoic Acid
- Para-Amino Phenol
- Para Toluene Sulphonic Acid
- Pectin From Raw Papaya
- Pectin From Apple Pomace
- Pectin From Mango Peel
- Pectin From Oranges
- Pectin From Citrus/Lemon
- Perfume (Lemon & Others)
- Perfume Spray Deodorant (Non-Alcoholic)
- Pest Control
- Pesticide Preparation Using Neem Fruit & Seeds (Margosa)
- Pet Bottles From Pre-Form
- Pet Granules (Dana)
- Pet Preform From Resin For Pet Bottles
- Petroleum Jelly
- Phenol
- Phenyl Acetic Acid
- Phenyl
- Phenyl (Black) In Liquid Form
- Phthalic Anhydride
- Phosphoric Acid From Rock Phosphate
- Phosphorus By Chemical Process
- Photo Emulsion For Rotary Screen Printing
- Phthalocyanine Blue
- Pigment Emulsion For Textile
- Pigment Gum
- Plant Growth Reagen Based Chlorothyltrimethyl Ammonium Chloride
- Plant Harmones Based On 2,4-Dichlorphenoxy
- Acentic Acid & Naphthalene
- Plastazote Polythylene Foam Used For Fibre Cable Joint
- Plasticine (Modelling Clay)
- Plastic Waste Reprocessing
- Plaster Of Paris Bandages
- Polyester Resin (G.P. Grade Laminate Grade, Electrical Grade)
- Polyol From Propylene Oxide
- Poly Vinyl Acetate
- Polyvinyl Acetate Emulsion
- Polyvinyl Alcohol
- Polyurethene Foam
- Potassium Dichromate/Bichromate
- Potassium Iodate
- Potassium Nitrate
- Potassium Permagnate
- Potassium Per Sulphate
- Potassium Sulphate (Fertilizer Grade)
- Potassium Per Oxy Di-Sulphide
- Potassium Silicate By Ion Exchange Process
- Potassium Silicate
- Potassium Stearate
- Processing Of Datura Stramonium Into Hyosyamina And Atropin
- Power Alcohol
- Pvc Resin From Ethyl Alcohol
- Pyridine & Its Derivatives
- Rapid Fast Dyes (Only Process)
- Reactor (Chemical)
- Resorcinol
- Reclamation Of Used Engine Oil (By Clay & Vacuum Distillation Process)
- Refinery Petrol/Diesel Etc.
- Reclamation Of Spent Bleaching Earth
- Reclamation Of Nickel Spent Catalyst From Vanaspati Industry
- Rectified Spirit From Molasses & Mahua Flowers
- Rectified Spirit From Rice Straw
- Red Oxide Paint/Primer (Anti Corrosive) Based Organic Red Pigments
- Refinery Petrol/Diesel Etc.
- Removal Of Antimony From Lead Scrap
- Resorcinol
- Rice Bran Oil (Rbo)
- Rosin Sizing Agent

Market Survey Cum Detailed Techno Economic Feasibility Report on all Projects are available Contact.
"ENGINEERS INDIA RESEARCH INSTITUTE". 4449, Nai Sarak (D), Main Road, Delhi-110006 (India)
Ph. : 09811437895, 9811151047, 91-11-23918117, 23916431, 23947058, 64727385, 45120361
E-mail : eiriprojects@gmail.com, eiribooks@yahoo.com • website: www.eiri.in, www.eiriindia.org • www.eiribooksandprojectreports.com

ALL FOLLOWING PROJECT REPORTS ARE READILY AVAILABLE

- Alluminium Printing Plate For Offset Printing Machine
- Aluminium Foils
- Aluminium Wire And Rods
- Brass And Aluminium Hinges
- Hard Anodizing On Aluminium
- Pilfer Proof Caps
- Piston Assembly (Aluminium Alloy)
- Pressure Die Casting (Aluminium)
- Paper Coated Aluminium Wire
- Pressure Cooker

FISH FARMING AND FISHERY PRODUCTS

- Aquaculture Prawn Farming (Fresh Water)
- Chitin & Chitosan From Prawn Shell Waste
- Chemicals From Prawn Fish Head
- Developing Trout Fish Preservation & Storage And Marketing Infrastructure
- Fish Farming
- Fish Canning And Pouching
- Fish Processing (Blast Freezing Process)
- Fish Net
- Fish Oil Soap
- Fish Meal
- Hdpe Fishing Net
- Plastic Milk Crate And Plastic Fish Crate
- Trout Fish Farming, Canning & Preservation With Aqua Feed Manufacturing (Integrated Complex)

SURGICAL AND DISPOSABLE MEDICAL PRODUCTS

- Ayurvedic/Herbal Pharmacy
- Blood Bags
- Bandage Cloth Weaving On Power Loom
- Crepe Bandage
- Disposable Surgical Caps & Masks
- Dextrose Saline (I.V.Fluid) In Plastic Bottle
- Dextrose Saline (I.V.Fluid)
- Disposable Needles For Syringes
- Disposable Plastic Syringes
- Diagnostic Centre
- Electronics Blood Pressure Measuring Instument
- Hospital Cum Nursing Home
- Homeopathic Medicines
- I. V. Fluids (Ffs Technology)
- I.V. Set-Cannula
- Intravenous
- Medical College
- Plastic I.V. Bottles

- Plaster Of Paris Bandages
- Pharmaceuticals (Tablet, Capsule, Syrups And Ointments)
- Repacking Of Medicines
- Surgical Cotton & Bandage
- Surgical Examination Gloves
- Surgical Bandage
- Surgical Adhesive Tape On Cloth Surface
- Surgical Methylated Spirit
- Sodium Phosphate Enema
- Vetenary Medicines

ALCOHOL, BEER, IMFL, COUNTRY LIQUOR, WINE & OTHER RELATED PROJECTS

- Alcohol From Rice Straw
- Alcohol From Molasses
- Alcohol From Potatoes
- Alcoholic Beverages And Vinegar From Coconut Water
- Alcoholic Drinks From Ethyl Alcohol By Mixing Of Various Flavours (Flavoured Alcoholic Beverages)
- Beer Plant (E.O.U.)
- Country Liquor
- Cider Plant
- Ethanol (Biofuel)
- Grape Wine
- Herbal Beer
- Mineral Water (Packed In Bottles, Glasses, Jars)
- Rectified Spirit For Potable Alcohol
- Industrial Alcohol & Medical Alcohol
- Rectified Spirit From Rice/Paddy Straw
- Indian Made Foreign Liquor
- Imfl (Whisky) From Potatoes
- Octalol (Octyl Alcohol) From Molasses
- Potable Beer (Alcoholic) Based On Potato & Barley/Malt
- Vodka From Potatoes
- Whisky
- Wine From Dates

PULP, PAPER, STRAW/GREY BOARD, KRAFT PAPER,PACKAGING, PAPER CARRY BAG, PAPER FROM AGRO WASTE & STATIONERY ETC.

- Ammonia Paper
- Automatic Book Binding
- Adhesive (Fevicol Type)
- All Pin & Gem Clips
- Ball Pen
- Ball Pen Refill Ink
- Ball Pen Ink Remover
- Carbon Paper
- Card Board
- Carbon Less Paper
- Cellphane Paper
- Computer Continuous Stationery
- Computer Forms & Security Printing Press
- Corrugated Board & Box (Printed & Laminated)
- Corrugated Board And Boxes From From Card Boards
- Corrugated Cartons From Plain Papers
- Corrugated Paper
- Corrugatred Packing & Material (Bulb & Tubes Packing)
- Desk Top Publishing
- Defoaming Agent For Paper Plant
- Drinking Straw Paper
- D.T.P Cum Offset Press
- Egg Trays From Pulp
- Ecg Paper
- Exercise Note Book, Register And Pad
- Flexographic Ink
- Greeting Card By Offset Press
- Hand Made Paper Filter Paper
- Hard Board
- Hard Board From Bagasse
- Injection Ampoules Packaging Boxes
- Insulatiing Paper
- Kraft Paper
- Kraft Paper From Bagasse
- Laminated Packaging Paper With Printing
- Lamination & Coating On Paper
- M.G. Paper From Waste Paper
- Mill Paper From Waste Paper
- Mill Board From Rice & Wheat Straws
- Mill Board From Waste Paper
- Mini Paper Plant From Sisal
- Mini Paper Plant
- Multi Wall Paper Sacks
- News Paper For Children
- News Print Paper From Rice Straw/Bagasse
- News Paper Childrens
- News Print Paper

ENGINEERS INDIA RESEARCH INSTITUTE
EiRi

Market Survey Cum Detailed Techno Economic Feasibility Report on all Projects are available Contact.

"ENGINEERS INDIA RESEARCH INSTITUTE". 4449, Nai Sarak (D), Main Road, Delhi-110006 (India)
Ph. : 09811437895, 9811151047, 91-11-23918117, 23916431, 23947058, 64727385, 45120361
E-mail : eiriprojects@gmail.com, eiribooks@yahoo.com • website: www.eiri.in, www.eiriindia.org • www.eiribooksandprojectreports.com

PHARMACEUTICALS & DRUGS TECHNOLOGY WITH FORMULATIONS

ISBN. 81-86732-52-7 # ₹ 950/-

Tablet & Capsules, Lubricants & Disintegrants, Pan Coating, Oral Preparations Mixtures, External Preparations, Ear Drops, Mouth Washes, Nasal Drops, Ointments, Creams & Eye Preparations, Antibiotics, Formulations, Packaging, Tablets including Amoxycillin, Analgin, Ibuprofen, Injectables, Liquid Orals, Capsules & Dry Syrups, Eye & Ear Preparations etc.

MODERN PACKAGING TECHNOLOGY FOR PROCESSED FOOD,BAKERY, SNACK FOOD, SPICES & ALLIED FOOD PRODUCTS

ISBN. 81-86732-28-4 # ₹ 600/-

Latest methods of Packaging Technology of fruits/veg. growers ,Spices mfrs., Snack food mfrs., Bakery Mfrs., and Edible oil mfrs. etc. Suppliers of Plant and Machinery have also been incorporated.

BOOKS ON SYNTHETIC DETERGENTS, SOAPS & DETERGENTS

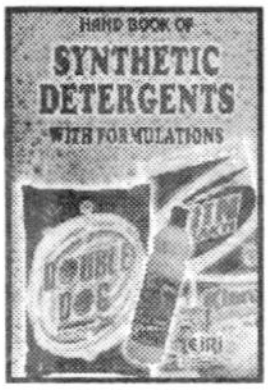

HAND BOOK OF SYNTHETIC DETERGENTS WITH FORMULATIONS

ISBN. 81-86732-43-8 # ₹ 900/-

Group of Synthetic Detergents, Synthesis of Detergents, Manufacture of Synthetic Detergents with Formulae, Testing of Detergents and Soaps, Project Profiles, Suppliers of Machinery and Raw Materials, Acid Slurry, Sirf Excel Type Detergent, Ariel Type Detergent, Dry Mix Process, Dry Clean Unit and much more others etc.

MANUFACTURE OF HOUSEHOLD SOAPS, TOILET SOAPS & OTHER SOAPS WITH FORMULATIONS

ISBN. 81-86732-53-5 # ₹ 750/-

Soap base manufacture, Solid, household and toilet soaps manufacture, Production of soap base, Perfuming, Manufacturing process & formulations, Miscellaneous formulae, Scourig bar, Detergent cake & powder, Toilet & herbal soap, Laundry soap, Liquid soap, Complete plant Suppliers, Suppliers of chemicals, Present manufacturers etc.

BOOKS ON ESSENTIAL OILS, PERFUMES & FLAVOURS

MODERN TECHNOLOGY OF ESSENTIAL OILS

ISBN 81-86732-71-3 # ₹ 850/-

Essential Oils Technology, Essential Oils and Flavours, Production of Essential Oils & Oleoresins, Herb & Oil Yield in Different Ocimum Species, Kewda Essential Oil and Attar, Mint Oil, Lemongrass, Palmarosa Oil, Musk, Java Citronella, Bio-Chemical Studies, Patchouli Oil, Rose-Scented Geranium, Basil Oil etc.

ESSENTIAL OILS PROCESSES & FORMULATIONS HAND BOOK

ISBN. 81-86732-39-X # ₹ 650/-

Essential Oils by Steam Distillation, GC-MS studies, Essential Oil from Cinnamomum, Kewda flower distillation, Composition of essential oil frombottle brush, Composition of essential oil from flowers of Keora, Manufacturers/ Exporters of Essential oils & Aromatic Chemicals with Machinery.

HAND BOOK OF ESSENTIAL OILS MANUFACTURING & AROMATIC PLANTS

ISBN. 81-86732-27-6 # ₹ 650/-

Rose oildistillation, extraction of essential oils, Uses of indigenous aromatic plants, essential oil bearing plants status,fractionation of essential oil, essential oil of hyptis suaveolens poit, super critical fluid extraction, ginger oil, Jasmine, rose etc..

HAND BOOK OF PERFUMES WITH FORMULATIONS

ISBN. 81-86732-42-X # ₹ 750/-

Creating a Perfume, Flower Perfumes, Colognes, Raw Materials, Classification, Packaging of Perfumes, Testing of Perfumes, Aromatic Perfumery Compounds, Scent & Perfume, Spray Perfume, Suppliers of Raw Materials .

HAND BOOK OF PERFUMES & FLAVOURS

ISBN. 81-86732-30-6 # ₹ 600/-

Perfume, Formulary of Perfume & Flavour, Natural Odours Simulated with Aromatic Chemicals, Simulated Flower Scents, Simulated Marine Scents (Algae), Plant & Equipment Suppliers, Suppliers of Raw Materials, Suppliers of Perfumes. Project profiles etc.

HAND BOOK OF FLAVOURS TECHNOLOGY

ISBN 81-86732-98-5
₹ 750/- or US $ 100/-

The book cover flavour analysis, Chemistry of flavours, Off-flavours in foods, Manufacturing processes of flavours, Plant materials used in flavouring, Principal Essential Oils used in Flavourings, Application of flavourings in food processing, Quality control, Non-Alcoholic Flavours, Flavours fruit (whiskey, vodka, Grape, Butter Scotch & Rum), Terpeneles Menthol Crystals.

ENGINEERS INDIA RESEARCH INSTITUTE Mobile : 9811437895, 9811151047

4449, Nai Sarak, Main Road, Delhi - 110 006 (INDIA) Ph. 91-11- 23918117, 23916431, 23947058

BOOKS ON PRINTINGS, OFFSET, SCREEN, FLEXO & GRAVURE TECHNOLOGY

HAND BOOK OF
PRINTING TECHNOLOGY
OFFSET, SCREEN, FLEXO, GRAVURE, INKJET & DIGITAL
ISBN 81-86732-75-6 # ₹ 975/-

Typographic, Pre-Press Processes, Camera, Scanning, Offset Plate Making, Presses, Offset Press, Proof & Proofing Techniques, Newspaper Printing: Gravure & Packaging, Screen Printing, Plant Economics, Suppliers of Machineries & Raw Materials etc.

...OK OF
...RINTING
...LOGY
...6732-82-9
... US $ 50/-

Desktop Publishing, Proof-Reading, Pre-Press Processes, Camera, Scanning, Offset Plate Making, Presses, Offset Press, Proof & Proofing Techniques, Newspaper Printing, Plant Economics, Suppliers of Plant & Machineries, Suppliers of Raw Materials etc.

HAND BOOK OF
SCREENPRINTING WITH PROCESSES & TECHNOLOGY
ISBN. 81-86732-63-2★ ₹ 350/-

Screen Printing Methods, Screen- Process Stencils, Screen Printing Stencils, Chemicals Adhesives, Screen Printing On Glass, Colour Combination, Silk Screen Photo Stencil Preparation, Plant Economics Suppliers of Plant & Machinery & Raw Materials.

HAND BOOK OF
PRINTING PROCESSES TECHNOLOGIES & INDUSTRIES
ISBN. 81-86732-07-1 # ₹ 375/-

The book covers latest technology of almost all the printing technology viz; screen, offset, velvet cloth, sheetfed offset. Project profiles on various printing industries are also provided. Suppliers of machinery are also given.

BOOKS ON PLASTIC COMPOUNDING, PROCESSING, MOULDS, POLYMER, FIBRE GLASS, PVC & PET PRODUCTS

PLASTIC COMPOUNDING MASTER BATCHES, PET & OTHER PLASTIC PROCESSING INDUSTRIES
ISBN. 81-86732-49-7 • ₹ 750/-

Extrusion, Injection, Blow & Rotational Moulding, Additives for Polymers, PVC Compounding, Colour Master Batch, PET, Suppliers of Machineries, Suppliers of Raw Materials etc.

PLASTIC PROCESSING AND PACKAGING INDUSTRIES
ISBN. 81-86732-11-X
₹ 975/- or US$ 100/-

Introduction, Plastic Processing, Injection & Blow Moulding, Compounding & Processing of PVC, PU, Project profiles and directory section. The book is covering with the 54 fully detailed chapters etc.

TECHNOLOGY OF
PVC COMPOUNDING AND ITS APPLICATIONS
ISBN 81-86732-88-8
₹ 900/- or US $ 100/-

PVC Resins Processing of PVC, Additives for PVC, Compounding, Compounding of PVC, Testing of Resins and Compounds, Speciality Plastic Compounds & Masterbatches, PVC compounds, Xlpe cable compound, jelly filled telecommunication cable compound & sheating compound, Plastic Granules Applications of PVC, Suppliers of Machineries/Raw Materials etc.

MOULDS DESIGN & PROCESSING HAND BOOK
ISBN. 81-86732-23-3
 # ₹ 495/- or US$ 50/-

Classification of Moulds, Production Schedule of Plastic Injection Mould, Steel for Injection Mould, Trouble, Injection Mould Design, Compression/Transfer Mould, Blow Mould Design, Standard Mould Parts, Conversion Table etc.

Technology of PET Bottles
PREFORM AND PET RECYCLING
₹ 850/-
US$ 85/-

Processing and manufacturing technology of PET Bottles, Preform and market study with Project Profiles of PET bottles, preform & others. Suppliers of Machinery & Raw Materials etc.

ENGINEERS INDIA RESEARCH INSTITUTE Mobile : 9811437895, 9811151047
4449, Nai Sarak, Main Road, Delhi - 110 006 (INDIA) Ph. 91-11- 23918117, 23916431, 23947058

BOOKS ON THINNER, PLASTIC FILMS, PLASTIC WASTE RECYCLING, ROTATIONAL MOULDING, MAIZE, INJECTION MOULDING, PLASTIC MATERIALS & POTATO

MANUFACTURING TECHNOLOGY & FORMULATIONS HAND BOOK ON THINNERS, PUTTY, WALL & INDUSTRIAL FINISHES AND SYNTHETIC RESINS

ISBN978-81-89765-32-3

₹ 900/- **Pages- 339**

The book covers Thinners, Inorganic Pigments, Titanium Dioxide Pigments, Organic Pigments, Extender Pigments, Putty, Glaxing, Compounds Caulking, Compounds and Sealants, Paint Driers, Paint Additives, Architectural Paints, Industrial Finishes etc.

ROTATIONAL MOULDING TECHNOLOGY HAND BOOK

ISBN- 978-81-89765-25-5

₹ 750/- Pages- 212

The book covers Innovative Rotomoulding, Technology of Rotational Moulding, Rotational Moulding Process, Roto moulding Technology Details, Materials that can be Roto moulded, Roto moulding Machines, Design Consideration for Roto mould Containers, Rotational Moulding Process Control, Rotational Moulding of Nylons, Moulds Fabrication for Roto moulding, Roto moulds for Cast Aluminium, Pin-holes and Bubbles in Roto moulded Products, Rotational Moulding of Liquid Polymers, Powdering Thermoplastic and Quality Consideration, Plastic Water Storage Tanks (HDPE), Sintex Type etc.

PLASTIC WASTE RECYCLING TECHNOLOGY

ISBN 978-81-89765-30-9

₹ 750 **Page No. 238**

The book covers Introduction, Details of Polymers , Types of Plastics, Identification of Plastics, Recycling of Plastic Waste, Recycling of Thermosets, Chemical Recycling, Recycling Commodities Plastics, Recovery of Chemicals from Plastic Waste, Factors Affecting Recycling Process, Automatic Scrap Recycling, Reclaiming Polyamide Spin Fibres, EPS-Recycling from Post-Consumer Expanded Polystyrene, New Patented Processes, Environmental Health and Future Prospects, Recycling Polyester Resins, Polyurethane Waste Recycling, Recycling and Government Policies, Identification of Plastics, Plastics and the Environment, Recycling An Industrial Approach etc.

INJECTION MOULDING OF PLASTICS

ISBN 978-81-89765-20-0

₹ 750/- Pages-319

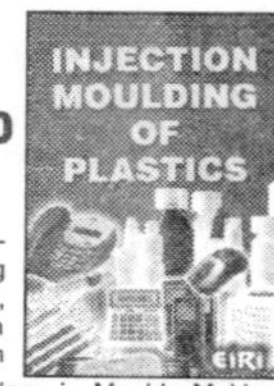

The book covers Injection Moulding, Setting-up-Mould and Machine, Effect of Processing on Mechanical Properties, Mouldflow, Computer Controlled Automatic Injection Moulding Machine, Maintenance of Injection Moulding Machine, CAE and CAD Technology in Moulds Making, Injection Moulding process, Specialised Injection Moulding Process, Troubleshooting in Injection Moulding, Injection Moulding of Thermosets, Injection Moulding Machine, Design for Injection Moulds, Designing Moulds for Thermoset Processing, Injection Moulded Plastic Components, Plastic Moulded Toys, Plastic Injection Moulding Products, Plastic Injection Moulding Items etc.

HAND BOOK OF PLASTIC MATERIALS AND PROCESSING TECHNOLOGY

ISBN 978-81-89765-26-2

₹ 750/- Pages 231

The book covers Introduction of Plastic Materials, Polyethylene, Linear Low Density Polyethylene (LLDPE), Polypropylene, Copolymers of Ethylene, Polystyrene, Acrylic Plastics, Poly (Methyl Methacrylate), Acrylic Fibres, Poly (Vinyl Acetate), Poly (Vinyl Chloride), Polytetrafluoroethylene (PTFE), Coumarone-Indene Resins, Polyacetals and Polyethers (Acetal Resins), Polyamides, Polyimides, Polyesters, Polyurethanes, Polycarbonates, Epoxy Resins, Cellulose Plastics, Phenolic Resins, Amino Resins, Silicones, Additives for Plastics, Polybutylene Terephthalate, Polyethersulphone, Nylon, Polyvinylidene Fluride etc.

POTATO AND POTATO PROCESSING TECHNOLOGY

ISBN- 978-81-89765-29-3

₹ 750/- Pages-264

The book covers Introduction, Origin, Description of Plant and Flower Parts, Nutritive Value, Growth and Development, Agro-Techniques, Management of Water, Weed Management, Seed Production, Handling of Post Harvest Potato, Prospects for Potato Exports, Quality Parameters that influence Export Quality of Potatoes, Areas Suitable for Producing Seed Potatoes, Areas Suitable for Producing Processing Potatoes, Grading of Potatoes, Packing of Potatoes, Potato Storage, Quality Requirements, Potato processing , Dehydration of Vegetables, Potato Based Textured Snacks, Potato Chips/Wafers etc.

TECHNOLOGY OF PLASTIC FILMS

ISBN 978-81-89765-28-6

₹ 650/- Pages 165

The book covers Introduction, Theoritical Aspect of Die Design, Plastic Packaging Films, Oriented Packaging Films, Orientation Techniques, Technology of Commercial Shrink Films, Stretch Films and Laminates , Properties of Heat Shrinkable Films, Coextrusion, Different Types of Die, Detailed Drawings of 100 MM Mandrel Type Dies, Chilli Roll Casting of Film, Internal Cooling of Blow Films, Side Fed Co-Extrusion Film Dies, Materials of Construction for Dies, Temperature Control in Dies, Die Maintenance & Care, Production of Blow Films, Polythylene Film Manufacture and Control, Water cooled Polypropylene Film, Orientation of Film, L.L.D.P.E. Film Extrusion, Coextrusion Dies for Manufacturing Flat Films etc.

TECHNOLOGY OF MAIZE AND ALLIED CORN PRODUCTS

ISBN 978-81-89765-17-0

₹ 650/- Pages-258

The book covers Corn, Types of Corn, Botany of Corn, Cultivation Practices, Carbohydrates and Related Compounds, Quality Factors, Traditional Food Products from Corn, Corn Milling, Products and their Uses, Processing Ready-to- Eat Breakfast Cereals, Popcorn, Formulated Puffed Snacks, Manufacturing Corn Chips, Maize Products, Maize Starch, Sweet Corn, Baby Corn, Extruded Snacks, Corn Flakes, Liquid Glucose, Maize/Corn Oil, Malto Dextrin from Maize, Plant Economics of Non Roasted Corn Flakes (POHA), Starch from Maize, Snack Food, Yeast Dry Powder from Maize, Suppliers of Maize/Corn Processing Machineries, Present Manufacturers/Exporters/Suppliers of Maize and Maize Products.

ENGINEERS INDIA RESEARCH INSTITUTE Mobile : 9811437895, 9811151047
4449, Nai Sarak, Main Road, Delhi - 110 006 (INDIA) Ph. 91-11- 23918117, 23916431, 23947058